Praise for Books from PlanningShop

Entrepreneurship: A Real-World Approach

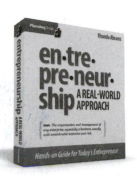

" What separates Rhonda Abrams from the crowd? She is an expert in building successful small businesses. And she continues to create timely, meaningful and (most importantly) useful content for academics, students, and business owners like myself. This book is the definitive guide for anyone who either wants to be an entrepreneur or just wants to grow their own business. "

— *Gene Marks,* New York Times *small business columnist*

Business Plan In A Day

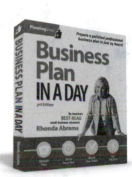

" A business plan is something every business needs, but too many fail to create one because it seems intimidating. Rhonda Abrams is on a mission to change that. With this book she shows you how to create a professional business plan that will seem like it took weeks to write instead of 24 hours. "

— *Anita Campbell, Publisher of* Small Business Trends

" I'm growing my business this year by purchasing a commercial building, and I needed a real estate loan to make the purchase. *Business Plan In A Day* was THE source I used for writing my plan, and the bankers and brokers I spoke with all commended my plan as being very strong and well-written. Thanks to you, I've secured my loan and the transaction is going through. I feel so fortunate to have found this book. "

— *Lisa Stillman, Garden Walk Massage Therapy, St. Louis, MO*

Bringing the Cloud Down to Earth

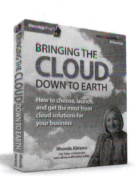

" No matter how you refer to it, working in the Cloud is a fundamental business practice these days and Abrams has done a terrific job of making this sometimes confusing subject relevant and practical for businesses of all shapes and sizes. "

— *John Jantsch, author of* Duct Tape Marketing *and* The Referral Engine

Successful Marketing: Secrets & Strategies

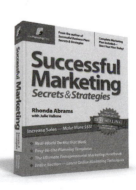

" Successful Marketing encourages students to think through standard marketing concepts while applying them directly to their business idea. "

— *Meredith Carpenter, Entrepreneurship Instructor, Haywood Community College*

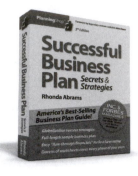

Successful Business Plan: Secrets & Strategies

66 [*Successful Business Plan* is] user-friendly and exhaustive…highly recommended. Abrams' book works because she tirelessly researched the subject. Most how-to books on entrepreneurship aren't worth a dime; among the thousands of small business titles, Abrams' [is an] exception. 99

— *Forbes Magazine*

66 There are plenty of decent business-plan guides out there, but Abrams' was a cut above the others I saw. *Successful Business Plan* won points with me because it was thorough and well organized, with handy worksheets and good quotes. Also, Abrams does a better job than most at explaining the business plan as a planning tool rather than a formulaic exercise. Well done. 99

— *Inc. Magazine*

66 We are again using *Successful Business Plan* in my business honors course this semester. Must be working, as Penn State was just named (by Kaplan and *Newsweek* magazine) as the 'hottest school in the U.S. for student entrepreneurs!' 99

— *Greg Pierce, Penn State University*

66 *Successful Business Plan* enables my Entrepreneurship students at the University of Vermont to develop really great business plans. The book's easy-to-follow, step-by-step format makes preparing a plan logical and understandable. Over the years…several students have actually launched their businesses successfully. Our son used the book at St. Michael's College in Vermont to develop a plan for airport fitness centers, winning the school's annual business plan competition for business majors…with a hefty cash prize! His plan was so thorough, especially the financials, that he was flown to the West Coast to present his plan to a prospective buyer. The bottom line, there is no better road map to business plan success than *Successful Business Plan*! 99

— *David Kaufman, University of Vermont*

66 If you'd like something that goes beyond the mere construction of your plan and is more fun to use, try *Successful Business Plan: Secrets and Strategies*, by Rhonda Abrams…this book can take the pain out of the process. 99

— *"Small Business School," PBS television show*

" *Successful Business Plan* is easy to follow and comprehensive. From the first chapter to the last, it guides you through the business planning process with a proven systematic approach. **"**
— *Sean S. Murphy, Ernst & Young LLP*

" As a 20 plus year veteran SBDC director, consultant and entrepreneurship instructor, I have assisted thousands of individuals and business owners through the planning process. Having reviewed tens of thousands of plans and critiquing hundreds of planning texts, programs and tools, *Successful Business Plan: Secrets & Strategies* remains my hands-down favorite text/workbook/guide. The content and construction is comprehensive, practical and 'do-able' for the serious small business owner/entrepreneur. **"**
— *David Gay, Illinois Small Business Development Center at College of DuPage*

" In my opinion, your book is the definitive guide for successful business plans. I particularly appreciate and recommend the use of the Flow-Through Financial worksheets. Each is a great device to illustrate the connection between the qualitative and quantitative elements of a plan. **"**
— *Gene Elliott, Business Consultant, New Mexico*

" I've been using and promoting *Successful Business Plan* since 1993, and it's great! I've taught business plan writing in several local SBDCs, as well as nationally, through the Neighborhood Reinvestment Training Institute. My course is designed and delivered around your book. **"**
— *Ransom S. Stafford, Business Consultant, Twin Cities, MN*

" One of the best books on business planning. The overall quality of this book is excellent, but three things make it stand out: First, it contains worksheets that walk you through the information gathering process. Fill them out, and even the financials—always the hardest part of a plan—will fall right into place. Second, it has a sample plan that reads like a real business plan, written by a real person for a real business. You can use much of the wording in your own plan. Third, it has tips from successful managers, leaders, and business owners, large and small. I was especially fascinated reading the tips from ex-49'er head coach Bill Walsh. You can't go wrong following his advice on planning and organizing! **"**
— *Economic Chamber of Macedonia*

" *Successful Business Plan* is thorough, well-organized, and a very useful tool for business planning and development. It's an excellent guide to the details involved with creating a solid, useful business plan. "
— *Jim Jindrick, The Institute of Electrical and Electronics Engineers and the University of Arizona*

" I chose *Successful Business Plan* because of its ease of use, its clarity, and its good examples. I have used the book for a number of years now. "
— *Jean Morris, The Culinary Institute of America*

" It has a clearly defined, comprehensive approach. "
— *Zane Swanson, Emporia State University, KS*

" Here at the SBDC we offer clients an eight-week business planning counseling program called Business Plan Expedited (BPE). BPE is structured around *Successful Business Plan*—the end result is a well-written business plan that can be used as a part of a business loan application package. I specifically chose this text because I used it, per recommendation from my graduate school advisor, for my MBA project in graduate school 13 years ago! "
— *Indria Gillespie, Sierra College SBDC*

" Your book has been both an inspirational read as well as a comprehensive guide for starting my business. Being relatively inexperienced with entrepreneurship, your book has not only given me the ability to create a solid roadmap for planning, but has also provided an encouraging and easy way to cope with the enormous amount of information and organization needed. I particularly enjoy the various quotes from business professionals who have had experience in business planning. They give precious insight and different viewpoints that I would not have seen. Thank you for writing this book! "
— *Simon Lee, entrepreneur*

" It combines, in a very clear way, both aspects of business planning and effective writing of business plans. The book is very well written. The forms are very useful. "
— *Eyal Yaniv, Bar Ilan University, Israel*

PlanningShop
Palo Alto, California

NEW! *3rd Edition*

Six-Week Start-Up

A step-by-step program for starting your business, making money, and achieving your goals!

Rhonda Abrams

Six-Week Start-Up:

A step-by-step program for starting your business, making money, and achieving your goals!™

©2013 by Rhonda Abrams. Published by PlanningShop™

ISBN: 978-1-933895-41-3

Library of Congress Control Number: 2013913331

Coca-Cola is a trademark of The Coca-Cola Company. The Coca-Cola logo is used by permission.

Third Edition:

Editor: Anne Marie Bonneau
Proofreader: Mark Woodworth
Cover and Interior Designers: Arthur Wait, Diana Russell Design

Services for our readers:

Colleges, business schools, corporate purchasing:

PlanningShop offers special discounts and supplemental materials for universities, business schools, and corporate training. Contact: info@PlanningShop.com or call 650-364-9120.

Free business tips and information:

To receive Rhonda's free email newsletter on starting and growing a successful business, sign up at www.PlanningShop.com.

PlanningShop
555 Bryant Street, #180
Palo Alto CA 94301 USA
Phone: 650-364-9120
Email: info@PlanningShop.com
Web: www.PlanningShop.com

PlanningShop™ is a division of Rhonda, Inc., a California corporation.

"This publication is designed to provide accurate and authoritative information in regard to the subject matter covered. It is sold with the understanding that the publisher and author are not engaged in rendering legal, accounting, or other professional services. If legal advice or other expert assistance is required, seek the services of a competent professional." —*from a Declaration of Principles, jointly adopted by a committee of the American Bar Association and a committee of publishers*

Printed in the United States of America

10 9 8 7 6 5 4 3 2 1

Who this book is for

This book is a step-by-step guide for getting a successful business up and running fast. It covers all aspects of launching a business, from licenses to bookkeeping to marketing to setting up shop. Everything is presented in a step-by-step format with checklists, worksheets, and top-notch advice from one of America's most highly regarded business writers.

This book is for you if:

- You're currently in the process of starting your own business and want to get things done as efficiently as possible, yet still do them right.

- You want to make certain you take care of all the details of getting a business under way, organize the process, and get some good advice.

- You're going to start a business soon and need a plan on how to go about it.

- You have an idea for a business but don't know where to start.

- You already run a business but would like to improve operations, marketing, or take care of essential aspects of growing a company.

- You're a student in an entrepreneurship or small business class and need to launch a complete business in a limited time period.

About Rhonda Abrams

Entrepreneur, author, and nationally syndicated columnist **Rhonda Abrams** is widely recognized as a leading expert on entrepreneurship and small business. Rhonda's column for *USA Today*, "Successful Strategies," is the most widely distributed column on small business and entrepreneurship in the United States, reaching tens of millions of readers each week.

Rhonda's books have been used by millions of entrepreneurs. Her first book, *Successful Business Plan: Secrets & Strategies*, is the best-selling business plan guide in America. It was named one of the top 10 business books for entrepreneurs by both *Forbes* and *Inc.* magazines. She is also the author of more than a dozen other books on entrepreneurship and has sold more than a million copies of her books. Rhonda's other books are perennial best sellers, with three of them having reached the nationally recognized "Top 50 Business Best-Seller" list.

Rhonda not only writes about business—she lives it! As the founder of three successful companies, Rhonda has accumulated an extraordinary depth of experience and a real-life understanding of the challenges facing entrepreneurs. Rhonda first founded a management consulting practice working with clients ranging from one-person start-ups to Fortune 500 companies. An early Web pioneer, she founded a website for small business that she later sold. Today, Rhonda is CEO of the publishing company PlanningShop, which focuses exclusively on the topics of business planning, entrepreneurship, and new business development. PlanningShop is America's leading academic publisher in the discipline of entrepreneurship.

A popular public speaker, Rhonda regularly addresses leading industry and trade associations, business schools, and corporate conventions and events. Educated at Harvard University and UCLA, Rhonda lives in Palo Alto, California.

TABLE OF CONTENTS

Week 6 ✓ Open Your Doors! 239

Index 305

Worksheets

Introduction

In six weeks you can change your life!

Where will you be six weeks from today?

Six weeks from today, you can have your own business up and running, and you can be on the road to success.

You've had the dream of owning your business for some time; you even have an idea for your business concept. Now, I'm giving you the blueprint.

I'm going to help you get all the nitty-gritty details of starting a business out of the way so you can spend your time on things you really want to do—make your products, provide your service, be creative, make money, and have fun!

With checklists and very specific advice, this book walks you through the process of starting your business, step by step. I've detailed the critical components of getting a business—a successful business—under way and created an easy-to-follow program for dealing with those components.

Starting a business can seem overwhelming—there's so much to do, so much to figure out. How do you set prices? What licenses do you need? How do you choose a location? Where do you find customers? Where do you get the money?

All these details seem paralyzing.

I know, because I've been there. I've started and built three successful companies. I still remember my first weeks in business—deciding on a business name, getting my first business card designed, figuring out a way to land my first customer. I was flustered by buying my first computer and choosing the software to go with it.

I want to make it easier—much easier—for you. And I want to not only deal with all those details, but to make sure you have some fun along the way—staying motivated and getting energized.

So, in this book, I've organized the start-up process into a comprehensive program that breaks down the many tasks of launching a business into six, manageable weeks. During each week, you'll focus on just a few major issues; this makes it possible for you to manage the necessary details without feeling overwhelmed.

Each week consists of:

- **Main accomplishments:** These cover major issues you'll have to deal with when you start your business, such as money, laws and regulations, and operations.

- **Checklists:** Each accomplishment is broken down into a checklist of steps for you to mark off as you complete each one. This makes it easier for you to tackle each major accomplishment.

- **Worksheets:** To make completing your checklists easier, each week includes helpful worksheets and planning forms. Use these to guide you as you go along. Even after you've opened your business, you may want to keep these completed forms to refer to from time to time.

- **Make appointments with:** Each week includes a suggestion of which experts or advisors can help you complete that week's accomplishments and checklists.

You can undertake these accomplishments in any order—or break up checklists into separate weeks!

In addition, throughout this book, you will find:

- **Questions to Ask:** Lists of suggested issues to deal with when you meet with key contacts such as investors, attorneys, accountants, and many more.

- **Red Tape Alerts:** To give you a "heads-up" warning when an issue may have legal or tax consequences.

- **What Would Rhonda Do:** Insight and advice based on my real-life experience.

- **Check It Out:** To help you find useful information and resources online quickly.

- **Start It Free:** To help you find free versions of applications such as website builders, data storage, and accounting applications, so you can get your business up and running for as little money as possible.

This book covers everything from taxes to trade shows, accounting to advertising, customers to computers.

Of course, you might want to—or need to—take more than six weeks to get your own business under way. That's okay. Set your own pace. This

xvi | SIX-WEEK START-UP

book still serves as a plan—a "cookbook"—outlining the steps to launching your business—whether you take six weeks or six months.

Can I guarantee that in six weeks you'll be sitting on a beach counting your money? No. This isn't some late-night infomercial.

Instead, this is a realistic, do-able guide to getting your own business up and running.

If not knowing where to start has been holding you back from launching your business, or you feel overwhelmed by the details, or you're afraid you don't have the money to pay for the advice you need, then this book is for you.

Where do *you* want to be six weeks from now?

week 1

week 1

Main accomplishments:

#1 Clarify your business vision and concept

#2 Create your company identity

#3 Get organized

Make appointments with:

- Graphic designer
- SBDC counselor

Lay the Foundation...

CONGRATULATIONS! YOU'RE NOW OFFICIALLY STARTING your new business. During this first week, you'll jump right in with some of the fun stuff of starting a business—like choosing a business name and developing a corporate identity. But most of the week is devoted to establishing a strong foundation for your new company: making sure your business concept is solid, developing a network of advisors and supporters to help you build and grow your company, and taking care of the organizational details to make day-to-day business life more effective and efficient.

In other words, we're going to make sure you get off to the right start.

Even if you are starting a one-person business, you'll find it beneficial to develop a network of colleagues and associates, referral sources and supporters. No one succeeds alone—so right from Week One, you'll start building your network.

GOALS FOR STARTING MY BUSINESS

Specific Goals:

Enter the number or amount you hope to achieve for your business in one year, five years, and ten years.

	One Year	Five Years	Ten Years
Number of Employees	_____	_____	_____
Number of Locations	_____	_____	_____
Annual Sales	_____	_____	_____
Profits or Profit Margin	_____	_____	_____
Number of Products/Services	_____	_____	_____
Awards/Recognition Received	_____	_____	_____
Ownership Allocation	_____	_____	_____
Other:	_____	_____	_____
_____	_____	_____	_____
_____	_____	_____	_____
_____	_____	_____	_____

Priorities:

Rate your priorities for your business.

	Urgent	Important	I'll get to it sooner or later	Not on the radar screen	Not applicable to my business
Add Employees	☐	☐	☐	☐	☐
Add New Lines	☐	☐	☐	☐	☐
Increase Marketing	☐	☐	☐	☐	☐
Add Locations	☐	☐	☐	☐	☐
Expand Online	☐	☐	☐	☐	☐
Increase Salaries	☐	☐	☐	☐	☐
Increase Inventory	☐	☐	☐	☐	☐
Increase Profits	☐	☐	☐	☐	☐
Retire Debts	☐	☐	☐	☐	☐
Increase Reserve	☐	☐	☐	☐	☐
Acquire Other Companies	☐	☐	☐	☐	☐
Other:					
_____	☐	☐	☐	☐	☐
_____	☐	☐	☐	☐	☐
_____	☐	☐	☐	☐	☐
_____	☐	☐	☐	☐	☐

ACCOMPLISHMENT #1:
Clarify your business concept

My Checklist:

- ☐ **Identify your personal goals**
- ☐ **Spell out your business values**
- ☐ **Remind yourself of your source of inspiration**
- ☐ **Describe your business concept**
- ☐ **Identify your strategic position**
- ☐ **Decide whether you want partners**
- ☐ **Decide whether you want investors**
- ☐ **Consider potential exit strategies**
- ☐ **Discuss the impact of starting a business with your family**

If you were building a house, before you drew up the blueprints, laid the foundation, or even bought the land, you'd first have a vision of what you'd want that house to be: big or small, one story or two, in the city or in the country. You'd have a "vision" of your future home. The same is true when building a company: You need a vision of what you hope to achieve.

When you imagine your business, what do you hope for? To make a lot of money? Use your creativity? Have more flexibility in your life? Do you see yourself working alone or building a company with employees? Do you hope your company grows very large or do you want it to stay small?

As you launch your new company, it's important to clarify and evaluate your business concept. What is your long-term vision? What are your personal goals? What do you see as the business opportunity? From that, how do you define your business specifics—what it does, whom it serves, how it differs from the competition?

Some entrepreneurs describe themselves as "visionaries" because they can conceive of grand schemes or bold new inventions. They envision their companies clobbering the competition, defining new product categories, perhaps growing to hundreds of millions—if not billions—of dollars.

Check It Out

For a list of the most popular sole proprietor businesses in the U.S., go to the Census Bureau's nonemployee statistics: **www.census.gov/econ/ nonemployer**

MY PERSONAL GOALS: THE FOUR Cs

Make copies of this worksheet for yourself and your partners or key employees, if any.
Check the level of importance to you in each area.

	Extremely Important	Somewhat Important	Somewhat Unimportant	Not Important
Creativity				
Determining the design or look of products/packaging	☐	☐	☐	☐
Creating new products or services	☐	☐	☐	☐
Devising new business procedures/policies	☐	☐	☐	☐
Identifying new company opportunities	☐	☐	☐	☐
Creating new business materials	☐	☐	☐	☐
Devising new ways of doing "old" things	☐	☐	☐	☐
Other:	☐	☐	☐	☐
Control	☐	☐	☐	☐
Over own work responsibilities	☐	☐	☐	☐
Over own time, work hours, etc.	☐	☐	☐	☐
Over company decisions and directions	☐	☐	☐	☐
Over products/services	☐	☐	☐	☐
Over other employees	☐	☐	☐	☐
Over work environment	☐	☐	☐	☐
Over social/environmental impact of products/services	☐	☐	☐	☐
Over own future and business' future	☐	☐	☐	☐
Other:	☐	☐	☐	☐
Challenge	☐	☐	☐	☐
Long-term problem solving	☐	☐	☐	☐
Critical problem solving (putting out fires)	☐	☐	☐	☐
Handling many issues at one time	☐	☐	☐	☐
Continually dealing with new issues	☐	☐	☐	☐
Perfecting solutions, products, or services	☐	☐	☐	☐
Organizing diverse projects and keeping the group goal-focused	☐	☐	☐	☐
Other:	☐	☐	☐	☐

Cash

List approximate dollar ranges for the following. Measure wealth as the value of stocks or of the company.

Wealth desired in 2–5 years _____   Income needed currently _____

Wealth desired in 6–10 years _____   Income desired in 1–2 years _____

Wealth desired in 10+ years _____   Income desired in 2–5 years _____

But a business "vision" doesn't have to be revolutionary. The important part is that you identify what you see your business becoming: what it will do or make, how it will grow and compete, how big it will get.

Over time, your business vision will almost certainly change. As you gain experience and confidence, you may change the nature of your products or services, your personal goals may evolve, and the things that seem most important to you now may be much less so in the next few years.

Nevertheless, clarifying your current business vision and articulating your specific business concept gives you a stronger start as you begin building your company. Use the "Goals for Starting My Business" worksheet on page 4 as a starting place for defining your business goals.

 ## Identify your personal goals

What are your personal goals in growing your business? Some businesses fail, and others flounder, because their founders or executives are uncertain of what they really want to achieve, and they don't structure the company and their responsibilities in ways that satisfy their personal needs and ambitions.

The Four Cs

For most entrepreneurs, their personal goals can be summed up by the Four Cs: Creativity, Control, Challenge, and Cash. Of course, we each want all four of these to some degree, but knowing which we most want or need can help us structure our companies to best achieve our goals.

For instance, my very first clients were the owners of a small sportswear apparel company. The designer began the business because she was good at—and loved—designing clothes. Her primary motivation was being able to act on her creativity. But an apparel company doesn't run on designs alone. There is a myriad of purely "business" aspects of the company—sales, operations, manufacturing, etc. If she hadn't planned for it, she might have spent the majority of her time on such issues instead of designing. Fortunately, she had a partner to take over those responsibilities. She gave up some control—which wasn't a major concern of hers—to maintain her creativity.

Which of the Four Cs motivates you most?

- **Creativity.** Entrepreneurs want to leave their mark. Their companies are not only a means of making a living, but a way of creating something that bears their stamp. Creativity comes in many forms, from designing a new "thing," to devising a new business process or even a new way to make sales, handle customers, or reward employees.

If you have a high need for creativity, make certain you remain involved in the creative process as your company develops. You'll want to shape your business so it's not just an instrument for earning an income but also a way for maintaining your creative stimulation and making a larger contribution to society. But don't overpersonalize your company, especially if it's large. Allow room for others, particularly partners and key personnel, to share in the creative process.

■ **Control.** Most of us start businesses because we want more control over our own lives. Perhaps we want more control over how our good ideas are implemented. Perhaps we want, or need, more control of our work hours or conditions so we can be more involved in family, community, or even golf! Control is a major motivator for most entrepreneurs—usually more important than money. But how much control you need—especially on a day-to-day basis—directly influences how large your company can be.

If you need or want a great deal of control over your time, you'll most likely need to keep your company smaller. In a large company, you have less immediate control over many decisions. If you're a person who needs control, you can still grow your business larger. You'll need to structure communication and reporting systems to ensure that you have sufficient information about and direction over developments, to give you personal satisfaction. If you seek outside funding in the form of investors, understand the nature of control your funders will have and be certain you are comfortable with these arrangements.

■ **Challenge.** If you're starting or expanding a business, it's clear you like challenge—at least to some degree. You're likely to be a problem-solver and risk-taker, enjoying the task of figuring out solutions to problems or devising new undertakings. Challenge-hungry entrepreneurs can be some of the most successful businesspeople, but they can also be their own worst enemies—flitting from one thing to another, never focusing long enough to succeed.

If you have a high need for challenge in your business life, it's important to develop positive means to meet this need, especially once your company is established and the initial challenge of starting a company is met. Otherwise, you may find yourself continually starting new projects that divert attention from your company's main goals. As you plan your company, establish goals that not only provide you with sufficient stimulation, but also advance—rather than distract from—the growth of your business. (Or take up skydiving on the side!)

■ **Cash.** Every entrepreneur wants to make money. Perhaps it's just enough money to provide a decent income; perhaps it's so much money you can buy a jet. How much you want or need affects how you'll develop your business. Will you need investors, and when? Will you sacrifice control to grow the business quickly?

Keep in mind there are sometimes trade-offs between personal goals: Wanting more cash often means having less control; staying at the center of the creative process may mean you need to have a partner or grow slowly, once again trading off control or cash. Examine your personal goals and those of key personnel using "The Four Cs" worksheet on page 6.

Spell out your business values

As we build our companies, we have goals not only for what our business will help us achieve for us, but also for how our business will impact others: our employees, customers, the environment, our communities.

For many entrepreneurs, the business values they want their company to project are part of their inspiration for getting started in the first place.

Incorporating your values into your business will help you build a company that gives you greater satisfaction in the long term and, quite possibly, a more successful company as well. Having a company that ascribes to and practices certain positive values can be a competitive advantage in attracting and retaining employees and in developing customer loyalty.

Be cautious, however, that as you build your business around your values, you do not impose your personal beliefs (especially religious or political beliefs) on others.

To help clarify the values you'd like to incorporate into your business, use the "My Business Values" worksheet on page 10.

Check It Out

Many businesses foster social responsibility in their organizations through volunteer work. You can find opportunities for donating your time—and your team's—at Volunteer Match (**www.volunteermatch. org**).

MY BUSINESS VALUES

Describe what values are important to you in building your company as they relate to:

☐ Corporate Culture and nature of the work environment (management/employee relations and communication, work hours and flexibility, dress code, office location, decor, etc.):

☐ Business Ethics (customer treatment; relations with vendors, distributors, competitors; advertising, etc.):

☐ Employee Treatment (wages and benefits, layoff policies, promotions, empowerment, etc.):

☐ Community and Civic Involvement:

☐ The Environment:

☐ Other:

MY ROLE MODELS

Use this space to list the names of people you admire, whether they're in business or not.

Name and Job or Role	What traits of theirs do you admire?	How could you incorporate those traits in your business?

✔ Remind yourself of your source of inspiration

Check It Out

What are the qualities of a successful entrepreneur? Read Rhonda's "Think Like an Entrepreneur" article **www. planningshop.com/ thinkentrepreneur**

At some point in their business lives, all entrepreneurs are inspired—by an idea, a person, or an opportunity. That inspiration not only gets you started; it also keeps you going. You may reach a point down the road when you ask yourself, "Why did I start all this?" Reread what you've written here when you need to be "re-inspired," or just to get a reminder of what your goals were from the beginning.

The worksheets in this section are also the starting point for articulating your business concept and identifying your niche and customer base.

My role models

Do you want to be another Bill Gates? Do you see yourself as a future Oprah Winfrey? Or do you look up to your uncle who ran his own store or your older sister who has been self-employed for 10 years?

Many of us are fortunate enough to know of people in business whom we admire or would like to emulate. You may know them personally, or you may have read about their business practices or success.

Thinking about your role models can help you clarify your own business vision. If your business hero is Bill Gates, what about him do you admire? His ability to make a great deal of money? Build a huge business? His marketing and strategic capabilities? Or do you admire his technical knowledge?

Take a moment to think about whom your business role models are, by completing the "My Role Models" worksheet on page 11.

My "bright idea"

What excites you about your business idea? If you have two or three ideas, what do you like best about each one? Where did the idea come from? How has it evolved since you started the process of turning the idea into a business?

By looking at how you initially got the inspiration for your business, you can take the next step toward determining how you might get others excited about your business also. That's the start of taking an idea and turning it into a plan, which becomes a successful business. You will also

MY "BRIGHT IDEA"

Use this space to record your initial business idea(s). This will become a starting point for defining your business concept and why it can be competitive in the marketplace (on page 14). It will also be useful as you prepare your marketing materials and write your "Elevator Pitch" in Week Six.

☐ **What is your business idea?**

☐ **How did you come up with it?**

☐ **What excites you about it?**

MY BUSINESS CONCEPT

Answering the following questions will help you clarify your concept:

☐ Is yours a retail, service, manufacturing, distribution, or Internet business?

☐ What industry does it belong to?

☐ What products or services do you sell?

☐ What improved features/services or added value do you provide? What makes you unique or special?

☐ Whom do you see as your potential customers?

☐ What is your overall marketing and sales strategy?

☐ Which companies (or types of companies) do you think of as your competition?

☐ What do you think will make customers buy from you instead of your competitors?

find it useful to have a record of what initially inspired you, to which you can refer from time to time, especially as your business grows. Use the worksheet on page 13 to record your initial business idea.

 ## Describe your business concept

Meeting needs is the basis of all business. You can devise a wonderful new machine, but if it doesn't address some real and important need or desire, people won't buy it, and your business will fail. Even Thomas Edison recognized this fact when he said, "Anything that won't sell, I don't want to invent."

Identify needs

Now that you know what your spark and passion is regarding your idea, use the worksheet on page 14 to determine how your product or service will meet new or existing needs in the marketplace.

A concept's success often hinges on whether it does something newer or better than anyone else. Being new or better can take many forms:

- **Something new.** A new product, service, feature, or technology.

- **Something better.** This could be an improvement on an existing product or service—encompassing more features, lower price, greater reliability, faster speed, increased convenience, or enhanced technology.

- **An underserved or new market.** This is a market for which there is greater demand than competitors can currently satisfy, an unserved location, or a small part of an overall market—a niche market—that hasn't yet been dominated by other competitors. Sometimes, markets become underserved when large companies abandon or neglect smaller portions of their current customer base.

- **New delivery system or distribution channel.** For example, the Internet enables companies to reach customers more efficiently, creating opportunities for businesses to provide products or services less expensively, or with far greater choice, to a wider geographic area.

- **Increased integration.** This occurs when a product is both manufactured and sold by the same company, or when a company offers more services or products in one location.

BASIC BUSINESS DESCRIPTION

Use this worksheet to develop a description for your business.
For example, a finished description might read:

"AAA, Inc., is a spunky, imaginative food products and service company aimed at offering high-quality, moderately priced, occasionally unusual foods made with only natural ingredients. We view ourselves as partners with our customers, our employees, our community, and our environment, and we take personal responsibility in our actions toward each. We aim to become a regionally recognized brand name, capitalizing on the sustained interest in southwestern and Mexican food. Our goals are moderate growth, annual profitability, and maintaining our sense of humor."

Describe the following in one sentence:

☐ Core business concept:

☐ Core business values:

☐ Core business goals:

☐ Core financial goals:

☐ Corporate culture:

Now combine these sentences into one comprehensive statement. You will revisit and rewrite it several times, but you'll need a succinct business description for your business plan, investors, employees, and others, so get something on paper now.

Your concept should be strong in at least one area. If it isn't, you should ask yourself how your company will be truly competitive.

Outline specifics

OK, so you have your inspiration, and you've seen an opportunity in the market…now how do those translate into your particular business concept? Exactly what are you going to sell? To whom? How?

The "Basic Business Description" worksheet on page 16 helps you outline the specifics of your business as you see them at this early point. You'll be more successful if you have a clear concept of critical business aspects such as your target market, competition, industry, and so on.

Don't worry if you aren't entirely certain about the answers to your "Basic Business Description." Fill in the answers anyway. You'll use these specifics to guide the research you'll do in Week Two, and you'll continue to refine your business concept as you go along.

Identify your strategic position

The late Eugene Kleiner, one of the world's most successful venture capitalists, once told me that most companies don't know what business they're in. By this he meant that most businesspeople don't understand the true basis on which they compete. Yes, they know how to make their products and invent their technologies, but they don't really understand what makes their customers buy from them.

Today, defining a strategic position is as important for the proverbial "mom and pop" small business as it is for a high-technology company. It's not enough to hang out a shingle that says, "I sell shoes," or "I sell ecommerce technology." You must have something that's unique, that few others can offer, that makes your customers want to buy from you.

You have to understand how you meaningfully differentiate yourself from the competition—your strategic position in the marketplace.

Of course, the best strategic position is just to be better than the competition—the tennis racket you've invented enables players to hit harder, the graphic designs you create are more memorable. But those things are often a matter of judgment and hard to prove.

So, how do you develop a clear distinction between yourself and the competition? Your company's strategic position can be based on:

- **Serving a specific niche in the market**
- **Unique features of your product or service**
- **Exceptional customer service**
- **Price**
- **Convenience, or**
- **Anything that significantly distinguishes you from others who offer similar services or products.**

The more you understand about your own company—and how you differ from others—the better able you are to compete.

Decide whether you want partners

Hewlett and Packard. Ben and Jerry. Great partnerships often make great companies. But just as often, bad partnerships destroy good companies.

Nothing affects your day-to-day work life more than the people you work with. Yes, work can be satisfying when you have challenging tasks, play with cool technology, or make lots of money. But whether or not you feel like getting out of bed in the morning can be greatly influenced by whom you'll work with that day.

Partners not only affect your mood but your bottom line as well. They share, or may even control, ownership of your company. Spend time getting to know the business skills, attitudes, and aspirations of any potential partners—even if you've been friends or acquaintances for many years. Find out whether their goals, work style, and values fit yours.

If you are going to take on a partner, carefully consider why you want or need one. As you start your business, you may feel uncertain about being on your own, but that feeling of uncertainty may pass quickly. A partner will be around for a long, long time. Remember, partners own a piece of the business. Even if you bring in someone with only a minority interest as a partner, your future is tied to them.

Make certain your partnership expectations are realistic. Are your partners willing to work as hard as you? Do they bring the same level of talent or skill (although perhaps in a different area) as you? Do they have the same long-term view of where they want to be?

You have more leeway, legally, to ask questions of potential partners than of employees. Of course, make certain your potential partner is honest, but also examine their personal attitudes, how they handle stress, how much money they need and how soon, family or other demands on their time, and any other issues that may affect your working relationship.

The best way to take on a partner is with clear-cut definitions of responsibilities and authority. It's nice to believe you will make every decision together, but that's not realistic. Who, in the end, gets to call the shots? And be careful about going into business with a friend—often both the business and the friendship suffer.

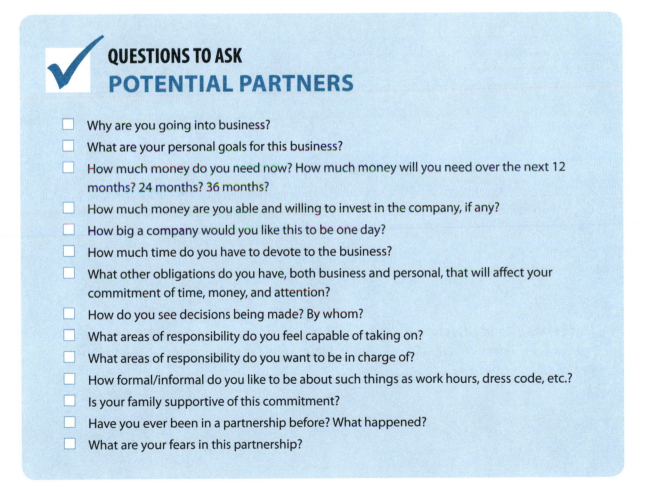

✔ QUESTIONS TO ASK
POTENTIAL PARTNERS

- ☐ Why are you going into business?
- ☐ What are your personal goals for this business?
- ☐ How much money do you need now? How much money will you need over the next 12 months? 24 months? 36 months?
- ☐ How much money are you able and willing to invest in the company, if any?
- ☐ How big a company would you like this to be one day?
- ☐ How much time do you have to devote to the business?
- ☐ What other obligations do you have, both business and personal, that will affect your commitment of time, money, and attention?
- ☐ How do you see decisions being made? By whom?
- ☐ What areas of responsibility do you feel capable of taking on?
- ☐ What areas of responsibility do you want to be in charge of?
- ☐ How formal/informal do you like to be about such things as work hours, dress code, etc.?
- ☐ Is your family supportive of this commitment?
- ☐ Have you ever been in a partnership before? What happened?
- ☐ What are your fears in this partnership?

DISCUSSING PARTNERSHIP TERMS

Use this worksheet to determine with your partners the terms of your partnership.
Then meet with a lawyer to draw up a formal partnership agreement.

☐ **Ownership Division.** Who owns what percent of the business?

☐ **Jobs/Responsibilities.** What jobs and responsibilities does each partner have? Can partners work for any other company or do any other work on the side?

☐ **Decisions.** How will general business decisions be made? What decisions does each partner have final authority on? Who has the final authority for decisions for the company as a whole?

☐ **Communication.** How will you communicate on a regular basis? How will serious disputes be resolved?

☐ **Exit Strategy and Dissolution Agreement.** What happens if one partner wants to leave the business or move? What if one partner wants to sell the company? What happens if a partner dies or becomes disabled?

☐ **Other:**

If you're going into business with other people, even a spouse or friend, formalize your arrangement with a written partnership agreement. Take the time to work out as many details as you can. Be certain to include a way to buy each other (or each other's heirs) out of the business. A messy "divorce" from a business partner is as difficult as a messy marital divorce—with potentially greater financial consequences. Drawing up an agreement now will help avoid difficulties if you later decide to go your separate ways.

Use the guide "Questions to Ask: Potential Partners" on page 19 to discuss the nature of your relationship. The worksheet "Discussing Partnership Terms" on page 20 outlines important issues that can later become part of a formal agreement, drawn up with the help of a lawyer.

Decide whether you want investors

You may have heard that it's best to start a business using OPM—"Other People's Money." But don't just rush out looking for investors. Choosing to get an investor is a big decision.

You are almost always tied to your investors for the life of your business. Remember, there usually isn't any easy way out of a relationship with an investor; in fact, if you have to come to a parting of the ways, your investors may have more ability to get rid of you than you will have to get rid of them. So proceed carefully!

Don't forget—investors legally own a piece of your business, and they have certain rights under the law. Not only are they entitled to a share of your profits but they have other rights as well. They are also entitled to a share of your losses for tax purposes. The involvement of investors makes dealing with legal issues, decision-making, taxes, and many other matters more complicated and expensive. And if things go wrong, having investors can make everything a lot messier.

If you decide you absolutely need investors, make certain you spend as much time as possible getting to know any potential investor—after all, you'll be tied to each other for a long time. It's unlikely you can ask as many probing questions of a potential investor as you can a potential partner, because investors usually view the investment process as an examination of you—not the other way around. Nevertheless, find out if they've invested in other companies before. If so, speak to other entrepreneurs who've worked with them. What are their financial and business motivations for investing? Are

Check It Out

To start your search for funding from an angel investor, check out the Angel Capital Association (**www.angelcapitalas-sociation.com**) or The Angels' Forum (**www.angelsforum.com**). The National Venture Capital Association (**www.nvca.org**) represents the venture capital industry in the U.S.

RED TAPE ALERT!

Even if you never use the word "partner," if you and a friend decide to start selling used golf balls online together, in the eyes of the law you've become partners. The best way for things to stay friendly between partners is to have a clearly defined partnership agreement before you begin the company. Prepare a legally binding contract spelling out the terms of your partnership: who owns what percent, how decisions are made, what happens to the company if one or more of the partners wishes to leave, how and whether additional partners can be added, and so on. It is also advisable to work out a "Buy/Sell" agreement, so the terms of how and to whom a partner can leave or sell their interest in the business are clear. You may want provisions limiting their ability to sell their interest to others and, in the case of a partner's death or disability, to have other partners buy out their heirs at a fair price—you don't necessarily want to wind up running the business with your partners' spouse or child.

those goals a good fit with your own? How much control do they want in the business?

Of course, when you need money to start a business, you may feel lucky to get the money you need from anyone. But over time, if you have a fearful, intrusive, or controlling investor, you may soon regret being involved with them.

If you decide you need investors, you'll find more information in Week Five, including Questions to Ask before you accept financing (page 232) and a worksheet with an Investor Comparison Chart (pages 234–235).

 Consider potential exit strategies

When you build a business, you don't spend a lot of time envisioning how you'll eventually get out of it. Oh, maybe you think one day you'll make enough money to retire, but while you can envision yourself sailing or gardening, what's happened to your company? You need an "exit plan."

An exit plan is a long-term strategy for transferring ownership of your company to others. The idea of thinking of an exit when you're just starting out may seem incongruous. After all, you hardly know what you're going to be doing next month; why try to figure out what you're going to do with your company 10 or 20 years from now?

If you're looking for an investor in your company, they'll want to know your long-term goals and will ask you to spell out an exit strategy. They want to know how they'll get their money back.

If you're going to have a partner, then discussing your exit strategy reduces the friction that comes when you have unspoken but differing exit assumptions. You may hope to grow the business substantially and later sell, while they may want to maintain the business at a modest level and perhaps someday have a relative take over.

Even if you own the company yourself and hope to have it last through the ages, an exit plan helps direct the growth of your company. If, for instance, you would ideally like to be acquired by a larger company, you might target your product development and marketing efforts in ways that would interest acquiring companies.

There are a number of ways you can exit your company or have the value of the company become "liquid":

- **Sell.** This is often the simplest way to get value out. All types of companies can be sold, not just retail or manufacturing enterprises. Professional practices are "bought into" by new partners, or a one-person consulting business can be sold to someone who wants a built-in customer base.

- **Be acquired.** Your company may be a good fit for a larger company that wants the part of the market, capabilities, or technologies you have developed.

- **Merge.** This is similar to being acquired, but the assets of the merging companies form a new entity.

- **"Go public."** When you issue shares in your company that are traded in a stock market—an initial public offering (IPO)—it is referred to as "going public." This doesn't necessarily mean you depart from management of the company, but you now have a way to get money for your ownership interest by selling some of your personal shares.

- **Arrange for family members to take over.** When Levi Strauss started selling blue jeans, he probably didn't envision a family-owned company bearing his name 160 years later. Even if you know you'd like this to happen, you need a plan. Your family members might not want to run your company, or be capable of doing so.

RED TAPE ALERT! A no-interest loan from a friend or family member may face what's called "imputed interest" by the U.S. Internal Revenue Service. If the IRS views the loan as a gift, the lender will have to pay taxes on the money if it's more than the maximum allowed by law. All lenders must charge an interest rate that reflects a fair market value.

- **Employee buyout.** An excellent way to keep your company together and to retain the jobs you've created is to structure a way for either key management or employees as a whole to buy the company. An "ESOP"—Employee Stock Ownership Plan—can help them finance the purchase and give you the cash you need.

- **Go out of business.** This is the easiest exit (assuming you have no debts or major employee commitments), but you also get the least financial reward. Sometimes though, you just want to close up shop and get on with the rest of your life.

 ## Discuss the impact of starting a business with your family

When you launch a business, it has an impact on everyone around you, especially your family. You'll almost certainly have to make financial sacrifices, spend less free time with those closest to you, and have more things on your mind than before you started. If you're married, owning a business may have legal and/or tax implications for your spouse.

Sit down and fully discuss your plans with the other people in your life who may be directly affected. Help them to understand what you see as the opportunities, while at the same time being clear about the potential risks and probable sacrifices.

Ask for their input, too. They may have suggestions of ways they can be supportive. In most small businesses, family members frequently lend a hand. Allow them to share some of their fears or concerns so you get a realistic idea of what's on their minds. Discuss ways to make certain that your family responsibilities are met even while you build your business. Make them feel a part of your new, exciting adventure.

Be careful, however, about asking for loans or investments from family or close friends—you may risk both the business and the personal relationship. Of course, there are exceptions: If the person understands the nature of your business, truly appreciates the risks, and is someone with whom you can communicate well, the situation may work. *Always* have loan or investment papers drawn up with the terms of the repayment or investment absolutely clear.

You can find more information about getting and working with investors in Week Five.

Make an appointment with an SBDC counselor

One of the best, least-known services provided by the U.S. Government to small businesses is a national network of Small Business Development Centers (SBDCs). There are over 1,000 SBDCs, located primarily at universities and community colleges.

SBDCs provide free one-on-one counseling and low-cost training programs to small businesses and start-up entrepreneurs. SBDC counselors are trained professionals; most have run small businesses themselves as well as having expertise in particular aspects of management.

Almost all SBDC locations also maintain libraries with books and other materials to assist you in planning and running your business.

SBDCs serve over 700,000 small businesses a year in face-to-face counseling and training sessions, and another 500,000 businesses turn to them for information, resources, and call-in assistance. They've been doing this for more than 30 years.

SBDCs offer assistance with many of the following:

- **Understanding local and state business laws and regulations**
- **Sources of market and competitive research**
- **Business plan development guidance**
- **Computer software training programs**
- **Budgeting**

Years ago, I turned to an SBDC for assistance in doing a trademark search (this was before the Internet made it easy to do a first-level search). The SBDC staff was helpful, supportive, and encouraging.

Check It Out

Great sources of advice for entrepreneurs include the publisher of this book, PlanningShop (**www.PlanningShop. com**), the Edward Lowe Foundation (**www. edwardlowe.org**), the National Association for the Self-Employed (**www. nase.org**), SCORE: Service Corps of Retired Executives (**www.score.org**), and the Small Business Administration of the U.S. Government (**www.sba. gov**).

Check It Out

Start here to find your local Small Business Development Center office. **www.asbdc-us. org**

SBDC counselors can assist you not only as you start your business, but as you grow your business as well.

I highly recommend checking out your local SBDC sooner rather than later. You can find a link to a list of SBDCs online or check your local White Pages listings. Set up an appointment with a counselor to discuss your business and business research, and for ongoing guidance as your business grows.

ACCOMPLISHMENT #2:

Create your company identity

My Checklist:

- ☐ **Choose a name**
- ☐ **Check out trademarks**
- ☐ **Secure a domain name**
- ☐ **Consider logos, taglines, and colors**
- ☐ **Get a graphic designer**

Right from Week One, you're going to be eager to begin working on one of the most challenging and creative aspects of starting your own business—developing your company identity: name, image, logo, tagline, and so on.

Coming up with a company identity can be fun, creative, and exciting. But if you're not careful, it can also paralyze you. You may think that finding just the *right* name or logo is absolutely critical for success.

Please don't let this process overwhelm you. While choosing the right name and image for your company *is* important, it doesn't determine your company's future. After all, not many people would consider names such as "Microsoft," "Safeway," or the "Walt Disney Company" as being particularly inspired or critical to the company's eventual success.

Nevertheless, creating your company identity certainly is an important part of getting your business under way. Your corporate identity helps customers remember you, understand what you do, and even develop a certain feeling about you. Your company name and logo make your business feel "real," both to you and to potential customers, suppliers, and others. Your identity is your brand image.

The key elements to a corporate identity are:

- **Name**
- **Logo**
- **Tagline**
- **Colors**

In addition, you might have other unique, distinguishing elements that make up your identity, such as clever or unusual packaging.

Once you've developed a certain identity, you'll use those elements consistently and repeatedly—on your business cards, stationery, signs, advertising, vehicles, uniforms, and website.

Creating an identity can be done very inexpensively or cost thousands of dollars. You may want to use the services of a graphic designer to help you create your logo and other aspects of your company's image.

 ## Choose a name

I collect cute business names: "All You Knead" (a bakery), "The Barking Lot" (a dog groomer), "Shear Ecstasy" (a hair salon). A clever business name can be an excellent marketing tool—helping make your company memorable—but coming up with a good name can seem frustrating. Big companies spend thousands of dollars researching names, and sometimes even they fail.

In small companies, *you* are the brand, and usually the best name for your company is your own, perhaps adding a descriptive phrase to clarify what you do. My first business was called "Abrams Business Strategies" since I developed business and marketing plans.

If you plan on growing your business substantially though, you may not want to use your own name, or any person's name. Having a name closely associated with the owner may later make a company harder to sell and can create expectations among customers that they will be getting personal attention from the owner.

BUSINESS NAME COMPARISON CHART

Questions	Name	Name
☐ What are the business names you have considered so far?		
☐ What about the name tells your customers what you do?		
☐ What about the name tells your customers what they get?		
☐ What about the name conveys a feeling? What kind of feeling?		
☐ Are the names already trade-marked by another business?		
☐ Are there companies with similar or confusing names?		
☐ Was the name trademarked in a different category? Which one? By whom?		
☐ Who likes the name? Why?		
☐ Who dislikes the name? Why?		
☐ Is the domain name (i.e., web address) available for this company name?		
☐ If the domain name is not available, is there another one that would work well with this company name?		
☐ Other comments/questions about each name:		

Name	Name	Name

A good company name achieves several goals:

■ **Communicates the correct information.** You want to avoid anything in your business name that could substantially confuse potential customers about what you do. So even if you think your name is crystal clear (e.g., Jim's Photo Services), ask a few other people if they can easily figure out what business you're in (e.g., do they think you take photos, process film, provide digital photo touch-ups?). A very clear company name, such as "Main Street Volvo Repair," immediately lets customers know what to expect, but watch out if your services later change or if you run into trademark problems—see below.

■ **Conveys the right feeling.** You generally want to choose a name with positive connotations: A day spa named "Haven" or "Oasis" transmits the sense that customers are going to escape the stresses in their lives. Even words such as "Main Street" or another location tells potential customers that the service is local and convenient.

■ **Won't get dated quickly.** Be careful not to choose names too closely identified with recent trends or that are too limiting. You are likely to change the scope of your products or services over time. Look at all those ecommerce companies that had to drop the words "dot com" from their company names. When Twentieth Century Fox Film Studios was founded in 1935 (merging Fox and Twentieth Century studios), the name "Twentieth Century" seemed associated with the idea of something young and new. Of course, by the end of that century, it no longer seemed fresh, and the company now uses just the name "Fox" for some of its entertainment units.

■ **Is easy to spell.** If a name is too hard to spell, it becomes harder for a potential customer to remember. Spelling becomes even more important when you use your company's name as part of your website domain name or if you're in a business where clients have to spell your company's name often.

■ **Is easy to pronounce.** People have a harder time remembering names they can't say easily, and they feel uncomfortable doing business with companies whose names they can't pronounce.

■ **Is memorable.** Obviously, if clients or customers have an easier time remembering your name, they're more likely to do business with you again. A memorable name isn't absolutely necessary or always even possible. In fact, a company with a straightforward name, such as "Des Moines Chiropractic Clinic" may develop a better business than a company with a cute name like "Back Attack."

In the end, however, one of the most important considerations is whether *you* like the name and feel comfortable with it. After all, you're the one who will see it and say it the most.

Most important, don't get stuck trying to decide on your name, slowing down the start of your business. At some point, you just need to make a choice and get on with it.

Use the worksheet on pages 28–29 to compare some of the names you're thinking of for your business, and their pros and cons.

 ## Check out trademarks

You're thrilled! You've settled on a name for your new breakfast cereal company: "Yummy Tummy." You've even invented a cartoon character, "Yummy Tummy Tillie," to symbolize your brand. You're ready to set the world on fire!

Not so fast. Before you can make your company a household name, you need to make sure you can use and protect that name. You don't want to invest money and time building "brand equity"—value associated with the name of your company—just to discover someone else is already using "Yummy Tummy."

That's where trademark laws come in. There are two primary kinds of trademarks:

- **Trademark**
- **Service mark**

When you acquire the rights to a trademark or service mark, you get legal protection from other companies' using your company's name, logos, taglines, or other distinctive marks on competing products or services.

Even when you are granted a trademark, you don't "own" the name in all instances. As part of the trademark application process, you'll indicate the specific category or categories of products or services for which you'll use the name. For instance, if you're using "Yummy Tummy" for breakfast cereal, someone else could get the rights to use the same name for unrelated products or services—a weight-loss program, for instance.

ABOUT TRADEMARKS

What is a trademark or service mark?

■ A **trademark** is a word, phrase, symbol, or design, or a combination of words, phrases, symbols, or designs, that identifies and distinguishes the source of the goods of one party from those of others.

■ A **service mark** is the same as a trademark, except that it identifies and distinguishes the source of a service rather than a product. The USPTO uses the terms "trademark" and "mark" to refer to both trademarks and service marks. [In Canada, a trademark can be used for either a product or a service.]

Is registration of my mark required?

No. You can establish rights in a mark based on its legitimate use. But in the United States, owning a federal trademark registration on the Principal Register secures the following advantages:

■ Constructive notice to the public of the registrant's claim of ownership of the mark;

■ A legal presumption of the registrant's ownership of the mark and the registrant's exclusive right to use the mark nationwide on or in connection with the goods and/or services listed in the registration;

■ The ability to bring an action concerning the mark in federal court;

■ The use of the U.S. registration as a basis to obtain registration in foreign countries; and

■ The ability to file the U.S. registration with the U.S. Customs Service to prevent importation of infringing foreign goods.

When can I use the trademark symbols TM, SM and ®?

Any time you claim rights in a mark, you may use the "TM" (trademark) or "SM" (service mark) designation to alert the public to your claim, regardless of whether you have filed an application with the USPTO. However, you may use the federal registration symbol "®" only after the USPTO actually registers a mark, and not while an application is pending. Also, you may use the registration symbol with the mark only on or in connection with the goods and/or services listed in the federal trademark registration.

—*from the U.S. Patent and Trademark Office*

WEEK ONE | 33

There are, of course, limits to what you can trademark. Indeed, it's often frustrating to find that you can't trademark the simplest names. That's because the U.S. Patent and Trademark Office requires a mark to be "distinctive" and not simply "descriptive." For instance, you can't get a trademark for a health resort called "Spa," because it's merely descriptive. But you almost certainly could trademark the name "Spa" for a brand of body lotions (assuming it wasn't already trademarked by someone else).

In fact, if you're inventing a whole new product category, you may need to come up with a generic way to describe the category in order to trademark your chosen name. A client of mine, Patrick McConnell, invented a dry-land snowboard, which he called the MountainBoard. To get that name trademarked, however, Patrick had to come up with a generic term—"all-terrain board"—to avoid his brand name's being viewed as merely descriptive.

Doing a trademark search

Getting the trademark process under way is fairly simple, but you'll want to discuss the trademark process when you see an attorney (Week Three), as well as discussing other protections of your "intellectual property"— such as copyrights and patents.

To get started on your name and trademark search, begin at the website of the U.S. Patent and Trademark Office. Find the section for Trademarks and follow the links for "Search."

Try different ways to search ("New User Form," "Structured Form," etc.) to see the various results. Begin by searching as broadly as possible—singular and plural forms of your words, similar words, alternate spellings, and so on. Results may show both "live" and "dead" marks. Dead marks are those that previous owners have let lapse.

Keep in mind that even if a particular name or mark does not show up as being taken, this does not necessarily mean you will be able to trademark the name/mark. Some names may already be in use in interstate commerce but may not have been officially registered. Other names/marks may not be allowed to be registered as trademarks. So don't print up thousands of dollars worth of brochures just yet!

And remember, you may run into difficulty if you use a name that is similar to a bigger, better-known company even if you think you can get a trademark. McDonald's, for instance, has been very effective in keeping

Check It Out

Start your trademark search at the U.S. Patent and Trademark Office website, **www.uspto.gov**

In Canada, you can do a trademark search on the website of the Canadian Intellectual Property Office, **www.cipo.ic. gc.ca**

others from using the "Mc" as a prefix for many different kinds of products and companies. A juice bar company was able to keep other juice bars from using names starting with the letter "J" just by taking them to court. Often, it's the company with the biggest bank account and most lawyers, rather than the ones with the law on their side, that controls a name or trademark.

If you are going to spend a great deal of money investing in a name and trademark, you might consider using a professional trademark search firm or hiring a trademark attorney to conduct a more complete search.

 ## Secure a domain name

An important part of choosing a business name and getting a trademark is researching the website addresses that are available. Before the Internet, you might have happily been able to do business in one state without being confused with a business using the same name in another one. Today, however, you need a "domain name" that is utterly unique, not just in your city or state, but in the world.

A "domain name" is the name by which your website is identified and found. It is also known as your company's URL (which stands for universal resource locator).

To find out if your preferred URL has already been claimed by another company, you can check with any of the companies that host websites or with the Network Solutions website, www.networksolutions.com. (Network Solutions was one of the original official keepers of the domain name registry.) Type into the WebAddress search box up to 10 names you'd like to use, including the suffix (three-letter code such as .com, .net, .org) you'd prefer. For example, if your desired company name is Widget Manufacturers, type in widget.com.

Don't be disappointed if your desired business name (even your trade-marked name) has already been taken. Today it's increasingly difficult to find a website name that exactly matches your business name. With so many companies vying for valuable virtual real estate around the world, chances are good that another organization has already claimed what you would consider the perfect URL. And then there are "cyber squatters"—those people (or organizations) that have bought domain names with the intent of selling them to businesses that might want them later. It might not seem right, but even if you get a trademark for your business name,

Check It Out

Sites you can use to register your domain name include Network Solutions (**www.network-solutions.com**), Google Apps (**www.google.com/enterprise/apps/business**), and Intuit (**www.intuit.com/domain-name-registration/**).

someone else may legally own the right to that domain name, especially since companies can have the same trademark name in different categories.

Try to find a domain name that is as close as possible to your desired company name. Use the entire company name, for example, widgetmanufacturing.com, or adding a "co" or "inc" to the end of the name—i.e., widgetmanufacturinginc.com—if the basic URL is taken. And you can choose a different suffix, such as widget.net, to distinguish your URL from one with the more popular .com suffix.

Although a domain name is only as good as the marketing budget—and the business—that it is attached to, it is, for most, a critical part of doing business. Some people even modify their company names slightly to make sure they can get a domain name that works for them. And, of course, you can always investigate who owns your perfect domain name (by typing it into your browser) to see if it's for sale, and make an offer if it is.

Ultimately, however, the success of your business won't rise or fall on your domain name. You will have many other means for spreading the word about your business—business cards, brochures, networking events, advertising, word-of-mouth, and so forth. If customers like you and your company, they'll find you online.

 ## Consider logos, taglines, and colors

Your company identity consists of more than just your company name. The colors you choose, the typeface you use, and what kind of tagline and logo you develop (if any) convey a message to potential customers. Right from the beginning of your business, you should consider what message you want to send and select a corporate identity appropriate for the type of business you're starting. You should then use those elements of your corporate identity consistently throughout all your marketing and communication materials.

Logos

All of us are familiar with logos: the Nike "swoosh," McDonald's golden arches, Apple Computer's apple-with-a-bite, Target's red bull's-eye. A logo is an image associated with your company, giving the public another way to remember you.

Visual images make your company more memorable. There's a reason for this: People learn things and remember things in many different ways.

When prospective customers see your logo as well as see or hear your company's name, they're using more of their brains to process the information—both the verbal and the visual kind. So you make more of a mental impact when people associate you with both words and images.

A good logo conveys something positive about your company. The Target logo, for instance, is simple and elegant. It tells customers that Target stores are where they'll find exactly what they want at exactly the right price. The bull's-eye logo also suggests competitiveness, accuracy, and efficiency, traits that shoppers—and shareholders—will appreciate:

If you don't have the money to have a logo designed, an inexpensive way to add a visual element to your business name is to just add geometric elements: lines, squares, diamonds, and so on. In my first business—business consulting—I used three sideways triangles, suggesting to prospective clients that I would help them move their business forward:

A logo doesn't have to be a drawing or illustration—you can make an "illustration" of just words. This is called a "logotype," and it can be very effective. Think of Coca-Cola:

When we were developing a logo for this content company—PlanningShop—we wanted an image that would convey the message that products from PlanningShop enable people to "complete" their business planning projects. We decided that the concept of the last piece of a puzzle would visually convey that feeling of completion. Here's what we came up with:

PlanningShop™

Use the "Creating My Identity" worksheet on page 38 to make notes or drawings of possible logos for your business.

Taglines

Many companies use a motto or tagline either to better explain the nature of the business or to create a feeling about the company or product.

A tagline helps customers remember what is unique about your business:

- **"Personalized service at practical prices"**
- **"Legal services for the real estate industry"**

Taglines don't have to be "catchy" to be memorable to your target audience. "Manufacturers of packing materials for technology products" may seem boring but be very effective if you make and sell boxes for computers. This lets your potential customers know—and reminds current customers—that you specialize in exactly what they need.

Taglines can become the basis of your advertising and marketing pieces. Of course, you would use your tagline in all your advertising. But even if you don't have much of a marketing budget, you can use your tagline on your business cards, packaging, and stationery, even at the end of emails.

You don't have to have a tagline, and you certainly don't have to choose one before you even open your doors. But developing a tagline helps you clarify what makes your business special and enables you to sum up your competitive position in just a few words.

Colors

Many people start their businesses without giving colors much thought, and yet most of us intend to use some colors in our business—in our decor, on our business cards, brochures, packaging, website, and so on. What often happens is that you end up using one color for one thing (let's say a brochure), another color for something else (for your stationery, perhaps) and yet another color elsewhere (maybe your website).

The result? You lose the opportunity to develop a strong brand image for your company and perhaps even risk confusing your customer.

Instead, come up with a consistent use of color—your "color palette"—to give you another tool that reminds customers who you are and conveys a feeling about your company.

Some colors are associated with certain feelings. Blue is considered calming and reassuring, so banks and financial institutions often use blue.

Check It Out

The Color Marketing Group forecasts color trends for the next 12–18 months for a variety of industries. **www. colormarketing.org**

CREATING MY IDENTITY

Use the space below to begin developing your corporate identity. You may want to draw pictures, as well as use words and phrases, to develop the look, feel, and message you want to convey. You will continue this process in Week Six.

☐ Business name

☐ Tagline and keywords for marketing material

☐ Logo

☐ Colors

☐ Distinct product design

☐ Distinct packaging

☐ Decor, employee clothing, or other unique identifying features

While red is considered lucky for some ethnic groups, it's viewed as a sign of danger or action to others, so consider your target market. Other colors have developed different associations: pink is viewed as feminine, pastels are associated with babies. Colors also go through fads, so be careful to choose a color that won't be dated too quickly.

Since referring to colors just by generic names ("blue," "teal blue," and the like) is very imprecise, professionals use a system to identify particular colors. You'll want to learn the "PMS" numbers (which stands for "Pantone Matching System") of the specific color(s) you choose so you can give future printers and designers the exact colors you want.

Since you're likely to use your color palette on your website, keep in mind that some colors do not display well on computer monitors. Check your colors on several different monitors before finalizing your choice.

Be careful also about how many colors you use in your business. If you use too many, it can become expensive to print your stationery, business cards, packaging, and so on.

Write down your thoughts for logos, taglines, colors and other aspects of your corporate identity on the "Creating My Identity" worksheet on page 38.

Meet with a graphic designer

If you can afford it, you may want a graphic designer to help you create your corporate identity: logos, website, stationery, and so forth. Obviously, when you hire a graphic designer, you should look at their portfolio (samples of previous work for other clients) to see if you like their style and if they have the right background for you. But once you've committed yourself to working with a designer, the next step is to help them understand your vision.

Have the designer read the business concept and description statements you developed on pages 14 and 16. Give the designer a sense of your goals and values so they can consider them in the design. Show them other visual images you like so they can get a sense of your tastes and preferences.

Use the guide "Questions to Ask: Graphic Designers" on page 40 as a starting point. The more information you give your designer to work with, the better they can develop a corporate identity that works for you.

✔ **QUESTIONS TO ASK**
GRAPHIC DESIGNERS

Ask about:
- ☐ Their experience.
- ☐ How they handle the design process.
- ☐ Who's going to do the work? The person you meet, assistants, or others?
- ☐ What fees/costs are involved? What deliverables will you receive?

Ask for:
- ☐ At least three to five design options included in the initial fee.
- ☐ Both black-and-white and color digital versions of your identity system.
- ☐ Digital templates for all aspects of your identity system you select: business cards, stationery, fax cover sheets, etc.
- ☐ Color palette and numbers, both for print and for the Internet.
- ☐ A signed agreement giving you ownership and copyright of all designs (very important!).

Tell them:
- ☐ What the company name represents and what your company does.
- ☐ Whom your target market is: their ages, industries, and concerns.
- ☐ How you want your customers to feel about you.
- ☐ Whether you want a traditional or more innovative approach.
- ☐ What color palettes you like or dislike.
- ☐ Whom your competitors are and how you're different.

ACCOMPLISHMENT #3:

Get organized

My Checklist:

☐ **Set up files**

☐ **Create digital records**

☐ **Set up a contact management system**

☐ **Keep track of your company's "vital statistics"**

☐ **Keep track of expenses**

Starting any new, big project can seem overwhelming. There's so much to do, so many things to think about. Some of the challenges are fun: figuring out a name for your business, creating new products, thinking up innovative marketing ideas. Some of the tasks don't seem like much fun: setting up a budget, going to a lawyer, getting business licenses.

With so many things to do, it's easy to forget or overlook some of the most important things. So right from Week One, start keeping track of all the basics and get organized so you don't lose critical information you'll need later.

 Set up files

Trust me: You're about to get a lot of stuff. You're quickly going to accumulate a whole lot of tangible stuff (reports, brochures, samples, contracts) as well as intangible stuff (information, data, advice, prices, and the like). You'll gather information on customers, competitors, suppliers, and distributors. You'll be researching and evaluating computers, facilities, and vendors. You'll be given names and numbers of people who can help you. And you'll be spending money—money you can later deduct as business expenses *if* you keep track of it and retain receipts.

All this stuff can overwhelm you. Instead of feeling like you're making progress, you'll feel completely over your head. And if you don't stay on top of your stuff, it can directly affect your chance of success—and your bottom line!

So, set up both physical files—to hold all that tangible stuff, including receipts—and digital files on your computer to hold all that intangible stuff: your notes, contact info, price comparisons, and so on.

Get in the habit—right from Week One—of putting the stuff you gather (tangible or intangible) in the appropriate file as you go along. If you wait until later ("I'll put this stuff away this weekend"), those piles of paper will just get larger and larger and larger…

In addition, I'd recommend getting a good-size box (like a large plastic storage tub) to keep all your bulkier items (such as samples, large brochures, research studies) in one place and easily retrievable.

Create digital records

In addition to all the physical staff you're going to accumulate, you're going to pile up information even faster.

Although you can start by keeping track of information such as what you paid for office supplies in a notebook, pretty soon you're going to find it hard to quickly find and retrieve critical information. The answer: Put it in electronic form so it can be easily searched for and found when you need it.

Since it's likely that you'll do a lot of online research—regarding competition, pricing, sources, and so on—you'll discover it's much easier to keep track of this data if you've got a system set up right on your computer.

One way to do this is to utilize the "folder" organizational structure used by most office automation software products. Start right away by setting up computer folders and files as you gather information. For example, you can create a folder called "Suppliers" and inside that folder put all documents—whether word processing, spreadsheets, PDFs, or other types of files—containing the data about suppliers that you unearth during your research.

Set up a contact management system

People who do not seem particularly important during the early stages of your business may be very useful at a later date. It's a horrible feeling to realize a few months down the road that you met the perfect supplier or distributor, or the person who could introduce you to the right investor, but you've lost the little slip of paper with their name, phone number, and email address.

Moreover, you'll want to start building your database of potential customers, referral sources, and friends so you can later invite them to your "Grand Opening" and send them your email newsletters (Week Six). Believe me, when it comes time to start your marketing program, you'll be glad you have an easy way to identify and contact people you want to communicate with.

So, right from Week One, establish a system for retaining and retrieving individuals' contact information. The best way to do this is with a "contact management" or "customer relationship management" (CRM) software program.

Contact management is so important that big corporations spend hundreds of thousands—even millions—of dollars on huge, powerful CRM systems. You don't have to. You can get by with a much simpler contact management application.

A contact management program can be as simple as an electronic "address book" such as one included as part of an email program, like Microsoft Outlook. As a start, that's a good way to make sure you don't lose important contact information.

However, you'll probably quickly outgrow the contact capabilities included in email programs and will want to get a dedicated contact management software application.

Start It Free

Take a look at free CRM solutions from Insightly (**insightly.com**), Zoho (**zoho.com/crm**), and Apptivo (**apptivo.com**).

Two of the benefits of cloud-based CRM programs for new entrepreneurs are that you pay as you go and that these applications can grow with you. So when you just start out and only have a short list of contacts, you can subscribe to a plan that suits your needs and your budget. Later, after you've grown, you simply upgrade to a larger plan—without interrupting your access to one of your company's most valuable assets: your contacts. Two popular cloud-based CRM applications to choose from are Salesforce CRM and SugarCRM.

At the very least, set up a file on your computer for contact information. Don't just let business cards stack up.

Keep track of your company's vital statistics

Throughout the life of your business, there's certain information you're going to be asked over and over again, such as your Tax ID number and your date of incorporation. You'll save a lot of time and aggravation later if you start recording all important dates, numbers, and data relating to your company right from the start.

Get in the habit of writing down—in one place—all of your company's "vital statistics." Otherwise, you'll find it's annoying to have to dig through files to find the same information repeatedly.

You'll find a worksheet to keep track of all the vital statistics about your business in Week Three on page 93.

Keep track of expenses

Start It Free

Look online for free expense trackers like **mint.com** and **expensify.com.**

In Week Five, you'll deal with money matters, but don't wait until then to start keeping track of the money you spend. After all, many of your expenses may be tax deductible, and you'll want to save every penny you can when you're first opening up shop.

You can choose to wait until Week Five to ask your accountant for a recommendation of a bookkeeping software program, but at the very least, start right now to keep track of each and every expenditure you make.

week 2

week 2

Main accomplishments:

#1 Learn more about your industry

#2 Research your target market

#3 Check out your competition

#4 Find suppliers

#5 Consider strategic partners

#6 Broaden or establish your network

Make appointments with:

■ Attend a community, entrepreneur, or industry organization meeting

Get the Info You Need

THIS WEEK YOU'RE GOING TO SHARPEN YOUR SKILLS at finding critical business information—whether it be about your industry, target market, competitors, or other business information you'll need.

Don't be put off by the word "research." It probably conjures up the image of term papers and school projects; this kind of research isn't like that. Instead, this week, you'll get shortcuts to finding reliable information to help you build your business and make decisions.

The emphasis is on finding such information fast, easily, and hopefully free (or at least pretty darn cheap).

Start with the "Learn more about your industry" section because many of the skills and sources you'll use will be the same for other types of research (for instance, your target market or suppliers).

To begin, get out your computer; most of the information-gathering will occur online. And get ready to find the information you need to build your company!

ACCOMPLISHMENT #1:
Learn more about your industry

My Checklist:

☐ **Make a list of your research questions**

☐ **Contact your industry association(s)**

☐ **Do online research**

 ## Make a list of your research questions

Once you start looking for information, you're likely going to find more information than you need—or not find the right information at all. A good way to speed up the process of finding information is to start by making a general statement that defines the basis of your business.

For example, if you are planning to start a company that provides online psychological therapy, your general statement might be: "There is a profitable way to provide psychological counseling via the Internet." Next, make a list of questions that logically follow from and challenge that statement. Here are some questions you might ask about the online therapy business:

- **What companies are already providing such a service?**

- **What is the market size for all kinds of psychological counseling?**

- **What indications are there that consumers would be willing to get counseling online?**

- **What portion of the existing psychological counseling market can you reasonably expect to transfer to online counseling?**

- **How many consumers who do not currently get counseling could you reasonably expect to be attracted to online counseling?**

- **What other companies are currently providing such online counseling services? How many are there? How many clients do they have? What is their ability to keep out new competitors? What do they charge?**

- **What are the costs involved in conducting an online therapy business?**

- **What are the key technology issues necessary to conduct such counseling, securely, online?**

- **What laws or regulations would affect the offering of such services?**

Begin your list with the "My Research Questions" worksheet on pages 50–51. Ask yourself tough questions—it's much better to uncover unpleasant truths now rather than after you've invested your time and money.

After drawing up your list of questions, start looking for answers. Organize your market research data in the files you set up last week. Refer to it frequently as you design your marketing plan, look for funding, and launch your operation.

As you prepare your questions, jot down any ideas about where you might find answers. See "Research Sources" on page 53 for ideas.

 ## Contact your industry association(s)

When looking for information for your new business, the very first place to start is with an association serving your industry or related industries. No matter what industry, trade, or profession you're in, there's almost certainly at least one association covering yours. Why? Because there are over 37,000 industry and professional associations in the United States!

You'll find industry, trade, or professional associations to be a highly valuable source of information. Most associations conduct research or collect data on trends of their industry. They monitor market size and demographics, costs, regulation, and a variety of other issues specific to their industry.

Typically, suppliers to an industry also often participate in that industry's associations. They'll exhibit at trade shows and be listed on the association's website or other directories. That makes your industry association an easy place to locate suppliers.

Most important, associations exist to help promote, train, and certify people in that industry. They'll hold trade shows, seminars, conventions, provide coursework, and offer joint marketing opportunities.

Let's say, for instance, you're thinking about starting a dog grooming business. You're going to want information about suppliers, costs, training, certification, marketing, and as much other information as you can get your paws on. A number of organizations exist to help pet groomers.

Check It Out

Every type of industry in North America has been assigned a NAICS code. You will often be asked for this code when researching business information. To search for your industry's NAICS code, go to **www.census.gov/eos/www/naics**

MY RESEARCH QUESTIONS

For each of the following categories, list questions affecting the future of your business.
Use these questions to guide your research efforts.

Industry

☐ Which industry does my business fall under?

☐ Which trade associations serve that industry?

☐ What does the data show about the financial performance of that industry in recent years?

☐ What does the research show about trends in that industry?

☐ Other:

Target Market

☐ What geographic area do I plan on serving?

☐ What is the demographic profile of the customers I plan on serving? (e.g., age, gender, income, education level)

☐ How many people fit that demographic profile in my target geographic area?

☐ What trends affect my market?

☐ What data (if any) indicates buying habits or preferences of my target market?

☐ Other:

Competition

☐ Who are the leading competitors in my market or geographic area?

☐ What do my competitors charge?

☐ What are their strengths? Shortcomings?

☐ What primary methods do my competitors use to attract customers?

☐ What, if anything, has caused previous competitors to close?

☐ Other:

Suppliers/Vendors

☐ What kind of equipment, materials, and services will I need?

☐ Which leading or recommended vendors provide those?

☐ What are the costs involved?

☐ Other:

Other

☐ Which laws or regulations (e.g., environmental, planning, etc.) typically affect my type of business?

☐ Which companies could make potential strategic partners?

☐ Other:

Three good ways to find an industry association online are:

1. **A general online search engine,** e.g., Google, Yahoo!, Bing. Type in the keywords associated with your industry.

2. **An online directory,** e.g., Yahoo! or Google. Look in subdirectories for "Business and Economy," or Business-to-Business, or Business Directories. Check "Professional Organizations" as well as "Trade" or "Industry" Associations.

3. **The "Gateway to Associations"** (asaecenter.org/Community/ Directories/Associationsearch.cfm). This national association of associations maintains an online directory of trade and industry associations. A caution, however: This link may change because the site is frequently redesigned. You may need to dig around. Look for "Directories" and/or "Gateway to Associations." Nevertheless, it's often a better jumping-off point than a general search engine or directory, which may result in thousands of unrelated results or commercial "organizations" that aren't genuine trade associations at all.

Finding trade associations can be difficult because they often use names that aren't obvious. For instance, if you type in the word "dog groomer," you might not find what you want. So check other words, such as "pet groomer" or "veterinary."

When you search for associations, you may find a dozen or more, so start with groups that contain the name "National," "International," or "American," rather than local organizations. Don't be afraid to look at national trade organizations outside of your country as they often have information such as standards, glossaries, other site listings, and so on.

✔ Do online research

In addition to your industry association, you'll find a substantial amount of industry information and data online. Of course, you'll want to make certain the information is accurate and up-to-date. Be careful to rely on information from trustworthy sources, such as recognized market research companies. If possible, when using data from media sources (such as newspapers and magazines), find the original source of the data; journalists, after all, have limited space and have to edit information, often leaving out data that might be important for your planning.

Check It Out

Check out USA.gov's alphabetical list of associations: **www.usa.gov/ directory/tradeassc/ index.shtml**

Or Yahoo!'s list: **www.dir.yahoo.com/ Business_and_Economy/ Organizations/Trade_ Associations/**

RESEARCH SOURCES

Type of information	Source	Website
U.S. Government	Census Bureau	www.census.gov
	Federal Statistics Online	www.fedstats.gov
	American Fact Finder	www.factfinder.census.gov
	2007 Economic Census	www.census.gov/econ/census07
	Government Printing Office (access to all federal documents and regulations)	www.gpoaccess.gov
	Louisiana State University's links to federal agencies	www.lib.lsu.edu/gov/index.html
Canadian Government	Statistics Canada	www.statcan.gc.ca
	Canadian Census	www12.statcan.gc.ca/census-recensement/index-eng.cfm
U.S. Census Bureau state and local information	County Business Patterns	www.census.gov/econ/cbp
	Quick Facts	http://quickfacts.census.gov/qfd
	Link to State Data Centers	www.census.gov/sdc
State/Local/Regional information	Each state government has a website	www.state.[two-letter state code].us e.g., www.state.ca.us for California www.state.md.us for Maryland
	Library of Congress links to state and local government sites	www.loc.gov/rr/news/stategov/stategov.html
	Links to state and local government sites (this is a private company)	www.statelocalgov.net
	Small Business Development Centers	www.asbdc-us.org (click on "Resources")
S.E.C. Annual reports	S.E.C. Edgar database	www.sec.gov/edgar.shtml
Company information	Hoover's	www.Hoovers.com
	Dun & Bradstreet	www.dnb.com
Supplier information	ThomasNet	www.ThomasNet.com
	eBay Business and Industrial	http://business.ebay.com
	Yahoo! business-to-business	http://dir.yahoo.com/Business_and_Economy/Business_to_Business
	Tradekey B2B directory	www.tradekey.com
	B2B Yellow Pages	www.b2byellowpages.com
Trade associations and trade shows	Center for Association Leadership	www.asaecenter.org
	TSNN—Trade Show News Network	www.tsnn.com

The key to finding industry-specific information is to be patient and diligent. You'll have to go to many sites and look around. When you find a site of interest—let's say an industry association site—follow links from that site (look for links saying things like "Related Links").

Another key is to visit websites of industries or associations you plan to market to. For instance, as a dog groomer, you might look for any local dog-owner websites or local petstore websites. They may give you ideas for marketing opportunities as well as help you learn more about your local market. Sometimes, you can buy membership lists, giving you a built-in database of sales leads.

Look for established market research companies in your field. In technology, for instance, some of the major market research companies are IDC, Gartner, and Forrester. If you're in the fashion industry, that would be the NPD Group. To find market research in your industry, do a search using your favorite search engine by using the name of the industry plus "market research."

Don't forget to check for news stories about topics related to your industry. You can look at general and specific media sites and use their search and archive capabilities.

You'll find lots of information online, but I'm also a big believer in the real world. Follow your online information hunt with real-world activities, particularly attending trade shows. Get out there and talk to people, including suppliers, potential customers, even competitors. Who knows? Perhaps other dog groomers will give you a leg up on your research, and you'll find that business isn't such a dog-eat-dog world after all.

ACCOMPLISHMENT #2:
Research your target market

My Checklist:
- [ ] **Define your target market**
- [ ] **Determine if there are enough customers**

WHO ARE MY CUSTOMERS?

Describe whom your customers are in each of the following categories. You'll find that the number of customers in each category grows the closer you get to the "end user."

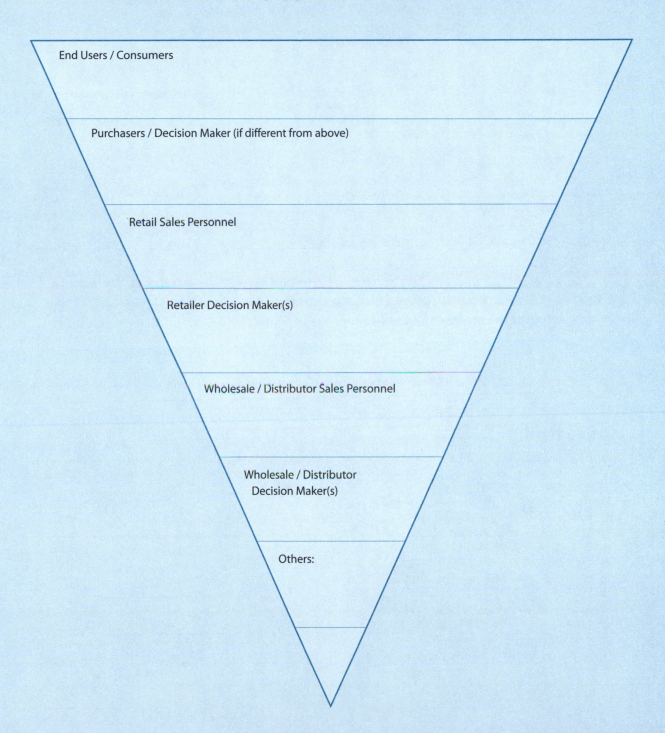

End Users / Consumers

Purchasers / Decision Maker (if different from above)

Retail Sales Personnel

Retailer Decision Maker(s)

Wholesale / Distributor Sales Personnel

Wholesale / Distributor
Decision Maker(s)

Others:

MY CUSTOMER PROFILE

Rank the characteristics of your customers that are most important in determining how receptive they'll be to your product or service. For the characteristics that have no bearing on whether or not they'll buy from you, leave the space blank.

☐ Gender   ☐ Education level   ☐ Children in household

☐ Age   ☐ Race or ethnicity   ☐ Home ownership

☐ Income level   ☐ Religious affiliation   ☐ Recreational activities

☐ Occupation   ☐ Marital status   ☐ Proximity to your business

Rank the characteristics of your product or service that are most important to your target customers.

☐ Price   ☐ Convenience   ☐ Product features

☐ Service   ☐ Reliability   ☐ Design

☐ Status   ☐ Other:_____   ☐ Other:_____

Now describe your customers according to the characteristics you have identified. Start with the characteristic you ranked as most important, providing details on how you think that characteristic will influence your customers' buying decisions.

☐ Characteristic #1 _____
_____
_____

☐ Characteristic #2 _____
_____
_____

☐ Characteristic #3 _____
_____
_____

☐ Characteristic #4 _____
_____
_____

☐ Characteristic #5 _____
_____
_____

✔ Define your target market

If I asked you to tell me whom your customers—or potential customers—are, how would you answer?

Let's say you've created a new breakfast cereal for children: "Yummy Tummy Oats." You've packed it with good things: vitamins, minerals, great nutrition. You figure you're going to wipe out the competition because every parent wants a nutritious breakfast for their child.

There's only one problem: Who's your customer? Is it Mom or Dad pushing the grocery cart down the cereal aisle, comparing the nutrition information on the side of the box?

Or is it the end-user (the "consumer") of your product—the kid—who couldn't care less about nutrition but wants cereal that tastes sweet, has cartoon characters on the package, and packs toys inside?

Or is it the cereal buyer for the grocery store chain? He cares little about nutrition or cartoon characters. His concerns are more down-to-earth: how much money you're going to spend on advertising, how quickly you'll replenish inventory, and whether you'll pay him a "stocking fee" to obtain shelf space. Parents and children aren't going to have a chance to buy or eat "Yummy Tummy Oats" if you don't meet the supermarket buyer's needs first.

On top of that, if you don't have your own sales and distribution force, you may first have to find a cereal distributor and convince them to carry your product.

The parent. The child. The store buyer. The distributor. That's a lot of "customers" you have to satisfy with each box of "Yummy Tummy Oats."

You give yourself a competitive edge by thinking of each of these "customers" and planning for their needs and motivation.

Being responsive to the details that are important to distributors, retailers, sales representatives, and others helps you plan your marketing materials, operations, packaging, even the nature of the product itself. If yours is an industry where sales reps must purchase their samples, for instance, you can set yourself apart by supplying samples free. If retailers can fit more square packages on a shelf than round packages, you'll be more competitive by choosing a square package.

Even if you think you'll market "directly to consumers" online, you'll discover there are still many entities between you and your "customer" in cyberspace. In the case of "Yummy Tummy Oats," your intermediary might be the online grocery store, the health food site, the children's site, or the search engine that will help customers find you. So you'll still have more than just parents and kids to please.

As you begin to define your customers, both the end-users and the intermediaries, describe all of their various attributes: age, location, industry, purchasing patterns, buying sensitivities, "psychographics" (what motivates them), and the like. Be realistic about how people actually behave—not how they should behave.

Use the worksheets on pages 55 and 56 to describe your customers. The first worksheet allows you to consider the types of "customers" you have. The second worksheet gets you started describing the characteristics of each of those. You may need to make copies of the customer profile worksheet—one for each type of "customer."

 ## Determine if there are enough customers

Ever wonder why there seem to be three or four fast-food joints at the same intersection? Or why, all of a sudden, not one but three big office supply stores open in a community?

The answer is they all rely on similar statistics to analyze a market. They look for certain factors: population density, characteristics of nearby residents (age, gender, income), number and type of local businesses, and so forth.

Big corporations hire consulting firms to compile these statistics. You've got an even bigger consulting group doing it for you—free! The United States Government, particularly the Census Bureau, compiles all kinds of information useful for businesses, and it has put much of it online.

First, a few key websites to remember:

■ **Fedstats** (www.fedstats.gov): The main portal for finding government statistics. The government really has tried to make this accessible, but if you don't know what you're looking for, it may be hard to find at this site.

■ **The U.S. Census Bureau** (www.census.gov): Bookmark this! This gives you access to all Census data about people, businesses, trade, and much more.

SIZE OF MY MARKET

Determine if the market is large enough to bring you sufficient sales.

- [ ] Estimated size of my market: _____

- [ ] Is this number growing or declining? _____

- [ ] By what amount per year? _____

- [ ] Estimated number of competitors in my market: _____

- [ ] Is this number growing or declining? _____

- [ ] By what amount per year? _____

Realistic assessment of the opportunity for additional competitors in my market:

- [ ] Outstanding   - [ ] Good   - [ ] Moderate   - [ ] Poor

- **County Business Patterns** (www.census.gov/econ/cbp): Eureka! This site has the nitty-gritty about businesses in your own area, down to zip code level. This is an easy-to-use database with detailed info. When viewing the data, be sure to click the box with the word "Detail" to get more information. If you want to know what's going on in your home town, this is the place.

- **Quick Facts** (http://quickfacts.census.gov/qfd): This is an easy way to access a wide variety of information about population characteristics at the state or county level.

- **American FactFinder** (www.factfinder.census.gov): A gateway site of the Census Bureau that leads you to specific information on people, housing, and economic and geographic data.

- **The "Economic Census"** (www.census.gov/econ/census07): Compiled every five years, the Economic Census gathers very detailed information on business activity, by industry and subsectors of industries, down to the zip code level. These can provide you with very specific information for your target area.

- **The Census Bureau's State Data Centers** (www.census.gov/sdc): The U.S. Census Bureau maintains this site, linking to each state's main statistic sites.

■ **Statistics Canada** (www.statcan.gc.ca). The entry page for data about Canada compiled by the Canadian Government. Search by subject, such as "Families, household and housing," "Income, pensions, spending and wealth," and "Population and demography," or search by resource, such as "Articles and reports" and "Data tables."

While this all seems daunting—you'll have to click through many pages to find what you want—you can find amazing information.

For instance, if I was thinking about opening a dry cleaning business in a particular neighborhood in Phoenix, I might want to find out how many dry cleaners already existed there and how well they were doing. Here's what I'd do:

1. Start from the County Business Patterns page: www.census.gov/econ/cbp.

2. Next, in the zip code field, put in the zip code of the area of interest—let's say 85013.

3. Then look for the industry classification that includes dry cleaning. In this case, it would be "Other Services," and be sure to click "Details."

4. Scroll down to "Dry cleaning & laundry services" to see how many dry cleaners or laundromats are in that zip code and how many employees they had.

5. Finally, click "Compare" to see how that zip code stacks up to other zip codes in Phoenix in terms of dry cleaners.

Of course, all this is just a starting point. You've got to drive or walk around the neighborhood, look at the competition, talk to other merchants. You still have to use your own good judgment. But if you're looking for hard numbers, the government's got them. McDonald's uses them, why not you?

And don't forget to visit the same online sources you used to gather industry data to gather more data about your target market. Go to the websites of industry associations, market research firms, media outlets, and so forth.

As you compile data on the size of your market, fill in the worksheet on page 59.

ACCOMPLISHMENT #3:
Check out your competition

My Checklist:

- ☐ **Identify your competitors**
- ☐ **Analyze your competition**
- ☐ **Compare competitors' pricing**

✔ Identify your competitors

In general, I'm not a big believer in spending much time or energy worrying about what the other guy is doing. Over the years, I've learned that success for a small business depends much more on what you do, rather than on what your competitors do.

Yes, big businesses spend millions of dollars fighting over each percentage point of market share (just think Coke versus Pepsi, Hertz versus Avis). But for a small company, that's not very productive.

But that doesn't mean you can just ignore the competition. From time to time, you should investigate who's out there, what they offer, and what they charge.

If you approach this competitive analysis exercise as an opportunity to learn, you may find ways to enhance your products or services, or at least to improve your marketing.

Competition comes in as many as six forms:

1. **Direct competitors.** The ones who keep you up at night. These other small companies resemble yours: close to customers, ambitious, and trying to reach the same target market. Most markets have enough business to go around, but you'd better know what your direct competition is doing.

2. **Online competitors.** These days, your competition isn't just on the next block, or even within your state. You could find yourself battling it out for customers with someone from the other side of the world. With time and geographic boundaries collapsing more each month, you have to take these online competitors very, very seriously. And

if you run a bricks-and-mortar store, you'll no doubt also experience "showrooming"—customers walking into your store, checking out your merchandise, then going online to buy the items more cheaply. You'll need to develop strategies for combatting this practice.

3. **The big guys.** The Walmarts, Home Depots, Lawyers 'R' Us— national companies or franchises with huge marketing budgets. Don't just dismiss these as being inferior because they're big—a lot of them have adopted customer service practices that used to be the hallmark of small business. These are very real competitors to you, especially if you plan to compete on the basis of price.

4. **Other ways to spend money.** When thinking about competition, you also have to consider all the other ways customers can spend their time and money. I can remodel my bathroom or go on a vacation. I can buy new electronic gadgets or new clothes. As a new business, you don't have the marketing dollars to compete against this kind of nebulous competition.

5. **Inertia factors.** Alternatively, your potential customers can simply decide not to spend their money on anything at all. Especially during tough economic periods, it can be difficult to persuade people to part with their hard-earned cash. And even in the best of times it can be hard to get people to *care* enough to spend their money.

6. **Potential future competitors.** Then there are the competitors you will face tomorrow. Note that these might differ from what you expect. Keep your eyes open—competition can emerge from the unlikeliest places.

In most situations, you'll concentrate your energy on looking at what your direct competitors are doing—whom they are, what their competitive strengths and weaknesses are, and how much they charge.

You can identify these direct competitors by looking through directories (online directories, trade association directories, business databases, and the like) and advertisements. You can also ask suppliers and distributors to name the major competition in your area. See if your competitors are exhibiting at trade shows. And you can even do a survey of potential customers, asking them to name your competition.

Check It Out

To find out information on industries, trends, your competitors, and more, consult publications such as the *Wall Street Journal* (**www.wsj.com**), *Business Week* (**www.businessweek.com**), *The Economist* (**www.economist.com**), and *Forbes* (**www.forbes.com**).

MY COMPETITORS

Use this worksheet to identify your competitors. What businesses compete with you directly? What other forces influence how or if your customers will spend their money on your product or service? Be realistic and honest in this assessment.

Competitor	Their Advantages/Strengths	My Advantages/Strengths
☐ Direct Competitors:		
_____	_____	_____
_____	_____	_____
_____	_____	_____
☐ Online Competitors:		
_____	_____	_____
_____	_____	_____
_____	_____	_____
☐ The Big Guys:		
_____	_____	_____
_____	_____	_____
_____	_____	_____
☐ Other Ways to Spend Money:		
_____	_____	_____
_____	_____	_____
_____	_____	_____
☐ Inertia Factors:		
_____	_____	_____
_____	_____	_____
_____	_____	_____
☐ Potential Future Competitors:		
_____	_____	_____
_____	_____	_____
_____	_____	_____

COMPETITORS' PRICE COMPARISON CHART

	Product/Service #1	Product/Service #2	Product/Service #3
Competitor A:			
☐ Competitor's price:			
☐ Competitor's costs (if known):			
☐ Basis for competitor's advantage (if any):			
Competitor B:			
☐ Competitor's price:			
☐ Competitor's costs (if known):			
☐ Basis for competitor's advantage (if any):			
Competitor C:			
☐ Competitor's price:			
☐ Competitor's costs (if known):			
☐ Basis for competitor's advantage (if any):			

✔ Analyze your competition

"Let's go shopping!" While those are three of my favorite words, this spree is limited: We're going to check out what the competition is up to.

The easiest way to begin your competitive analysis is online. Here's the plan of attack:

1. **Direct competitors' websites.** Drill down way beyond the home page. Be sure to read the "About Us" section and any press information, as well as descriptions of their products or services. Here are some of the things to look for on your competitors' sites:
    - **Descriptions of products/services**
    - **Prices**
    - **Client/customer lists—testimonials**
    - **Staff—to see what size company they have and their qualifications**
    - **Their strengths**
    - **How they position themselves—self-descriptions**
    - **Which segment of the market they appear to be targeting**

2. **You can also see if any of your competitors have been written about in the press** recently by checking their names at the Google News directory. Go to http://news.google.com.

3. **At the Google home page,** do searches on the names of your competitors and the generic description of your product or service category and location (if appropriate). Use alternative phrases as well. In other words, if you want to find out who's competing with you in the landscape business in Mobile, also try phrases like "lawn care" and Alabama. Go also to the Yahoo! directory, http://dir.yahoo.com.

4. **If you target specific industries as customers, check out the websites of those industry associations** by searching for listings of exhibitors at past trade shows (you might need to check under "events" or "conventions"). That will give you an idea of whether your competitors are actively marketing to the same industry.

5. **If you're willing to spend a bit of money,** and your competitors are pretty well established, you can order a Dun & Bradstreet report on them. Go to www.dnb.com. This highly regarded agency was designed to help businesses check on the credit-worthiness of potential business customers. But it also gives you the opportunity to purchase a report containing financial and credit information about your competitors.

Finally, not all competitive analysis can be done online. Check to see if your competitors advertise in the newspaper or local Yellow Pages. You might phone or visit a competitor to see what they offer and how much they charge. Don't request proposals or bids—just ask for a simple brochure or have a quick discussion on the phone. Better yet, join a local chapter of your trade association and get to know your competitors personally. Then, you can sit down and discuss what they're doing face-to-face. You may be surprised to find that some are actually helpful—and even a source of potential referrals!

In the best of all possible worlds, the fact that you have competition should cause you to constantly improve your products and services. That way, you'll make more money—and can really go shopping!

Use the worksheet "My Competitors" on page 63 to identify and assess your competitors.

Compare competitors' pricing

One of the most important things you'll want to know when gathering data on your competition is what they charge. After all, setting prices is one of the most critical aspects of starting a new business. This is especially true in service industries, where prices can vary greatly from one provider to another.

Of course, finding out what others charge is not always easy. If you're lucky, they post their prices directly on their websites or in their written materials.

In other cases, such as when you open a retail store or restaurant, your competitors' prices are visible when you go into their place of business. Just visiting their establishment enables you to check their prices.

Unfortunately, it's much more difficult to determine pricing patterns in professions and trades where prices are set on a one-on-one basis or negotiated. In these situations, you'll most likely find out about pricing patterns by asking others already in the field, by talking to potential clients, and by participating in trade associations. In some cases, you may be able to speak with customers of other businesses in your industry about pricing.

Keep track of the information you find about competitors' pricing patterns on the worksheet on page 64.

ACCOMPLISHMENT #4:
Find suppliers

If you're opening a toy shop, how do you find the toys to put on your shelves? On the other hand, if you're manufacturing toys, how do you get your toys onto toy shop shelves?

In the business world, whether you're buying or selling, you're likely to need a "middle man"—a person or company that puts buyers and sellers together. While "middle men" may be much maligned, in reality they serve very valuable functions.

With the advent of the Internet, the business world was supposed to become "dis-intermediated"; in other words, we were supposed to be able to get rid of the middle man. Now, after all, manufacturers are able to sell directly to end users, without the need for all those people in the middle—wholesalers, distributors, retailers, and others. Theoretically, this should make everything less expensive because there would be fewer hands taking a cut, and making a profit, at each step of the way.

But while this dis-intermediation has occurred in a few instances (buying a Dell computer directly from Dell), for the most part, manufacturers don't want to be bothered with selling goods on a "one-off" basis, then having to deal with fulfilling small orders and all those pesky customers. And buyers don't want to wade through dozens—even hundreds or thousands—of choices.

No, we need middle men: wholesalers, distributors, and independent sales representatives. They serve as the marketing, sales, and service arm for manufacturers.

In turn, middle men also serve buyers as "editors" (selecting the best choices from the myriad of options), and provide individualized service and order fulfillment, especially for smaller customers.

But if you're new to business, where do you find these valuable intermediaries and vendors?

- ■ **Word-of-mouth:** The best way to find a supplier or distributor is the old-fashioned way—asking someone who's knowledgeable for a recommendation. When I first started my publishing company, I asked another publisher for names of book distributors and printers. I didn't

Check It Out

Will you manufacture products to sell internationally? Then you'll likely want to follow procedures to get your products or processes certified as meeting quality standards set by the International Organization for Standardization or ISO (**www.iso.org**).

use their distributor, but their printing company was my primary vendor for many years.

If you don't know anyone in the same industry, ask others in related industries (for instance, ask a printer for the names of graphic designers or vice versa) or those who might have a similar need (such as for shipping services or sign painters).

- **Trade associations:** Trade associations are an excellent source for locating suppliers. Besides holding annual or regional conventions and trade shows where suppliers exhibit their products and services, many associations publish supplier directories, both in print and online. Use the methods listed in the section "Learn more about your industry" to find an association serving your industry.

- **ThomasNet:** Consult ThomasNet, the ultimate resource for locating suppliers and vendors. Its website features a free, searchable database of products manufactured in the United States. You'll find this site particularly useful for hard-to-find industrial products. Go to www.thomasnet.com.

- **Tradekey B2B directory:** Tradekey is one of the world's largest online marketplaces for importers and exporters. It connects worldwide wholesale buyers with importers and exporters, distributors, and agents in more than 220 countries. Go to www.tradekey.com.

- **B2B Yellow Pages:** You can find suppliers in some 70 industries that offer products, services, and information for your business by visiting the B2B Yellow Pages. A special section on "B2B Shopping" helps you find the best products, prices, and shopping comparisons for business supplies and more. Go to www.b2byellowpages.com.

- **eBay Business and Industrial:** Most people think of eBay for consumers, but eBay also has a section for industrial supplies and products sold in large lots. Go to http://business.shop.ebay.com.

- **Yahoo! business-to-business (B2B) directory:** Most online directories maintain separate categories for business-related topics. Yahoo!, as one of the oldest directories, has an extensive list. You can find it at http://dir.yahoo.com/Business_and_Economy/Business_to_Business/.

POTENTIAL STRATEGIC PARTNERS

List here potential strategic partners, how you can help each other,
and how you can secure the relationship.

Potential Strategic Partners	Mutual Benefits	Ways to Start a Relationship

ACCOMPLISHMENT #5:
Consider strategic partners

You don't have to do everything alone. A strategic partnership is a relationship with another company for purposes such as distribution, product development, promotion, or add-on sales. A strong strategic partner that is already serving your target market can give you a real edge in reaching that market.

For example, you might use a partnership for:

- **Distribution agreement:** This is an agreement whereby one company carries another's product line and sells its products or services. This is the most common type of strategic partnership.

- **Licensing:** One company may grant permission to another to use its product, name, or trademark. Instead of selling your product or service directly, you might license it to another company to sell under its name and brand. Examples abound in the entertainment industry where, for instance, toy manufacturers will license a movie's brand and create toys around the movie's main characters. Professional athletes often also license their likenesses for promoting consumer goods.

- **Cooperative advertising:** This type of advertising occurs when two companies are mentioned in an advertisement and each company pays part of the costs. This is a frequent practice in many industries. Start with your trade association when looking for such opportunities. Manufacturers also often put together co-op advertising packages for their distributors and retailers.

- **Bundling:** In this type of relationship, one company includes another company's product or service as part of a total package. You keep your own identity, but get the advantage of being included in their package.

Securing a major company as a key partner can not only give your company specific competitive advantages, but also add credibility with customers and funders.

Use the worksheet "Potential Strategic Partners" on page 69 to identify those with whom you might form a strategic partnership in which you both benefit.

ACCOMPLISHMENT #6:
Broaden or establish your network

My Checklist:

- ☐ **Attend a community, entrepreneur, or industry organization meeting**
- ☐ **Build your online connections**

There's one piece of advice I always give entrepreneurs as they're starting out in business: Join an organization. You can't build a company if you're sitting in your office by yourself; you need to be part of a community or an industry or, better yet, both.

Since I began my business, I've participated in many groups—entrepreneurs' clubs, industry associations, women's business groups, local Chambers of Commerce, and more. I've never sat down and figured out how much I've spent on memberships, meetings, and meals, but I'm sure it adds up to quite a sum. And I can say, without a doubt, it's been worth every penny.

After all, it was at a referrals group that I first learned how to give an "elevator pitch" (the short description of my services). And that's where I found many of my clients during my early years in business. In fact, it was through someone at an entrepreneurs' group that I made the connection that led to my first book contract. And that changed my life!

Entrepreneurs are even more fortunate now. There are many more resources to help you launch your business, learn your industry, and make important contacts than when I was starting my company.

What will you get out of joining an organization?

- **Community:** Working alone or in a very small business, it's easy to feel isolated. Joining organizations helps you become part of a larger community.

- **Connections:** If you're looking for the name of an attorney or graphic artist, trying to find a supplier, or just need advice on how to handle a problem or price your services, you'll have connections to others with experience.

- **Education:** Many groups, especially entrepreneur and industry associations, provide valuable information and training. They can help you stay on top of current trends.

- **Friends:** You can meet people who become your personal friends, regardless of any business connection or benefit.

- **New business:** Of course, it's ideal if you get clients or referrals as a result of joining an organization. But I should warn you, if that's your only goal, you're likely to drop out fairly quickly.

✔ Attend a community, entrepreneur, or industry organization meeting

Every community has its share of organizations. Some types of groups you can join:

- **Entrepreneurs' groups:** You're likely to find lots of entrepreneur groups, both formal associations and informal get-togethers. Don't forget the grand-daddy of them all—the Chamber of Commerce.

- **Industry associations:** With more than 37,000 industry and professional associations in the United States, it's likely there's a local chapter of interest in your community.

- **Group-specific entrepreneur associations:** You'll find business organizations aimed at women, minorities, religious groups, gays and lesbians, youth, immigrants, and more.

- **Civic organizations:** In big cities, you'll find organizations dedicated to civic or world affairs, politics, and so forth. You're certain to find service groups such as Rotary International, Kiwanis, or Lions Clubs in your town. Established business leaders are more likely to belong to civic organizations than to entrepreneur groups.

Check the following to find out if there's a group that's right for you in your town:

- **Business section** of your local newspaper for calendar of meetings/events of entrepreneur groups.

- **Community calendar** of your local newspaper for civic organizations.

- **Small Business Development Centers** for a list of local entrepreneur groups. To find a contact for an SBDC office in your state, go to www. asbdc-us.org/About_Us/SBDCs.html.

Check It Out

Find a trade association for you at **www. planningshop.com/ associations**

ORGANIZATIONS TO JOIN

Use this worksheet to research networking, trade, business, charity, and social organizations you will join or in which you will participate.

Organization	Meeting Time & Place	Dues

- **Websites of trade associations.** Find an appropriate industry association by using the methods in the section "Learn more about your industry."

- **Chambers of Commerce directory** online, www.uschamber.com/chambers/directory.

- **Websites of women's groups,** particularly National Association of Women Business Owners (www.nawbo.org) and Forum for Women Entrepreneurs (www.fwe.ca).

- **Websites of civic organizations.** Check an online directory, such as Yahoo!'s directory of community organizations, or the site of the specific group, e.g., www.rotary.org or www.kiwanis.org.

Once you have found groups that interest you, you'll want to evaluate the following:

- **Types of businesses represented and fit for your target market.** Since you'll be looking for clients or referral sources, you'll want to make sure members are the types of people who have a need for or can use your products or services. For instance, if your target market is small businesses, you might join a Chamber of Commerce, since its members are mostly small businesses. If you're hoping to gather with professional colleagues for mutual benefit (like trade education, resources, influence, and discounts on services), choose an association that serves your industry.

- **Number of members.** Bigger groups work well when you want to find as many potential clients, or leads, as possible and your products or services can serve many types of people. Smaller groups are better when you're targeting a specific industry or need only a few big clients, whom you'll have a better chance of meeting and landing in a close-knit environment.

- **Convenience.** Check to see when the group meets, where, how often, and at what cost to ensure that you can be a regular participant.

- **Networking opportunities.** Do the meetings and events allow time for you to easily meet and get to know other members, or is the time structured solely for educational sessions? Will you have other opportunities to tell members about your business (for example, by making presentations, giving your elevator pitch, or being featured in emails or newsletters)?

- **Cost.** Some organizations can be extremely expensive, particularly for-profit networking and leads groups. Check the prices not just of membership but also of attending events (including meals and parking) and compare them with those for other groups you might join. Also find out how many meetings you can attend as a guest before joining.

When deciding whether to join a group and when evaluating it after you've joined, be sure your goals are realistic. What do you hope to achieve by joining? How much business do you expect to attract? If you want to get the most out of an organization, don't just go to one or two meetings; attend regularly, volunteer, or serve on a committee. That's how people will get to know you, and both you and the organization will be more likely to succeed. As with any form of marketing, you need repeat exposures to make an impact.

Use the worksheet on page 73 to keep track of organizations you'll join.

 ## Build your online connections

Once considered the province of the young and wired, social networks such as Facebook, Twitter, LinkedIn, and Pinterest are now required reading. Businesses today realize they must have a presence on these sites, especially if their desired customers are there.

Social networking sites are a dynamic way to stay on top of the people, trends, and news that affect your business. Use these sites to gather business intelligence, connect with former colleagues, get in touch with potential customers, mine for information, and market your product or service. Create profiles on the sites that make sense for you and post useful information, updates, words of wisdom, and offers as a way to stay visible and remain top-of-mind with potential customers (more in Week Six).

Finally, consider joining an online entrepreneurship forum. There are literally thousands of free and for-a-fee "virtual" forums online where entrepreneurs congregate to discuss issues and ideas surrounding their particular industry. These groups can be great sources of information on suppliers and vendors, best practices, educational opportunities, and the like. Post a specific question and receive credible answers from people "who have been there"—sometimes in just a matter of hours. In some cases, you'll find you're hobnobbing with the top names in your industry!

Keep in mind, however, that just as in the "real" world, these forums typically have codes of conduct and generally accepted rules of etiquette. Most, for instance, frown on blatant advertising of one's business or products. It's always a good practice to spend a week or two "lurking"— reading other participants' postings, learning who's who, getting the lay of the land—before you venture in with your own postings.

Also, as with the real world, consider the source before you apply anyone's advice to your business. While most forums I've participated in have been good sources of information and camaraderie, the Internet unfortunately provides an accommodating home for both unscrupulous people and plenty who, innocently enough, simply offer poor advice.

There are undoubtedly many ways to find online forums; here are some good places to start your search:

- **Your industry association website:** Many associations run members-only forums on their websites. If yours offers such a service, sign up and jump in.

- **Yahoo! Groups (http://groups.yahoo.com):** Yahoo! hosts all sorts of online groups. Many are for people with particular interests, hobbies, health concerns, and so on. But there are professional groups also, so spend some time looking around for one that fits your business type.

- **Google Groups (http://groups.google.com):** Almost everyone loves Google's search engine, but the company is also host to one of the largest and oldest repositories of online forums. You'll find discussion groups on just about every topic under the sun. Spend some time on the Groups home page looking for topic areas that relate to your industry or business specialty.

So this week, get out there and mingle! Take the plunge. Spread the word about your business. Face any fears of meeting new people or engaging in an online dialogue. No matter what type of business you're starting, your networks will prove to be critical to your success. So start building them now!

week 3

week 3

Main accomplishments:

#1 Deal with legal and licensing matters

#2 Build your team and employee structure

Make appointments with:

☐ Attorney

Cut Through Red Tape

Yuck! No one enjoys dealing with the red tape—the paperwork and legal requirements—of starting and running a business. But, unfortunately, it has to be done, so this week we'll get it out of the way.

The key activity is meeting with an attorney. After that, you may have to run around to city, state, or other government offices to file paperwork to get permits, licenses, and so on.

If yours is a simple business, this may all go pretty quickly. But even if yours is a one-person business and you work out of your home, don't think you can just forego the legal issues altogether. An ounce of legal prevention now can prevent a ton of legal trouble later.

Aside from dealing with legal issues, this week you'll get started on building your team. Taking advantage of the time you spend with a lawyer, you can ask for advice on personnel matters—hiring, benefits, taxes, and other issues to make sure you follow the law—and then hire the right people, treat them fairly, and manage them well.

You'll also plan whom you need on your team, including what kind of advisors you may want or need. You can even get the hiring process under way!

ACCOMPLISHMENT #1:

Deal with legal and licensing matters

My Checklist:

☐ **Choose a legal form and ownership structure for your company**

☐ **Discuss ownership of your company**

☐ **Apply for business licenses, permits, and identification numbers**

☐ **Discuss collecting sales tax**

☐ **Draw up basic contracts and other legal agreements**

☐ **Protect your intellectual property**

The origin of the term "Red Tape"

In England, at least as far back as the 17th century, stacks of legal documents were tied in red cloth ribbon. By the 19th century, "red tape" had come to connote any kind of bureaucratic or legal complication.

Taking care of your company's legal health is like taking care of your personal health: An ounce of prevention is better than a pound of cure. Time after time, entrepreneurs end up in legal battles costing thousands of dollars that could have been avoided with a $300 trip to an attorney.

Make your first visit to a lawyer right at the beginning of your business life. Look for an attorney who handles general business law, especially with new or small companies. Ideally, he or she will have experience with companies in your industry, but that is certainly not necessary unless you are in an industry that is highly regulated. The best way to find a lawyer is by asking for referrals, especially from others in your field.

When I went into business for the first time with my own consulting practice, I spent two hours with a lawyer. We not only wrote a simple letter-of-agreement I could use with clients, but we also discussed how to price my services, collect overdue fees, and minimize taxes.

Most lawyers charge by the hour, but some have set fees for specific tasks such as incorporation. Don't hesitate to interview your prospective lawyer and ask about costs before engaging their services. You have the right to choose someone you're comfortable with and can afford.

Then, establish a good working relationship with a business attorney and become used to consulting with them before you make major business decisions.

In addition to making that vital trip to a lawyer's office, you can also consult a number of other resources to help you with legal and licensing issues. These include:

- **Small Business Development Centers** (see page 25): Your local SBDC office is likely to be able to help you understand the specific business regulations you'll have to deal with in your community. The SBDC will also have contact information for city, county, and state offices (such as a County recorder or city planning department).

- **BusinessUSA (www.business.usa.gov):** Setup and maintained by the U.S. Government, this site serves as a one-stop platform through which businesses can access the resources and services they need, including business laws, both federal and state.

- **Individual state business portals:** Individual U.S. states all have their own websites. Many of these also have set up gateways or "portals" to assist those who want to do business in that state. These portals compile a great deal of information in one place. Here are a few tricks to find your state's business gateway:

  - Try www.state.[your state's two-letter abbreviation].us. In other words, for California, the website would be www.state.ca.us; for New York, www.state.ny.us. Once at your state's site, look for "Business," "Starting a Business," or similar.

  - At a search engine, type in your state and the words "business resources." In other words, for Iowa, type in "Iowa business resources." This may turn up additional state business sites.

- **Individual city or county websites:** Many cities and counties, especially in large metropolitan areas, maintain business information on their websites. Use a search engine to find your city or county website.

Choose a legal form and ownership structure for your company

When starting a business, one of the first choices you need to make is which legal form your business will take.

QUESTIONS TO ASK
WHEN CHOOSING AN ATTORNEY

☐ What is your specialty or particular area of expertise?

☐ Have you ever worked with businesses in my industry?

☐ Do you have any clients who are in similar businesses? Competing businesses?

☐ Is there any reason you'd have a conflict of interest representing me?

☐ What is your workload like? Are you generally available when clients call?

☐ Will I be working with you or with an associate or other attorney?

☐ How much do you charge per hour? How do you charge for additional expenses (pass-through, add on a percentage, etc.)? How much do you charge for the services of associates or paralegals?

Now, this may sound like a question that shouldn't be important to a very small business. After all, if you're going to be a consultant or a graphic designer or an electrical contractor, why bother dealing with the government? Who needs to pay a few hundred dollars in corporation or legal fees?

But choosing a legal form affects how much you pay in taxes, who can invest in your company, and most importantly, your personal financial security.

Three things to keep in mind when choosing a legal form are:

■ **Liability:** Legally, corporations are considered individual entities. As such, the corporation—not individual shareholders—is responsible for the actions of the business. In other words, if something goes very wrong and a corporation is sued, only the assets of the corporation are at stake—not the owners' personal assets. (There are some exceptions to this rule, but generally, your personal liability is *greatly* limited.) Obviously, having liability limited to the company's assets is quite desirable, since it means your personal assets—your home, investments, savings—can't be seized if your company has a legal judgment against it.

■ **Double taxation:** No one likes paying taxes, and you certainly don't want to pay taxes twice—once on income for the business and then again when that income is distributed as profits to you. Instead, look for a legal form that allows for the profits of the company to "pass through" to the owners, without having to pay corporate taxes first.

- **Ownership:** Some legal forms of business limit the number or type of people who can invest in your company. If you're seeking a large number of investors or international investors, find a corporate structure (for instance, a "C" corporation) that permits such stockholders.

When you meet with your attorney, these are the legal structures you can consider:

- **Sole proprietorship:** A business owned by one person with no formal legal structure. ADVANTAGES: It's simple! Just start your business; there's no additional paperwork. You don't file corporate income taxes—just a Schedule "C" with your personal income taxes. DISADVANTAGES: You have no personal liability protection. If your business is sued, you could lose everything you own—and in some cases, your spouse could lose his or her assets also.

- **Partnership:** A business with more than one owner who actively engages in the management of the company. ADVANTAGES: No required legal forms (although you'd be well advised to draw up a partnership agreement). No double taxation—profits pass through to the partners. DISADVANTAGES: Each partner has unlimited personal liability, even for actions taken by other partners. Be warned: If you go into business with others, you've got a partnership in the eyes of the law whether or not you've drawn up any paperwork.

  There is also a "Limited Partnership" form, in which the General Partners actively manage the affairs of the company and the "Limited Partners" are passive investors, not permitted to participate in the management of the company (and have limited financial exposure).

- **Limited Liability Company (LLC) or Limited Liability Partnership (LLP):** A legal form that provides liability protection for the company's owners without requiring incorporation. LLCs have become the form of choice for many small companies. A Limited Liability Partnership (not to be confused with a "Limited Partnership," above) is almost the same as an LLC but is used for certain professional practices, such as firms of attorneys or accountants. ADVANTAGES: Personal liability protection for all owners and pass-through profits without corporate

Check It Out

After you've chosen a legal form for your business, you can file the necessary forms online through MyCorporation (**www.mycorporation. com**) or LegalZoom (**www.legalzoom.com**).

TYPES OF LEGAL FORMS OF U.S. BUSINESS ORGANIZATIONS

Legal Form	What Is It?	Advantages?
☐ Sole Proprietorship	An unincorporated business owned by one person. If you don't set up a legal structure, and no one else owns any part of your business, you have a sole proprietorship.	Simple. No legal forms or costs to establish. No double taxation.
☐ General Partnership	A business with more than one owner. All partners actively participate in the business.	You have the time and talents of more than one person. No double taxation.
☐ Limited Partnership	A business with an owner or owners who manage the business (general partners) and other partners who do not (limited partners).	Protects the personal assets of limited partners, who aren't responsible for the debts and obligations of the business. Limits investors' financial exposure.
☐ Limited Liability Company (LLC) or Limited Liability Partnership (LLP)	A popular legal form that provides much of the protection of incorporating with most of the simplicity of a sole proprietorship. LLPs are LLCs for certain professional practices.	Protects personal assets against most business losses. No double taxation. Relatively simple, inexpensive to establish and maintain. Can distribute profits and losses disproportionately.
☐ "C" Corporation	A corporation is a legal entity, separate from its owners. Major investors often want companies to be C corporations.	Protects owners' personal assets against corporate losses and obligations. Can issue stock. Unlimited number of stockholders. Costs of benefits for employees and owners are deductible.
☐ "S" Corporation	A type of corporation that allows pass-through taxation instead of double taxation. S corporations are less popular since the introduction of LLCs.	The personal liability protection of a corporation with the pass-through taxation treatment of a sole proprietorship.
☐ "B" Corporation	A type of corporation, allowed for in a few states, that is organized for the public benefit as well as for the benefit of the shareholders.	Gives directors of a company more legal protection and responsibility for making decisions motivated by achieving a public good rather than merely maximizing profits.
☐ Not-for-Profit, "501(c)(3)" Organization	An organization, agency, institution, charity, or company with charitable, educational, or other public benefit goals, that has been certified as tax exempt by the IRS.	No federal income taxes; usually exempt from state and local taxes. Donations are tax deductible. Has members and Board of Directors rather than shareholders.

Disadvantages?	Tax Treatment	Watch Out For
The business owner, and possibly their spouse, has unlimited personal liability for the debts, obligations, and judgments against the company.	Pass-through profits and losses. The business owner can deduct losses against other personal income.	In community property states, spouses may be liable for business debts as well as having an ownership interest in the company.
Each partner can enter into contracts and incur debts for which all partners are responsible and have unlimited personal liability.	Pass-through profits and losses to the partners who pay tax at their individual rates. Partnership pays no taxes but must file a Form 1065.	If in business with others, you have a partnership whether you draw up documents or not, and partners have a share of the business and other rights.
Limited partners cannot participate in running the company. General partners are all liable for the company's obligations.	Limited partners can deduct "passive" losses against "passive income" only, and the amount they can invest is capped.	If a limited partner participates in any way in the management of the company, they can lose their liability protection.
Each owner can enter into contracts and incur debts for the entire LLC. Must file Articles of Organization with your state; often requires annual state fees.	Pass-through profits and losses to each owner. LLCs pay no taxes but must file a Form 1065.	Can be cumbersome converting from an LLC to a C corporation in order to accept VC financing or to be acquired by a large corporation in return for stock.
Double taxation. Must file articles of incorporation with your state. Annual state fees. Requires record-keeping, annual meetings, and a Board of Directors in most states if more than one stockholder.	Double taxation: Corporation and shareholders each pay tax on income. However, if the corporation keeps significant cash reserves, this can have lower tax consequences than pass-through taxation.	Securities rules affect how you sell stock and to whom. Use a lawyer to help you determine whether to set up a C corporation.
Disadvantages over an LLC include limits on number and residency of stockholders, proportionate distribution of profits and losses, and more record keeping.	Pass-through taxation, but profits and losses must be allocated at same percentage as ownership.	Ask your lawyer if there is any benefit in choosing an S corporation over an LLC or C corporation in your specific situation.
Limited number of states allow this option.	Same tax treatment as other corporations.	Requires an annual "benefit report," detailing which public benefits the company has achieved, that meets independent, third-party standards.
Must not be operated for the financial benefit of any individuals; no profits distributed to individuals. Must meet IRS requirements.	Tax exempt.	May not engage in any political activity. Typically must raise money through contributions and grants. Board of Directors can oust founders or restrict salaries.

taxes. Another benefit: Profits can be distributed unequally—a 60% shareholder can take only 10% of the profits. This allows more flexibility for tax planning and for rewarding owners who bear more management responsibilities. DISADVANTAGES: LLC laws vary by state; you are likely limited in the number of owners (investors) you can have, and some states do not permit international investors.

■ **"S" corporation:** A type of corporation that provides personal liability protection but permits pass-through (rather than double) taxation. ADVANTAGES: Lawyers and accountants are very familiar with laws relating to "S" corporations. DISADVANTAGES: You cannot distribute profits unevenly as you can with LLCs. You also pay state corporation fees.

■ **"C" corporation:** A corporate form that allows for the most investors and significant liability protection. ADVANTAGES: No limit to the number of people who can own stock. Legal form for companies that are going to be publicly traded. DISADVANTAGE: Double taxation.

■ **"B" corporation:** Also known as a "benefit" corporation, these kinds of businesses have as their very purpose to create a benefit for the public as well as the shareholders. ADVANTAGES: Because company directors make decisions based on public good, not merely profits, they have more legal protection and control. DISADVANTAGES: Allowed in a limited number of states.

■ **Not-for-profit, "501(c)(3)" organization:** A tax-exempt organization, agency, institution, charity, or company with charitable, educational, or other goals based on public good. ADVANTAGES: No federal income taxes. Often exempt from state and local taxes. Donations are tax deductible. Has a Board of Directors rather than shareholders. DISADVANTAGES: No profits. Must meet IRS requirements.

A chart outlining the pros and cons of the different types of legal entities is included on pages 84–85.

Discuss ownership of your company

One of the key issues involved in choosing a legal form for your business is determining who owns it. In a sole proprietorship, you own it. In any other form, you share ownership, with either a partner or shareholders.

If this is your first time in business, you may imagine that you can get someone to invest in your company and then leave you completely alone. Wouldn't that be nice! The truth is, when someone invests in your company, they become a part-owner. And the minute someone owns a piece of your company, they acquire certain rights.

Some forms of ownership give investors more rights than others. Also, if you haven't set up either a corporation, an LLC, or a limited partnership, your investors are likely to become legally responsible for your company's debts.

You may also think you're protected from other shareholders meddling in the business as long as you keep more than 50% ownership in the company. Beware: Depending on your corporate form, whether you have a Board of Directors, in which U.S. state your company is incorporated, and other factors, shareholders not only have rights, they make binding decisions for the company, and can even remove you from management.

Before you begin parting with any ownership interest in your company —even taking on a good friend or family member as partner—discuss the ramifications with your attorney.

Corporations can issue stock

In the early days of your S or C corporation, when you have very limited money, you may be tempted to promise or hand out a small share of ownership to anyone who invests money in your company or provides you

RED TAPE ALERT!

Any time you deal with stock in your company, you face a host of potential legal and tax implications. Be very cautious about distributing or promising stock in your company and don't do it before you've discussed it thoroughly with a competent attorney and accountant! If, for instance, in the early days of your company, you give a consultant an amount of stock in return for a certain monetary value of service (e.g., 10,000 shares of stock for $5,000 worth of graphic design work), you may inadvertently be placing a value on all other stock that the company has issued or will issue, including the stock you and other founders own. This can have a significant tax impact on you and others. If you issue stock to company founders, or stock options to employees, be sure the correct paperwork, including a "Form 83B Election," has been done, or you may all incur significantly higher taxes.

PEOPLE YOU'VE GIVEN OR PROMISED STOCK

Track here people to whom you've given or promised stock. When starting a new company, you may use promises of stock in many ways—from raising venture money to getting your logo designed. Discuss with your lawyer how to draw up these formal agreements.

Name	Amount or Value of Stock

STOCK DISTRIBUTION PLAN

What percentage of the company do you want or need to give to others? In a young company, the number of shares is not as important as the percentage ownership those shares represent. Use this worksheet to plan the distribution of stock in your company.

	Number of Shares	Percent of Ownership	Vesting Period
☐ Founder #1			
☐ Founder #2			
☐ Founder #3			
☐ CEO			
☐ Chief operating officer			
☐ Chief technology officer			
☐ Chief financial officer			
☐ Other officer level employees			
☐ VP level employees			
☐ Director level employees			
☐ Manager level employees			
☐ Other longtime or key employees			
☐ Other employee levels			
☐ Investors			
☐ Consultants/professional service firms			
☐ Advisory Committee members			
☐ Board of Directors members			
☐ Strategic partners			
☐ Others			

with products or services. After all, it seems a lot cheaper to pay someone with stock than with cash. And it seems a promising sign that others feel that stock in your company will be worth something someday.

Anytime you issue stock, you have to deal with legal and financial considerations. Moreover, you're also diluting your own ownership of the company. When you give someone stock, they're getting a "share" of the company and a percentage of the ownership.

Corporations—not sole proprietorships or LLCs—are the only legal entities that can issue stock. For an LLC, instead of stock, you spell out what percent of ownership each partner or investor receives in the LLC documents. Corporations, however, cannot only issue stock, they can issue different classes of stock—preferred or common—with some shareholders getting better financial treatment than others. For instance, preferred stock shareholders may get paid before common stock shareholders if the company closes and remaining assets are distributed.

If you decide to issue stock in your company, before you start making promises of stock to anyone else, come up with a "Stock Distribution Plan." Investors, of course, will take a significant piece of the ownership, as will you and any other company founders. Set aside a pool of stock for key employees you'll recruit in the future and all other employees. You may also choose to give stock to consultants or other service providers, as well as grant stock to your Advisory Committee members, strategic partners, and others.

Decide at what point a person's stock "vests" or actually becomes theirs. Because your goal is to keep good employees with the business, you typically want their stock to vest over a period of years. If you set up a four-year vesting period, for example, employees might be entitled to one-fourth of their stock after the first year, and then another 1/48th of their stock each month (4 years times 12 months). That way, if they leave before their stock vests, they don't receive more than they deserve.

Use the worksheets on pages 88–89 to outline your stock distribution plan and keep track of whom you've promised or given stock.

BUSINESS LICENSES AND PERMITS

List the licenses and permits you need, including where and how to apply, requirements and fees.

License Type	Agency and Contact Info	Requirements	Fees
☐ Local licenses:			
☐ Local permits:			
☐ County licenses/permits:			
☐ State licenses:			
☐ DBA required:			
☐ Federal certification:			
☐ Other:			

✔ Apply for business licenses, permits, and identification numbers

Whoa! You may be ready to start your business, but the authorities may not want you to—at least not without making sure you have the proper licenses or permits. As frustrating as it may seem, you can't just rent an office or a store and set up shop.

The bureaucratic things you'll deal with fall into three general categories:

1. **Identification numbers:** to keep track of your business with government authorities. Example: federal identification numbers for income tax purposes, such as the Employer Identification Number (EIN) in the United States or the Business Number (BN) in Canada.

2. **Licenses (or certifications):** required to engage either in any business (in a specific locality) or in certain types of businesses or professions. Examples: a city business license, a contractor's license, license to sell alcoholic beverages, an optometrist certification.

3. **Permits:** required for particular, often more limited, actions. Examples: construction permits, special event permits.

Sometimes, these terms are used interchangeably, such as "permit" instead of "license" or vice versa.

To make matters more complicated, you *may* need to get licenses, permits, or identification numbers from different levels of government. These may include:

- **Federal**
- **State**
- **County**
- **City**

The requirements vary greatly depending on the type of business you're opening and the state, county, or city in which you plan to do business. That's why it's good to ask your attorney about these types of licenses.

Listed below are some of the most common issues you're likely to deal with in getting permits, licenses, and identification numbers.

Use the worksheet on page 91 to keep track of which licenses and permits you'll need.

VITAL STATISTICS

Use this worksheet to keep track of important dates, numbers and information about the legal status of your business or yourself. You may be asked to refer to these often.

☐ Date of incorporation:

☐ Corporation number:

☐ Formal company name:

☐ "DBA"/in what county filed/date/number:

☐ Federal Employer Identification Number ("EIN"):

☐ State Employer Identification Number:

☐ Federal business license or permit number:

☐ State business license or permit number:

☐ City business license or permit number:

☐ Better Business Bureau number:

☐ Unemployment insurance provider/date of instatement, renewal date:

☐ Other:

Federal tax ID number

One number you'll be asked for repeatedly is your Federal Employer Identification Number. This may also be referred to as your Employer Identification Number or Tax ID number or a variety of different abbreviations: FIN, TIN, FEIN, and so on. It's one of the most important identification numbers you'll need. Fortunately it's very easy to get.

You'll need a federal tax ID number if your business has employees, or is formed as a corporation, LLC, or partnership. Don't be misled by the word "Employer" in the name—you do not need to have employees to get a Federal Employer Identification Number.

Even if you're not required by law to have a Federal Tax ID number—for instance, if you're operating as a sole proprietor—you may still want to get one. That's because many of your customers—especially if they are other companies, institutions, or government entities—will ask for your Tax ID number. It seems much more professional to have a Tax ID number than to give them your Social Security Number. It's also a lot safer; this way you don't give your personal Social Security Number to strangers.

It's very easy to get a Tax ID number. You can apply online at www.irs.gov. You can also call 1-800-TAX-FORM to request IRS Form SS-4. Be prepared to answer the questions on that form, then call 1-800-829-4933 (toll-free), and the IRS can assign you a Tax ID number over the phone. There's no charge.

Because you'll be asked your Tax ID number frequently, as well as other key company information (for example, date of incorporation), start keeping track of your company's "vital statistics." Use the worksheet on page 93 to keep these handy.

State licenses, certifications, and ID numbers

Individual U.S. states may also assign you an identification or account number for various reasons. The usual are: corporation number for incorporated businesses, employer account number for employer businesses, certificate numbers for specific licenses.

You may also need licenses from the state or other authorities to operate certain businesses. States regulate many industries, from liquor stores to barbershops.

Check It Out

To apply for an EIN on the IRS website (**www.irs.gov**), click on "Tools" and look for "Online Employer Identification Number." In Canada, go to the Canada Revenue Agency (CRA) website (**www.cra-arc.gc.ca**); find "Businesses" and look for "Business Number (BN) registration" under topics.

Certain professions require you to pass a certification test in order to practice that profession in your state. For instance, to practice law in a state, you must pass an exam administered by that state's Bar Association and meet that state's Bar requirements. You may have to take tests for many other trades, such as a Realtor, hairdresser, or contractor.

As to federal involvement in issuing permits and licenses, generally, the federal government doesn't get involved with regulating local or state businesses. There are exceptions, of course, especially if you are involved in interstate transportation (such as interstate moving companies or trucking). And there may be federal requirements regarding your production processes, especially if you use hazardous or environmentally sensitive materials.

This may all seem overwhelming. Ask your attorney, or consult with a local Small Business Development Counselor, about the licenses you'll need in your community and for your type of business.

Reseller's license

There's one government permit you won't mind getting—a reseller's license or reseller's permit. If you are a manufacturer, wholesaler, or retailer, and your state collects sales tax, you may qualify for a reseller's license.

Such a license enables your company to purchase goods or materials for manufacture or sale without your having to pay sales tax, since you are not the ultimate consumer—your customer is.

In other words, if I own a sporting goods store, I can buy golf clubs from the manufacturer without paying sales tax because I will charge *my* customers the tax. If I'm going to use the clubs myself, I do need to pay the sales tax since the exemption is allowed only on goods I will resell.

Once again, each state has its own requirements and terminology. So check your own state's rules. Some states don't even require a license for you to get an exemption from sales tax—just a signed statement of intent to resell goods.

County and city licenses, permits, and ID numbers

Most cities or counties require some form of basic business license no matter what kind of business you're in. If you want to open up shop—whether a retail store, a dentist's office, or even a consulting practice—you have to get

> ## Check It Out
>
> Locate state and local government information at: **www.statelocalgov. net.** This is a private website, but easy to use. This is the Library of Congress guide to state websites: **www.loc. gov/rr/news/stategov/ stategov.html**

a business license from your county or city. This may feel like "Big Brother," but it provides your local government with information on what kinds of businesses are being operated in the community and who is responsible for the company. Of course, there are usually fees or taxes they collect too!

In addition to basic business licenses, cities frequently require permits to operate some kinds of businesses, install various types of business equipment, or make changes in buildings or facilities.

Use the worksheet on page 93 to keep track of all the state business licenses and permits you need.

"DBA" (Doing Business As) or fictitious business name

If you use any name other than your own personal name for doing business, you'll need to file a "doing business as" or fictitious business statement, usually with your county government. This enables the public to know who's actually operating a company. In some states, you may have to publish this information in a local newspaper.

In other words, if I own a flower shop called "Blooming Nuts," I must file a DBA, so people will know that I'm the nut behind Blooming Nuts.

But even if I use the business name "Abrams and Associates," I have to file a DBA, since that is not my full legal name (it's Rhonda Abrams).

Check with your attorney, SBDC, or county government regarding the fictitious name requirements in your area.

 ## Discuss collecting sales tax

As a buyer, when I purchase something from a local business, I pay sales tax. I may not like the extra cost, but it's a pretty seamless transaction—the seller just tacks on the appropriate percentage, and I pay the total amount. But what happens when I'm the seller?

How do you, as a businessperson, know whether you have to collect sales tax? Here's the short answer: Collect sales tax on most goods and some services that are delivered to a customer in any U.S. state in which you have any physical presence.

The long answer is much more complicated. Sales tax rates and rules vary from state to state, city to city. There's truly a hodgepodge of laws and taxing authorities. According to the National Retail Federation,

45 states and more than 7,500 cities, counties, and jurisdictions impose sales taxes.

States call these taxes by various names: sales tax, franchise tax, transaction privilege tax, use tax, and more. Some are the responsibility of the seller, others the buyer. But governments figured out that it was easier and more reliable to make the seller collect the tax than to get individual consumers to send in tax on every purchase. So, businesses are typically responsible for collecting sales tax and sending it to the state.

Generally, if you're going to collect sales tax, you must get a license from your state. On each taxable transaction, you calculate the applicable sales tax, collect it from the buyer, keep tax records, and then file a tax return and pay the taxes to your state. You'll pay monthly, quarterly, or annually, depending on your level of sales.

Each state makes its own rules as to what sales are taxable. Typically, most products sold to end users are taxable. Major exemptions include:

- **Prescription drugs**
- **Food, especially groceries and nonprepared food**
- **Animal feed, seed, and many agricultural products**
- **Products for resale—raw materials, inventory, and other items that are going to be sold, rather than used, by your customer**

Many states also exempt services from sales tax. But that varies greatly from state to state, and even within a state the rules as to what is taxable and what is not seem very inconsistent.

As for sales taxes on remote sales, meaning sales you make to customers outside of your home state, most likely you will be exempt from collecting these if your remote sales are less than $1 million a year. Remote sales include online sales and catalog sales—for example, to customers who live in a state other than your own, and in which you have no physical presence. A physical presence in a state can include a location, facility, employee, call center, warehouse, address, or even one independent salesperson.

At the time of the publication of this book, ecommerce sales tax laws were still in flux, and as you read this, rules and tools for collecting taxes are likely still developing. But keep this in mind: Most likely, you will have to deal with collecting taxes on sales you make outside of your state if you sell over $1 million a year remotely; most small businesses just launching will not reach that number.

Start It Free

TaxCloud (**www.taxcloud.net**) is an application that both online and bricks-and-mortar retailers can use to calculate, collect, and file sales taxes for free. The tax management application integrates with most accounting systems and online shopping carts, automatically calculating sales tax rates based on the origin of the shipment, the destination, and the class of goods. You can also use the site to simply look up sales tax rates for any city in the U.S.

One thing's for certain—if you're going to make sales in any state with a sales tax, talk to your attorney. You may also want to discuss this issue with your accountant (Week Five). It's not easy to figure out all the details on your own.

 ## Draw up basic contracts and other legal agreements

While the days of doing business with just a handshake may not be over entirely, doing so leaves you at risk. Ours is a litigious society, and the best way to avoid ending up in court—or in hot water—is to get things in writing.

You're likely to find you have a number of agreements or contracts that you'll use over and over. For instance, a consultant may have a simple letter of engagement; an electrician might have a standard contract. Have your attorney help you draft a standard template for these documents, into which you can just plug the specifics each time.

Some of the many types of legal agreements you may need are:

- **Contract**
- **Letter of agreement or engagement**
- **Leases**
- **Employment contracts**
- **Distribution agreements**
- **Project proposals**
- **Work-for-hire agreements**
- **Statements of work (SOWs)**
- **Nondisclosure agreements**
- **Noncompete agreements**

 ## Protect your intellectual property

What is the value of the Nike "swoosh?" The design of a Macintosh computer? The content of a Beatles song? We all recognize that these things have a value far beyond the "physical property" of the running shoes, computers, or CDs themselves because of the "intellectual property" of the swoosh, the design, or the wonderful music and lyrics of John Lennon and Paul McCartney.

Every company has certain intangible things that are, or can be, very valuable. Many of these come under the heading of "Intellectual Property"—assets that have value because of the knowledge, recognition, inventiveness, and so on, that they consist of. Indeed, some companies *only* have products composed of intellectual property—software developers, writers, inventors, consultants, and many more.

So just as you would protect the physical property of your company, you need to protect your intellectual property.

Trade secrets: Just about every company has ideas or knowledge that gives them a competitive edge, and which would be harmful if shared with others. If you're only starting out, your business concept may be one of your major assets. But "trade secrets" covers a huge range of things—from how you make a product to the preferences of your best customer.

The law provides a certain amount of protection to you for your trade secrets—but only if you take steps to keep such information secret. So be careful how you disseminate information: Mark documents "confidential," get others to sign nondisclosure agreements, put passwords and other security measures on "work-in-progress" websites or computer programs, and be careful whom you talk to!

Nondisclosure agreements: One of the simplest ways to protect your ideas is to get a signed nondisclosure agreement or confidentiality agreement before discussing your concepts with others. This is a typical procedure, and you'll often be asked to sign NDAs if you're trying to do business with another company. Venture capitalists will *not* sign NDAs, as they see too many new business ideas.

WHAT WOULD RHONDA DO?

TRADEMARKS

I'd be sure to avoid any name close to or potentially confusing with a big company's trademark. It may seem silly when a big corporation goes after a tiny company, but if a big company doesn't protect its trademark, the law says they can lose it. They have no choice but to sue. Even if you're legally in the clear, with a trademark issued to you, the reality is that in trademark issues, the side with the greatest ability and willingness to spend money on lawyers gets their way. McDonald's, for instance, vigorously goes after any company that uses the prefix "Mc" even for products or services that could not possibly be confused with food. So don't even think of naming your barber shop "McHaircut."

Noncompete agreements: Once a trade secret is learned, it can't be unlearned. So sometimes the biggest fear you have is that a valuable and knowledgeable employee will go to work for a competitor. To help guard against this, you may want to have employees sign an agreement limiting their ability to go work for a competing company (or start their own competing company) for a period of time. Noncompete agreements provide a measure of protection, but courts don't like enforcing them, so make certain they are carefully written and appropriately used. Some states, like California, may not enforce noncompete agreements.

Trademarks/service marks: In Week One you spent some time determining whether or not the trademarks and service marks you plan to use are available (see page 31).

The Internet makes trademark issues particularly baffling. A company may have happily and legally been doing business in one state for decades without being confused with a business using the same name in another state. Now one of these companies puts up a site online, and customers don't know who's who.

Check It Out

Although your work is automatically copyrighted at the time you create it, you may want to further protect yourself by registering your creation with the U.S. Copyright Office (**www.copyright. gov**). In Canada, register your copyright with the Canadian Intellectual Property Office (**www. cipo.ic.gc.ca**).

Since many companies can have the same trademarked name in different categories, your domain name may legally be taken by another trademark owner, leaving you without any recourse.

So now's the time to talk with your attorney about ensuring that your marks are protected—both online and off.

Copyrights: If you create works that others might want to copy—content, music, art, software, illustrations, and the like—you'll want to protect what you've created. This is where copyright law comes in.

Copyrights cover any type of work that is "fixed" and "tangible"—even if it's only computer code, words spoken on an audiotape, or images "fixed" on a movie.

Copyrights do not cover "ideas" no matter how unique, just the particular fixed expression of that idea. For instance, you can't copyright your idea to have a boy go off to a school for wizards, but you can copyright your novel telling the story of this boy.

Once you have a copyright, you retain the rights to that creation, and no one else can make a movie about your hero without your permission.

RED TAPE ALERT! Whenever others help you create any of your intellectual property, you want to make clear who owns what they develop. For instance, if you hire a graphic designer to create your logo, software developers to write computer code, or writers to create content, who owns the rights to all those creations? In most cases, you want to make sure you do! So in your contract or agreement, clarify the ownership of the work product, make certain that they are required to transfer any copyright or other ownership if necessary, and specify that you are hiring them on a "work-for-hire" basis, with all work product becoming your property. And have the agreement looked at by an attorney.

You also can't copyright "facts." So if what you're creating is purely the compilation of facts, you won't be able to copyright that.

Copyrights are easy to get. The rights to your creation are yours *at the moment you create it;* theoretically, you don't have to do anything to ensure your copyright. But that puts you at some risk. The easiest thing to do to protect your copyright is to add a simple copyright notice whenever you produce something. Just add the word "copyright," the © symbol, the year, and your name (copyright ©2013, Rhonda Abrams).

Patents: Copyrights are easy to get; patents are incredibly tough. Copyrights cost little; patents are very expensive. Copyrights are yours the instant you create the work; patents can take years to get. Patents are also difficult and costly to enforce—if someone violates your patent and starts selling a knock-off of your product, it may take a lot of money (in legal fees) and time to put a stop to it—and if they're overseas, enforcement will be even harder. So if you're building your business around a new invention, process, machine, recipe, or formula that needs to be patented, it'll be tough going.

If, however, you have a new invention or a new process that is indeed unique, "nonobvious" (a requirement for qualifying for a patent), and worth a lot of money, then pursue the patent process. The first thing you'll need—after you've come up with your invention or idea—is a good patent attorney. A good one will warn you of the costs and pitfalls before you get too far down the road. To find a competent patent lawyer, start by asking your business attorney.

Build your team and personnel structure

My Checklist:

☐ **Consider your support structure**

☐ **Decide whom you need on your team**

☐ **Figure out how much you can afford**

☐ **Examine the use of independent contractors**

☐ **Understand employment laws and consider your personnel policies**

☐ **Appraise your management style**

 ## Consider your support structure

You don't have to have employees to build a team. Even if yours is a one-person business, you'll want to find people to turn to for guidance as you start, run, and grow your company. Building a company can be lonely work. Advisors can be one of the most valuable assets an entrepreneur can have, providing support, contacts, and advice.

Business buddies/mentors: In my early years in business—when I worked alone and out of my home—I had my "business buddy," Jennifer. Jennifer was a good friend who had started a consulting practice at about the same time I did. Her work was similar to mine, although in a different industry.

Jennifer and I would share templates for writing proposals or sending invoices. We'd discuss how to bill or collect from our clients and swap solutions to client problems we were having. Sometimes the most important thing was just to have a conversation in the middle of the afternoon when one of us felt lonely or overwhelmed.

Finding a novice entrepreneur who's in the same stage of business as you can be a great way to get support. You'll have each other to think through ideas, learn from, and be each other's cheerleader.

MY SUPPORT SYSTEM

Use this worksheet to list the names of people or organizations you can turn to for support and advice. Include potential supporters from whom you may want to seek help in the future.

☐ Business buddies:

☐ Mentors:

☐ Entrepreneurs' groups:

☐ Blogs/online communities:

☐ Industry groups:

☐ Advisory Committee members:

☐ Board of Directors members:

☐ Others:

If you can, find a more experienced businessperson to serve as your informal "mentor." Many accomplished entrepreneurs enjoy helping others, and you can learn from someone who's already gone through the process of setting up a business.

Don't be afraid to ask for help. Many people are willing to be of assistance, especially if you're professional in your approach and realistic about what kind of help you need and what they're able to offer.

Advisory Committee: An Advisory Committee is an informal group with no legal authority, no legal liability, and no set rules about when to meet or how many people must be involved. In fact, they don't ever have to meet; your Advisory Committee can simply be a few people who've agreed to let you turn to them for advice.

The point of having advisors is to seek advice, so look for people whose advice you trust to serve on your committee. Ideally you'll find wise folks who are seasoned entrepreneurs from your industry. Be wary of asking potential investors, customers, employees, or, naturally, competitors. You don't need many advisors, and you don't have to ask everybody at once.

Most people willing to be an advisor aren't motivated by money—they're motivated to help you succeed. If you do want to reward them, and you're setting up stock in your company, granting stock would be a good form of compensation; that way, your advisors will share in your success. Of course, make sure your advisors get any company trinkets—t-shirts, coffee mugs, pens, and the like.

One of the best things about formally asking people to serve as members of your Advisory Committee is that they then have a sense of ownership and continuing interest in your company. They may initiate conversations with you, make suggestions, or provide useful connections. Setting up an Advisory Committee is a good way to get support from people you trust and admire.

Board of Directors: This is typically a legal entity required for an incorporated company (check with your lawyer for rules relating to corporations and Boards of Directors in your state). It has legal responsibilities established by the state and will probably be required to meet at least once a year and record minutes of its meetings.

Members of the Board of Directors have a fiduciary duty to protect the interests of the shareholders of the company—not to protect you. They can control the decisions about management of the company even if you own a controlling interest in the stock. They have legal liability for the company's actions, so they should take their role very seriously. In many companies, especially large companies, board members are paid—or at least reimbursed for their expenses incurred coming to board meetings or doing company business.

In some states, you may not need to have any members of the board other than yourself or the company owners or founders and you may not need any outside board members. But there are occasions when you might want to—or need to—invite outside people to sit on your board. For instance, if you have investors, especially venture capitalists, they'll expect to be on the board. If you are able to secure well-known individuals from your industry, or a related industry, you can gain valuable advice and insight as well as adding stature and connections to your company.

Whom should you ask to be on your board? Since the board makes legally binding decisions for the company, be very careful about whom you ask. The best board members are those who understand your business, are supportive of you (even when they challenge particular decisions), have a long-range view of your company's growth, and bring excellent connections to the business or financial world.

Use the worksheet on page 103 to sketch out how you'll build your support system.

Decide whom you need on your team

What kind of help will you need to succeed? Who will handle your financial affairs, make sales, plan operations, and produce your goods? What roles do you need to fill "in-house" and what jobs can you fill with outside contractors or suppliers?

Every company's need for staff is unique—a restaurant clearly has different staffing needs than a medical equipment manufacturer or an out-source design firm. Some companies—such as consulting firms—can be more flexible in their hiring arrangements, perhaps only hiring employees or using independent contractors after a client or project is secured. Others—such as manufacturers—usually need staff before they can actually make a sale. Even if you're a "solopreneur," here's something to keep in mind: If you want to grow a company with real value beyond the hours you put in, you're going to need help.

WHOM DO I NEED ON MY TEAM?

List the job titles needed in each area. Some suggestions for managers and officers are in parentheses, but you should hire only those your company really needs as it grows.

Key Personnel	Responsibilities	Desired Experience/Background
☐ **Top Management** (President/CEO)		
☐ **Administrative** (Office Manager, Administrative Assistants)		
☐ **Financial** (Controller, Bookkeeper, etc.)		
☐ **Marketing/Sales/PR** (VP Marketing, Salesperson, PR Director)		
☐ **Operations/Production** (Production Manager)		
☐ **Technology** (Chief Technology Officer, Website Developer, Tech Support)		
☐ **Human Resources** (Personnel Director)		
☐ **Logistics Staff** (Shipping Clerk, Janitor)		
☐ **Other:**		

Desired Attitudes/Habits	Desired Education/ Training	Skills Desired	Compensation

Hiring enables you to:

- **Serve more customers**
- **Produce more products or services**
- **Add additional skills and talents to your business**
- **Spend your time on the things you do best and like to do**
- **Make money when someone else is working**
- **Grow your company**

Whom do you need on your team? Brainstorm about the jobs you need done in your business. After compiling your list, indicate whether you want to keep these tasks for yourself, hand them over to someone else, or share these duties. This will start to give you an idea of the jobs you'd like to hire others to complete.

Check It Out

Small businesses with 1 to 24 employees typically hire a quarter of their employees on a part-time basis. For more small business statistics and information on services, visit the Small Business Administration (www.sba.gov).

You're almost certain to have a long, long list of things you'd like someone else to do. Prioritize what you'd like accomplished. Can they all be undertaken by the same person? In a small business, it's typical for people to wear many hats, but you still have to consider whether one real-live person can manage very different tasks. For instance, is it realistic to imagine that the person who handles your administrative paperwork can also do some bookkeeping, shipping, and basic work on your website? Probably. But is it realistic to think the person who's going to handle your administrative tasks can also manage your computer network, handle your back-end technology needs, and make sales calls? Probably not.

Also consider how much time you'll require from an employee. Based on your job requirements—and your budget—consider the range of your options for getting the help you need. Not all new hires need to be full-time employees. It might make sense for you to hire part-time workers, a short-term contractor or independent consultant, even college interns.

Common functions for small business employees include:

- **Administrative**
- **Sales/customer service**
- **Billing/bookkeeping**
- **Production**
- **Shipping**
- **Marketing**
- **IT/technology planning**

Use the worksheet on pages 106–107 to identify the positions you need to fill and the specifics of each job.

 ## Figure out how much you can afford

One of the biggest hurdles to overcome when deciding to hire is figuring out how much you can afford. Fear over making enough money is probably the biggest obstacle to becoming an employer. After all, if you don't make enough money in a month, you still have to pay your employees—it's the law. That means you might not have enough money to pay for other things—your rent, your suppliers, or yourself. But employees are an investment in your business—not simply a cost—and the goal is greater growth. As with every investment, you can address your concerns with some careful planning.

When figuring out how much you can pay an employee, take the following steps:

1. **Review your monthly cash flow.** Even if your business is profitable at the end of the year, you have to make payroll every two weeks or so. That means you need cash in the bank. Take a realistic look at your monthly dollars in and dollars out.

2. **Estimate your monthly profit.** Will you consistently generate enough income to support the type of employee you need, as well as yourself?

3. **Estimate expected additional income.** The goal of hiring employees is to make more money. How much will they realistically help you generate? In what time frame? Be conservative in these projections.

4. **Estimate how much you'll pay an employee.** Once you decide what role and tasks you want your new employee to assume, investigate comparable pay rates.

5. **Estimate monthly taxes and benefits.** Budget an additional 15–30% of their salary for payroll taxes and benefits.

6. **Estimate additional costs.** With the new employee on board, will you pay higher rent for more space? Have increased telecom or travel expenses? Greater use of office equipment? Make a guesstimate of these costs as well.

A good plan is to save up for payroll just as you save for other investments. Set up a separate payroll account with enough money to cover at least three months' worth of payroll and taxes. Expect to make payroll from monthly cash flow rather than this separate account, which acts as an emergency backup in case you have a bad month. This financial cushion allows you to hire with more confidence.

Use the worksheet on page 111 to calculate how much money you'll have available each month for wages.

 ## Examine the use of independent contractors

Most companies use outside providers to perform certain tasks. It's not necessary that you handle every function—even relatively critical functions—with people you employ on your own staff.

You can outsource all kinds of responsibilities, including bookkeeping, website design and hosting, payroll management, public relations, marketing, employee training, and even many aspects of production.

To provide these functions, you can use other companies or hire self-employed individuals—independent contractors.

Indeed, it may be that you—or your business—might serve as an outside provider of services or as an independent contractor for other companies. This is especially true if you provide services like those listed above.

Few areas of employment law are murkier than who qualifies as an independent contractor for tax purposes and who doesn't. And few areas of tax law can get a business—or an independent contractor—in more trouble with the IRS. Here's why:

As a business owner, you—naturally—want to reduce your costs as much as possible. When you hire someone to work for you, you can pay them in one of two ways:

- **as an employee:** paying additional payroll, Social Security, and unemployment taxes (and typically providing benefits); or

- **as an independent contractor:** paying no additional taxes (and typically not providing any benefits).

HOW MUCH CAN I AFFORD?

Use this worksheet to estimate how much money you'll have available each month to pay wages or salaries.

A. Current monthly profit	
B. Estimated increased monthly income	
C. Subtotal: Add (A) profit and (B) increased income	
D. Expected monthly salary/wages	
E. Estimated monthly taxes/benefits	
F. Estimated other monthly costs	
G. Subtotal: Add (D)wages, (E) taxes/benefits, and (F) other costs	
TOTAL: Subtract line G from line C.	

As an individual working for others, you can work:

- **As an employee:** receiving less money in your pocket due to withholding taxes but also receiving more legal protections and typically more benefits; or

- **As an independent contractor:** often getting more money in your pocket since there are no withholding taxes, but also receiving no benefits and little or no worker protection, and having to deal with the hassle and paperwork of handling and paying your own taxes quarterly or at the end of the year.

Employee vs. Independent Contractor: The Right Classification

EMPLOYEES...	INDEPENDENT CONTRACTORS...
Do not run their own business	Are independent businesspeople, especially if they are incorporated
Work in your office and use equipment you provide	Choose their work location and provide their own equipment, tools, and materials
Work hours specified by you	Set their own hours
Work per your instructions and may receive training from you	Decide how to perform their services, in what order, and usually receive no training
Are paid for their labor regardless of business performance	Can earn a profit or suffer a loss depending on the quality and quantity of services they provide
Work for you on a continuing basis	Typically manage multiple clients or customers and work for you on an as-needed project basis
Receive employee benefits	Are responsible for their own benefits
Are usually paid by unit of time	Are usually paid a flat rate or by project
Can quit or be fired at any time	Can be terminated or leave according to the terms of their agreement with you

Obviously, many businesses would prefer to treat "employees" as independent contractors and avoid all those pesky taxes and worker protections. Equally obviously, the federal government, states, and cities, want to make certain that anyone who actually does the work of an employee gets treated—and protected—as such, and that all payroll and Social Security taxes are paid.

So watch out! The IRS is particularly aggressive in pursuing companies that intentionally—or unintentionally—inappropriately pay workers as independent contractors instead of as employees.

There used to be a list of specific rules governing independent contractor status, but the IRS, responding to the legitimate needs of businesses for greater flexibility in hiring independent contractors, made the rules broader. Yet that leaves more room for misunderstanding.

In determining employee status, the IRS looks at three areas:

- **Behavioral:** Does the worker control how they do the work? Who controls:

  —**When and where the worker does the work?**
  —**What tools or equipment they use?**
  —**Who determines where they purchase supplies?**
  —**What order or sequence of work to follow?**

- **Financial:** Does the worker have a significant investment (e.g., own their own tools)? Can they make a profit or loss? Do they make their services available to others or work for other businesses?

- **Type of relationship:** How permanent is the relationship? Is there a written contract? Is the worker responsible for their own benefits? Is the work performed a critical and regular part of the business?

Because the rules are somewhat fuzzy, the IRS does provide some protection for businesses that make mistakes in treating employees as independent contractors—as long as those mistakes were made in good faith. They'll look to see whether a business relied on advice of an attorney or accountant, followed industry practice, and treated workers consistently.

But—and this is critical—there's absolutely *no* protection for a company that doesn't file the necessary tax forms. Each year, you are required to file a Form 1099-MISC, reporting payment to independent contractors over a certain dollar figure. If you fail to file 1099s and the IRS later

Start It Free

If you expect to receive a large number of resumes for your job opening, you may want to manage them online with a cloud-based tool like Zoho Recruit (**www. zoho.com/recruit**). This solution enables you to collect resumes from your website, track applicants, schedule and track interviews, and more. The free plan supports several job openings.

challenges you on the classification of independent contractors, you're in very hot water.

Check It Out

IRS Publication 15-A can help you make sure you stay well within the IRS's employment rules. www.irs.gov/pub/irs-pdf/p15a.pdf

As an employer, before using independent contractors, consider the impact on your workers' productivity. Legitimate, self-employed contractors are usually highly motivated to do a good job; they want to keep you as a client and have you refer others. The opposite happens when a business needs employees—with definite work hours, specific work, and supervisors directly managing them—but treats them as independent contractors. Such workers are demoralized, less productive, eager to find better employment, and more likely to call the IRS if you're not following the law.

If you plan on using independent contractors, be certain to ask your attorney (this week) about how to stay well within the law, and check with your accountant (Week Five) about filing all necessary tax forms.

RED TAPE ALERT!

Federal and state governments impose several laws on compensation, treatment, and protection of employees. Among the many regulations your business must follow are the following:

- OSHA safety rules and record keeping
- Minimum wage and hour laws and child labor laws
- Tax withholdings, including income, Social Security, and unemployment taxes
- Insurance requirements, including workers' compensation and "COBRA" requirements
- Anti-discrimination laws
- Immigration laws
- Family and medical leave laws
- Employee vs. independent contractor distinctions
- Exept vs. non-exempt employee distinctions
- Posters and record keeping laws
- Employee vs. independent contractor distinctions
- Exempt vs. non-exempt employee distinctions
- Posters and record keeping laws

✔ **Understand employment laws and consider your personnel policies**

As soon as you decide to hire your first employee, you'll need to understand critical personnel laws. There are many government protections for workers, as well as extra taxes and obligations on you as an employer. Things such as questions you can't ask in an interview, how many hours an employee can work without getting paid overtime, even how long a lunch break must be are all likely to be covered under federal or state labor laws. You want to avoid running into any trouble with government agencies just because you inadvertently violated employment laws.

Additionally, you'll need to come up with basic personnel policies: benefits, vacation, holidays, sick days, working hours, and so forth. Even in a very small company, a written set of policies helps create a sense of security and fairness for employees.

Developing company policies doesn't mean you need a five-inch-thick rule book. You can develop a simple set of policies, listing:

- **Number of vacation days earned each year, and how many of these days can be carried forward if not used**
- **Number of sick days each year**
- **Number of personal leave days, and whether these can be taken as partial days**
- **Paid holidays**
- **Working hours**

In a very small company—with highly motivated staff—you may be able to keep these issues flexible (as long as you follow the law, of course).

As you develop your company policies, be clear, allow flexibility when you can, and above all, be fair. Treating people fairly does not necessarily mean treating people equally: A salesperson may need a paid cell phone; a stockroom clerk may not. An employee with a terminally ill relative may need more flexible work schedules than others. Part of your job as an employer is to constantly examine your own actions for bias. Apply the same standards—not the same rules—to all.

Sometimes you can't be flexible—rules have to be followed. This is particularly true when company policy is dictated by law. When you have to follow inflexible rules, let employees know why. Is it for safety, to obey

Check It Out

Labor laws vary from state to state. Visit the U.S. Department of Labor for federal rules (**www.dol.gov**), then enter "state labor offices" into the search field to find links to your state's site. Visit **www.business. gov** for more helpful information.

MY PERSONNEL POLICIES

Always check with an attorney or human resources specialist before finalizing your personnel policies, as state and federal laws may affect your policies regarding overtime, work hours, family leave, and so on.

☐ **Work Hours**

Starting time: _____

Ending time: _____

Flex time policies: _____

Overtime policies: _____

Other: _____

☐ **Vacation Days**

Number of days per year: _____

When do they become available? _____

Increases after years of service? How many? _____

Can unused vacation days be accumulated? How many? How long? _____

What times of year can they be taken? How do they have to notify you? _____

☐ **Sick Leave**

How many paid sick days off per year? _____

Can they be accumulated? _____

Special circumstances? _____

☐ **Personal Leave**

Will you allow any paid personal leave time? How much? _____
_____

How much notice do employees have to give for personal leave? _____

☐ **Holidays**

Which holidays will be time off with pay? _____
_____

Any "floating" holidays? _____

Any other time-off policies, either paid or unpaid, sabbaticals, etc.? _____
_____

☐ **Reimbursement Policies?**

Which expenses will the company reimburse employees for? (e.g., travel, commute, parking, public transportation):
_____

How will those have to be documented/submitted? _____
_____

☐ **Insurance**

List the insurance coverage you'll offer and how and whether dependents are covered:

Health insurance: _____

Dental insurance: _____

Vision insurance: _____

Life insurance: _____

Disability: _____

Other: _____

☐ **Retirement Program**

Will you offer a retirement plan? _____

List details: who is covered, when the plans vest, what amount employees have to contribute, etc.:

_____

_____

☐ **Training/Education**

What ongoing training will you offer employees? _____

Will you reimburse/pay for noncompany-sponsored education/training programs/tuition?

_____

☐ **Benefits**

List any other special perks/benefits offered (e.g., cell phones, auto lease, birthdays off, etc.):

_____

_____

☐ **Employees Who Telecommute/Work from Home Offices**

What reimbursements do you offer them? (e.g., phone, Internet connection, cell phone, office supplies, electricity, furniture allowance, etc.): _____

_____

How do they get reimbursements (submit monthly form or give ongoing amount?): _____

How many days/weeks are they expected to be at the main office? _____

Other: _____

☐ **Performance Review**

How often will you do performance reviews? _____

On what basis will performance be judged? _____

Who will participate in reviewing employees? _____

Other: _____

laws, or to meet certain standards? Help people understand why a rule isn't silly.

Nordstrom, the upscale department store, became famous for its outstanding customer service. How does Nordstrom instill such dedication and loyalty in its employees? One factor may be its personnel policies. The Nordstrom personnel manual contains only one sentence: "Use good judgement in all situations."

Use the worksheet on pages 116–117 to establish the main policies your business will follow in dealing with employees.

Finding and hiring good people

Your business is only as good as the people who work for it. No matter how good your product, how necessary your service, or how innovative your technology, it's the people in your company that will ultimately determine your success. That's why it's important to find the right people, then train, nurture, and reward them.

When you have an immediate need for help, you might be tempted to hire anyone you can get, but it's often better to leave a position unfilled until you can find a person you consider capable and trustworthy.

Here's something to keep in mind right from the start: Hire for attitude, train for skills. You want people on your team with good work habits, a positive attitude, and an ability to get along with others. In most cases, you can teach a smart and willing person a particular skill (such as how to use a software program or operate a piece of machinery). It's much more challenging—and a lot more work—to instill the right attitude in the wrong person.

The key to successful hiring is to have a very clear definition of the position you're filling. Job descriptions spell out the critical duties, roles, and responsibilities of a specific job. When a candidate reads a well-crafted job description, they should be clear about what the position involves. This clarity should help them figure out whether the job suits their interests, skills, and background. A well-crafted job description helps you attract the candidates you want and weed out the ones you don't.

Check It Out

To prepare for an in-person interview, read Rhonda's tips for interviews that click. www.planningshop.com/hire/interviewtips

QUESTIONS TO ASK
POTENTIAL EMPLOYEES

Don't wait until a job applicant is sitting in the waiting room before figuring out what to ask. Take time well before the first interview and make a list of things you'd like to know about your candidate, such as whether they have the right experience, skills, education, and so forth. Ask specific questions in those areas, "What were your exact responsibilities?", "What computer programs did you use regularly?" And so on. Find out, also, what they liked and didn't like about their previous jobs and what they hope for in their new position. That gives you a better sense of whether they are a good fit for your job and your company.

During interviews, don't do all the talking! It's appropriate to explain the job and, in many cases, to try to "sell" the job to the candidate, but most of the time the candidate should be talking, not you. You may want others to also interview the applicant, especially the prospect's direct manager, and possibly coworkers and even people who will work for him or her.

In addition to direct work-related questions, it's important to ask questions that give you a sense of the applicant as a person and their attitudes toward responsibility, working in a team, how flexible they are when faced with change or uncertainty, and so forth. But be careful! Some questions are illegal to ask. You can't, for instance, ask a candidate about their marital status, plans for having children, religion, or age (in most cases). But it's perfectly legal to ask about hobbies, interests, and long-term goals.

And never, never discriminate on the basis of race, gender, age, national origin, and the like. It's not just illegal—you'll eliminate some terrific potential employees.

Consider the following criteria when writing a job description:

- **Skill sets desired.** Envision the daily tasks and activities your new hire will have to perform. What are the must-have skills? What would be nice to have?

- **Past experience needed.** Which critical aspects of the job would benefit from specific past work experience? Are you looking for a particular educational background or someone with specialized training? Do they need prior industry knowledge or experience performing certain job functions?

- **Personal characteristics desired.** Do you need an outgoing and friendly employee for a customer service job? A creative one for a marketing position? It's OK to include personal traits if they're key to finding a good fit, but avoid potential legal problems by focusing on qualities needed to do the job well, not qualities like age or gender.

- **Where you'll compromise.** Know if you'd be willing to provide on-the-job training for a candidate with the right personality and less experience. Make sure your job description emphasizes the things that are the *most* important to you.

As you jot down a list of job duties and responsibilities, think not only of the tasks you want help with right now, but of your long-term needs also. As your business grows and attracts more customers, what duties will you want this employee to perform? Forecast for your reasonable immediate future growth and plan ahead.

Here are other ways to increase the quality of job applicants:

- **Create an ongoing recruitment campaign:** Develop a network of referral sources, and remind everyone in your company to be on the lookout for great employees.

- **Be creative in your ads:** When you place a "help-wanted ad," create as much attention and interest as possible. Express the "personality" of your company in your ads.

- **Hire the unusual:** Increase your applicant pool by expanding your vision of a typical employee. Does your industry usually hire young people? Try recruiting retirees. How about looking for employees with disabilities? Or from different ethnic groups? Sometimes the best employees don't look like the ones you already have.

- **Be in the game on salary and benefits:** As a new company, you may not be able to pay more than big companies or give as many benefits, but you'd better be fairly competitive. You can't be so far apart that any applicant would feel like a fool for accepting your job.

- **Offer creative "perks":** We allow employees to bring their dogs to work; I give employees their birthday as a paid holiday. One of the best perks is flexibility. An applicant may want to start work at 10 a.m. to avoid rush hour and stay later, or come to work earlier and leave at

Check It Out

Popular online job sites include Craigslist (**www.craigslist.org**), Monster (**www.monster.com**), CareerBuilder (**www.careerbuilder.com**), and LinkedIn (**www.linkedin.com**)

3:30 p.m. to be home with the kids after school. Of course, this isn't always possible, but flexibility is a highly desired job benefit.

- **Act fast:** If you see someone you really like, be prepared to decide and make an offer. But don't ever hire out of desperation; it's better to keep a job open than be stuck with the wrong person.

- **Get a reputation as a great place to work:** Sure, all applicants look at tangible benefits. But in the long run, what encourages current employees to recruit others, reduces turnover, and attracts the best new applicants, is building a business where people feel good about going to work—a company with integrity, that shows respect for all, and that lets people also have fun. Do that, and they'll line up at your door.

Use the worksheet on page 123 to identify places to seek employees.

Hire Your First Employee guides you step-by-step through everything you need to make the decision to hire, find the right people, and lead and manage your team. It's available in bookstores throughout the U.S., or from PlanningShop, www.PlanningShop.com.

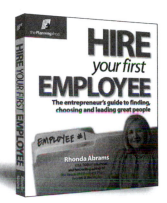

Compensation

To attract good employees, you have to offer salaries and benefits that are competitive with similar businesses in your area. Most employees' main financial concern is the salary or wage offered, but they will also decide to accept a job based on the total "package," including:

- **Base salary/wage**
- **Bonuses, based on either individual performance, group or company performance, or guaranteed bonus**
- **Overtime, which may be set by law**
- **Signing bonus, as an incentive in a very tight job market**
- **Commissions, given on sales made**
- **Profit sharing, a portion of the overall company profits**
- **Stock options or stock purchase plans, giving the employee a discounted means to purchase a direct financial stake in the company**

To determine the "going rate" for your new employee, do some research to determine how much other companies pay. Keep in mind that you want to look for comparable pay based on job duties, location, industry, and business size.

Check It Out

Research comparable compensation at **www.salary.com** or **www.salaryexpert.com**

Find out the average compensation for over 800 occupations from the Bureau of Labor Statistics, **www.bls.gov/oes**

RED TAPE ALERT!

Discrimination. It's not good business. It's not good behavior. And it's against the law. In virtually all situations, it is illegal to discriminate against employees because of race, religion, sex, or national origin. In many situations, it's illegal to discriminate on the basis of age, physical disability, or sexual orientation. You may not discriminate in hiring, promotion, pay, or treatment. Moreover, it is your responsibility as an employer to create an environment that is not hostile to any individual or group based on such factors. You must also make "reasonable accommodation" to employees' religious observance needs, such as allowing them time off on their sabbaths or holy days or wearing articles of religious attire (unless there is a significant safety concern). Ask your attorney about conforming to regulations laid out in the Civil Rights Act, Americans with Disabilities Act (ADA), and other anti-discrimination laws.

Benefits

When a potential employee—especially a well-qualified employee—considers accepting a job, they're going to weigh many things besides simply how much the job pays. They're going to look at the full range of benefits they receive—things such as health care, vacation, retirement, sick leave, and more. In human resource terms, this is called the "package," and employees always consider the total package of benefits they'll receive.

You'll be surprised at how few benefits you're actually required to offer by law. In most states, you don't even have to offer sick leave, let alone health insurance. So why bother? Consider the upside of providing good benefits:

■ A competitive benefits package, especially one with good health insurance, helps you attract and retain great employees. Offering insurance makes you more competitive with other employers.

■ Employees will often accept better benefits in lieu of a higher salary, which can translate to financial savings for you.

■ When it's tax time, you can deduct the cost of benefits.

■ Your own benefits—especially health insurance—costs substantially less when you purchase them as a group rather than on an individual basis.

RECRUITING EMPLOYEES

☐ What recruitment efforts will you use to find employees?

☐ What ongoing training will you offer employees?

☐ What features of your company and/or specific job do you want to mention in your ads or listings?

☐ What unusual or particularly appealing aspects of your company and/or specific job can you describe that would make you stand out from others?

☐ Other aspects to mention in ads or interviews:

List specific places you could advertise/look for employees:

☐ Newspapers: _____

☐ Online career/hiring sites: _____

☐ Social networking sites: _____

☐ Schools/colleges/universities: _____

☐ Career fairs: _____

☐ Trade organizations: _____

☐ Other organizations: _____

☐ Bulletin boards: _____

☐ Unemployment offices: _____

☐ Former employees: _____

☐ Personal network: _____

☐ Other referral sources: _____

☐ Competitors: _____

☐ Others: _____

- Many benefits, such as good health insurance, actually decrease absenteeism and improve employee health and wellness.

- Benefits are good for morale and enhance the caring, family-like environment of a small business. And, it's the right thing to do.

As a small business owner, you need to distinguish yourself from other businesses when competing for the best employees. So get creative! Perhaps you can provide more flexible work hours or paid time off. Many nontraditional benefits—such as season tickets for a local sports team, a bring-your-dog-to-work policy, or free team lunch on Fridays—won't cost you much but may help make your employees very loyal to you.

Training

Just as you have to continually improve your own skills, you want to continually improve the capabilities of your employees. The best companies make a strong commitment to ongoing training and education.

Often the easiest way to provide training, especially for a small company, is to pay for employees to attend outside seminars or classes. These are offered by a wide range of providers. As your company grows, you may want to develop some in-house training programs or bring in seminar leaders or speakers.

Don't just provide training for specific skills. While these may be necessary, it's also beneficial to educate employees in broader areas, such as overall business strategy, industry trends, etc. The smarter, more knowledgeable an employee, the more he or she can contribute to your success.

 # Appraise your management style

When you run a small company, you can't afford to waste resources, yet many business owners often squander one of their most valuable assets: their employees. I'm always surprised when I encounter an employer who views having employees as a necessary evil to be endured rather than a resource to be developed. If you waste the intelligence, energy, or skills of employees, it's like throwing money out the window.

Your attitude toward the people you hire goes a long way in determining their attitude about the job they do. The surest way to get the most from employees is to treat each one with respect. No matter what kind of work a person does, they like to have a sense that their opinion and input counts. When you allow your employees to think about how to solve problems, not just carry out specific tasks, you can unleash an amazing amount of creativity and energy.

But having employees is also a challenge. In addition to dealing with all the laws, paperwork, and policies, you've got to deal with employees as people—each with a distinct personality. That means some of your time will be diverted from specific tasks to personality issues—how people get along, communicate, and solve problems. You can view this as a distraction from your "real" work or you can recognize that this is part of the job of being a boss.

Being a boss is tough. It's one of the most demanding challenges of running a company. You have to inspire, lead, motivate, discipline, and reward. Some of the most important leadership skills are:

- **Communicating goals:** Let people know why they are doing something, not just how to do it; employees are far more motivated when they understand the purpose of a task.

- **Setting standards:** You are responsible for establishing—and demonstrating—the standards you expect others to maintain.

- **Being fair:** Make sure your standards are reasonable and fair, and that goals are actually reachable.

Manager vs. Leader—Wearing Both Hats Is Required

A MANAGER	A LEADER....
Tells employees what needs to be done	Sets high-level goals and strategy; establishes clear standards and values
Trains employees (or arranges for training) on how to do their jobs well	Keeps the business on track to reach those goals
Monitors/measures success on a daily procedural/process level	Monitors/measures success at the financial/organizational level
Helps prevent things from going wrong	Helps things go right
Fixes problems when they do occur	Empowers others to take action to fix problems

Start It Free

Once you have your team assembled, you'll need to find a way to manage projects and tasks. Mavenlink (**www. mavenlink.com**) offers a free version of its project management application that supports an unlimited number of team members. Do (**https://do.com**), another project management tool, also offers a free version. Need a fun way to nudge someone to complete a task? Send them a monkey through Monkey On Your Back (**www.monkeyon.com**).

- **Listening:** Learn to talk *with* and not just talk *to* your employees; enlist their suggestions and set goals together.

- **Making decisions:** The buck has to stop somewhere; employees look to their leaders to make choices and stick with them.

Rewarding and acknowledging

Everyone wants acknowledgment for a job well done. Few things are more dispiriting than to excel at a task and then have your hard work ignored. Moreover, it's only human nature to try harder to please those who appreciate us than those who ignore us.

Give credit to all employees who do their job well, with particular rewards for those who perform exceptionally. Give praise quickly and publicly. If you need to discipline an employee, do that privately. Find fun or creative ways to congratulate people. But often, just a public "thank you" or a round of applause shows that you've noticed their contribution. Take time to celebrate successes, especially with everyone in the company. It's a morale booster.

Recognizing that employee turnover is costly, especially in a small company, think about how to build an atmosphere where employees are likely to want to stay.

Here are five ways to retain employees:

1. **Trust them.** Give your employees responsibility and authority. Show them what has to be done and the standards you want them to meet. Then, let them do their jobs.

2. **Offer them the opportunity to grow.** Although some people might be content to perform the same tasks month after month and year after year, most people would prefer to learn new skills and be given more responsibility as time goes on.

3. **Communicate.** You reduce the chance for misunderstandings and increase the chance of success when everyone on your team knows what's going on. Even short meetings can be helpful and keep you and your employees in sync.

4. **Recognize effort and accomplishment.** Everyone wants to have their hard work acknowledged, even when things don't work out as planned. People thrive when they feel appreciated, and a simple

"thank you" can make your staff members feel that they're a valuable, contributing part of your team. Recognition has been shown to be an extremely positive motivator of employee behavior.

5. **Reward accomplishment.** Rewards reinforce behavior. Even small rewards—whether cash, promotions, time off, gifts, something as simple as a candy bar or certificate of achievement—show that you appreciate what they are doing for you and your business and keep employees wanting to do more.

So what kind of boss will you be? Will you have the skills to lead your company rather than micromanage your employees? Can you create an environment that encourages employees to do their best? Fill out the "My Leadership Skills" worksheet on page 128 to evaluate your own experiences and abilities as a leader.

Pay attention to choosing, training, developing, and rewarding the people on your team—because they are your most important resource. One of the best ways to motivate employees is to make your company an organization they're proud to work for. Everyone, including your employees, wants a sense of pride and purpose in what they do.

MY LEADERSHIP SKILLS

Rate yourself in each area below as either excellent, good, fair, or needs work.

Skill	Excellent	Good	Fair	Needs Work
☐ Decision making				
☐ Communicating goals				
☐ Setting standards				
☐ Listening				
☐ Consistently being fair				
☐ Patience				
☐ Creating a learning atmosphere				
☐ Training others				
☐ Motivating others to do their best				
☐ Constructively communicating problems/disagreements				
☐ Acknowledging and rewarding the contributions of others				
☐ Other leadership skills:				

☐ List things you'll do to improve your leadership and management skills (classes, training, books, etc.):

week 4

week 4

Main accomplishments:

#1 Find and secure a location

#2 Design your work and production space

#3 Research and purchase computers, software, and other technology

#4 Consider how you will distribute your products

#5 Design procedures for handling administrative tasks

#6 Deal with insurance

Make appointments with:

- [ ] Real estate agent
- [ ] Suppliers
- [ ] Insurance agent

Take Care of Operations

WHERE WILL YOU WORK, MAKE, OR SELL YOUR PRODUCTS? What kind of equipment do you need? How will you keep track of paperwork? Even something as basic as a desk and a chair can turn your business into a reality, but which desk? Which chair?

During this week, you'll deal with issues such as choosing a place to work, selecting furniture and equipment, purchasing inventory, and handling the day-to-day operations required to turn your vision into an operational business.

How you handle the operations and administration of your company directly affects your success. While these details may seem mundane, in fact, they may make all the difference in whether you are profitable, have sufficient cash flow to pay your bills, or stay out of trouble with authorities. The wrong location can doom a retail business; a poor manufacturing process can result in higher costs, lower quality, or too much waste. These issues are so important that you may want to develop a detailed operations plan or manual to outline your processes in greater detail.

Find and secure a location

How important is location to the success of your business? If you have a business serving a particular neighborhood or community, you need to be physically located in or near that area. If you're in retail, the choice of location is absolutely critical and may determine whether you have enough customers to stay in business. A factor as seemingly insignificant as which side of a particular street you're on can dramatically affect the amount of customer traffic you'll receive.

If you're a manufacturer, you'll need access to raw materials, a shipping system (whether that's trucks, air, ships, or rail), and a good labor force, but location may otherwise not be that important.

And then there are lots of companies that provide services from a distance (thanks in large part to the Internet) so business needs don't direct their choice of location at all.

Even if the site of your business isn't critical to your revenues—for example, if you deliver your services at client sites, or if you sell your products solely online—the choice of your neighborhood has an impact on how you and your employees feel about coming to work. A pleasant building, in a safe neighborhood, with nearby parking and friendly neighbors can make work more enjoyable. It can even help in recruiting employees.

Many entrepreneurs know exactly where they want to work—at home! Working at home can be a great advantage but it also presents some challenges especially if children or a spouse are there. Planning your home office—its space, storage, and policies—helps you make the most of this arrangement.

Some people run their businesses almost entirely from their vehicles—cars, trucks, vans. If you work from a vehicle, plan that "office," too.

Many new companies today launch in shared spaces, alongside other entrepreneurs at the same stage of business. This type of arrangement cuts down on expenses and can also foster important business connections.

In this section, the task of finding and securing your location depends on what kind of space you're planning for your business, either:

- **rented space**
- **office in a vehicle**
- **home office**
- **shared space**

Go to the section appropriate for your business to see the checklist associated with your needs.

OPTION A:
Rent space

My Checklist:

☐ **Decide on the necessary attributes of your location**

☐ **Meet with a real estate agent**

☐ **Compare properties**

☐ **Consider whether you need more than one location**

Decide on the necessary attributes of your location

Before you begin to search for rented space, prioritize your needs. Generally, this depends on what kind of business you're in—retail, manufacturing, service, or other type of industry—and your specific business activities. For instance, as a publisher, my company deals with heavy boxes of books daily. So when we looked for new facilities, even for our administrative offices, we wanted to find space either on the ground floor or with elevator access, so we didn't have to carry those heavy boxes up flights of stairs.

Don't forget less tangible issues, especially ones important to the quality of life for you and your employees. After all, you aren't starting your own business to hate the place where you go to work! In my case, I wanted offices where I could still walk to work from home, and where employees could bring their dogs. Those issues certainly narrowed our search.

Of course, you need to figure out about how much space you need and what your budget can handle. You may want to start small—with a short-term lease—until you establish yourself somewhat.

As you ponder the necessary attributes of your space, consider your needs, depending on the use of your facilities:

Office/Administrative: Virtually all businesses need at least some office space. Many businesses *only* need office space—professional, sales, or administrative offices. On the other hand, if the main purpose of your

Check It Out

Does renting an office by the month or a meeting room by the hour make sense for you? If so, check out Liquidspace (**https://liquidspace. com**), Regus (**www. regus.com**) or Premier Business Centers (**www. pbcenters.com**).

THINGS TO CONSIDER WHEN RENTING SPACE

Questions and terms to negotiate in lease	Notes
☐ **Cost of rent:** In addition to my rent, must I also pay the taxes, insurance, or even a percent of my income? Am I required to pay a portion of rent on "common areas"?	
☐ **Length of lease and subletting:** Can I get an option to renew? At what rent? Can I sublet some or all of the space?	
☐ **Layout:** Does the layout of the space suit my work style or production needs? Is there lots of wasted space I pay for?	
☐ **Leasehold improvements/remodeling:** Who is responsible for improving the facility—me or the landlord? Am I responsible for returning the facility back to its original condition when I move?	
☐ **Utilities:** What utilities are included in the rent? Are adequate utilities available—electricity, water, and heat?	
☐ **Janitorial/maintenance:** Who is responsible for cleaning and repairs? Who is responsible for waste disposal?	
☐ **Zoning laws and other use restrictions:** Are there any limits on how I may make use of the premises?	
☐ **Permits/planning departments:** What kind of permits will I need to operate my business or remodel? What are the costs and time involved?	
☐ **Storage:** Is there adequate space for storing supplies, raw materials, and inventory? Is it easily accessible?	
☐ **Furniture/equipment:** Does the space come with any furniture, equipment, or fixtures? If so, are those included in the rent?	
☐ **Safety/security:** Is the location safe for employees, customers, and my equipment and inventory?	
☐ **Expansion:** Is there sufficient space for me to grow? How soon will my needs exceed this space?	
☐ **Environmental:** What environmental limitations or concerns apply to this space? Is noise a factor—either noise I produce or noise from outside?	
☐ **Insurance:** What insurance does the owner have? What insurance must I provide? Will I have any difficulty getting adequate insurance for this location?	
☐ **Access/parking:** Is the site easily accessible for customers, employees, shipments? Are there adequate parking spaces provided? Is it near public transportation?	
Office space considerations	
☐ **Appearance:** Will I meet clients or customers at the office and need to make a positive impression? Does the office have a waiting area?	

Office space considerations (continued)	Notes
☐ **Privacy:** Does the office have sufficient privacy for my business needs?	
☐ **Meeting space/conference rooms:** Do I have sufficient access to conference rooms or other meeting space?	
☐ **Mail shipping and receiving:** Can I receive mail or shipments? Is it secure? What time does it arrive?	
☐ **Coffee/kitchen/eating areas:** Is there access to any coffee, food preparation, or eating areas? Is water convenient?	
☐ **Lighting:** Does the space have lighting adequate enough to prevent eye strain and fatigue?	
☐ **Wiring/data lines:** Is the space already wired for high-speed Internet access? If not, will it be difficult or expensive to install wiring?	
Retail space considerations	
☐ **History of others in the space:** How have other retail or restaurant businesses fared at this location?	
☐ **Fellow tenants/neighbors:** Are the retail neighbors compatible, with similar market demographics?	
☐ **Quality of the space itself:** Does it feel welcoming and make showing off my merchandise easy?	
☐ **Limitations on space, additional fees:** Are there any limits on my hours of operation, or requirements to pay additional fees or participate in certain promotions (common in malls or business improvement districts)?	
Manufacturing space considerations	
☐ **Docks/shipping facilities:** Can I receive/ship my expected materials/inventory? Does the location incur additional shipping fees?	
☐ **Utilities:** Are there adequate utilities for my production needs — water, electricity, natural gas, etc.?	
☐ **Waste disposal:** Is there adequate access to waste disposal, including any hazardous materials resulting from my production process? Costs?	
☐ **Proximity to suppliers and distributors:** How long will it take to replenish materials, to send my product to distributors and customers? Costs?	
Other lease provisions?	
☐ What other fees, duties, or limitations are part of the lease agreement?	

business is retail or manufacturing, your "office" may only be a small portion of your total site.

Since you are just starting out, and if your company has just one or two staff people, one approach to securing office space may be to rent an "Executive Suite" office or to find space to sublet from another company. This gets you up-and-running much faster, since it may be set up with furniture, Internet access, conference room, and the use of office equipment (copiers, printers, fax machine). It may also give you the flexibility of a short-term or month-to-month lease.

Retail: Location, location, location. One of the most important considerations for a retail business is the choice of location. Do you want to be in a mall? On a popular pedestrian street? In a particular neighborhood?

If your business is easily seen by passers-by (such as in a mall or well-trafficked street) you can save considerably on marketing and advertising costs. Of course, these locations typically charge higher rent. However, paying higher rent to get a more visible and accessible space may be well worth it.

In addition to being visible, your store must be accessible. If customers have easy access—either walking, driving, or taking public transportation—you have a competitive advantage over businesses that are hard to reach or find.

Manufacturing/Production: What do you make? Toys? Computer peripherals? Packaged organic vegetables? Obviously, the nature of your product dictates the kind of facilities you need.

Your production facilities can have a direct impact on your profitability. Are you set up to save on energy use and costs? Can you lay out your production processes efficiently? Are you near your customers or shipping facilities? How much does it cost to have waste removed? Understand all costs and benefits as you choose your space.

Also consider whether you need your own facilities or whether contract manufacturing facilities are available. Some industries have contract manufacturing or production facilities (such as contract kitchens) that give you the flexibility to start up without investing large sums of capital.

Warehouse/Storage: Some facilities are used primarily for storage. In these situations, you have many of the same concerns as manufacturing:

Check It Out

When setting up a retail shop, you'll need to know the demographics of the neighborhood. Sperling's Best Places (www.bestplaces.net) includes comprehensive information on county, city, and neighborhood demographics across the U.S. For more resources for researching a market, see pages 58–60 in Week Two.

shipping, docks, utilities, safety, access, security, and proximity to distributors. Be particularly cautious of environmental considerations that may affect the products or materials you store.

Use the worksheet on pages 134–135 for a more detailed checklist of issues related to renting space. It includes items of general concern if you are renting space, and items specific to the type of space you are renting.

 ## Meet with a real estate agent

Once you know what you need, you can begin shopping for space.

The first thing to do is to start driving—or walking—around the area that interests you. You might want to drive around a few different areas before settling in on your first choice. You're likely to find some "For Rent" signs if lots of properties are available.

However, commercial properties are harder to find than residential. They're not as likely to be listed online or in the newspaper, and often, there's not even a "For Rent" sign in available commercial property windows. There isn't a "Multiple Listing Service" as there is for home sales.

As a result, you will probably want to work with a commercial real estate agent, especially if you need a lot of space.

You'll have to be persistent. It's often difficult to get fast action from agents or landlords if you only need a small amount of space. So you have to stay on top of the process.

Find a real estate agent who specializes in either the location that interests you or your type of business. Ask other entrepreneurs if they have any agents to recommend.

Remember, most commercial real estate agents represent landlords and specific properties, so you may end up working with different agents for different properties. Make sure someone who's looking out for your interests reviews any leases or contracts you sign.

 ## Compare properties

Once you start looking for space, you'll need to know common commercial real estate rental practices and terms.

Typically, you'll be quoted rental prices on a "per square foot" or "s.f." basis. (If you're subletting or renting executive office space, you might be quoted a flat rate.) In most of the U.S., the square foot price is given on an annualized basis (e.g., $12 a square foot); in parts of the western U.S., it's quoted on a monthly basis (e.g., $1 a square foot).

Before you make your first call, familiarize yourself with terms brokers and landlords toss around. *Beware!* Definitions vary from landlord to landlord, so have them be clear about what's included:

- **Triple Net or NNN:** You, the tenant, are responsible for *all* costs of your portion of the building, including property taxes, insurance, utilities, and maintenance. In other words, you pay these costs *in addition* to your monthly rent.

- **Full service or Gross:** Your rent includes all—or some—of those triple net costs, so you need not pay them separately. It's most likely to include taxes and insurance. Ideally, it includes utilities, janitorial, and perhaps—if you're subletting—Internet access.

- **Modified Full Service:** The rental price includes some, but not all, of triple net costs. Typically, utilities and maintenance are excluded.

- **CAM or Common Area Maintenance or Load Factor:** An additional amount—usually a percentage of your base rent—you're charged for common areas you share with other tenants, such as halls, bathrooms, entryways. So while the space you're renting may be 1,000 s.f., your landlord may charge you for 1,200 s.f.—the extra 200 s.f. you're paying for is the CAM fee.

- **T.I. or Tenant Improvements:** In some cases, the landlord, at their own expense, will be willing to make improvements or changes to the space to accommodate a tenant's specific needs. The larger the space, the longer the lease, and the softer the rental market, the more willing a landlord is to make improvements. Make it *very* clear in the lease what improvements will be made—and paid for—by the landlord.

Whether you use your space for retail (a store), administrative (office), manufacturing (a plant), or storage purposes (a warehouse), you face many of the same considerations. The chart on page 139 and the checklist on pages 134–135 can help you as you shop. You may also want to use the checklist as a basis for negotiating terms with your landlord.

LOCATION/SPACE COMPARISON CHART

	Location One	Location Two	Location Three
☐ Address/contact info			
☐ Total sq. feet			
☐ Rent (per sq.ft., total)			
☐ Length of lease (option to renew, at what rent?)			
☐ What's included? (utilities, janitor, data lines?)			
☐ What am I responsible for? (utilities, janitor, data lines?)			
☐ Legal issues (permits, zoning, etc.)			
☐ Parking, access, and safety issues			
☐ Insurance issues			
☐ Advantages			
☐ Disadvantages			
☐ Other:			

That brings us to the question of how long a lease to ask for. This depends on the stability and stage of your business, the quality and price of the space, your future plans, and your comfort level with taking on a long-term obligation. As a new business, you may be better off with a short-term lease, even if rents increase in the future or you have to move. If you take a long-term lease, make certain you can sublet it.

And remember, before you sign any contract, including a lease, go over it with your lawyer first.

WHAT WOULD RHONDA DO?

SERVING ANOTHER LOCATION

Do you want to make sales in another city, but you lack the money to open and staff a second store or office? One approach I'd use is to get a "remote location number" from the phone company. With a remote location number, you get a local phone number in your target city and a listing in that city's local phone directory. However, all calls are immediately forwarded to your regular phone number. Voila! You can serve another community even though you don't have a store or office or even a phone there. You pay a small monthly fee plus toll calls from the target city to your local phone, if any. This is also a good idea if you're moving; you can keep your former phone number, along with your customers, in your former city. You can also get an additional phone number through Google Voice, and choose the area code you want. Most area codes in the U.S. are available. After choosing your number, pick which phones it will forward calls to. You can sign up for this free service at **www.google.com/voice**.

 ## Consider whether you need more than one location

In some instances, you may need more than one location for your business. If you are in manufacturing, you may find it less expensive or necessary to situate your manufacturing facilities in one city and your administrative or sales offices elsewhere. An apparel manufacturer may want a sales office in New York City, for example, while the actual production occurs in New Jersey.

In most types of business, technology has made it relatively simple to employ some remotely located workers, often far away from the main office. This may be a good option if you want to hire individuals with certain skills who are located far from your main place of business.

Be warned, however: Having more than one site presents a number of legal and logistical issues, in addition to the challenge of getting more than one business location up-and-running. After all, it's hard enough to start a business in one place; why give yourself the added burden of operating in more than one location unless you have a pressing need?

You will particularly run into legal and tax issues if you employ workers (even nonemployees) in more than one state. You may also have to deal with that state's payroll, business, and sales and income taxes. Each state may enforce different insurance regulations, and if you offer health insurance, you may need to get different providers for each state.

OPTION B:
Set up a home office

My Checklist:

- ☐ **Find the space to work**
- ☐ **Figure out your phone, fax, and Internet connections**
- ☐ **Plan how to meet with customers**
- ☐ **Decide whether you need a separate business address**
- ☐ **Understand home-based office tax deductions**

For many years, I ran my business from my home. I enjoyed working from home, and I never had more than what I jokingly called my "one-room commute." When I finally decided to lease office space, I left home with some regret. Running a business from home has many advantages, but it has its challenges as well. The key is to set up a home office right.

 ## Find the space to work

A home office can take many forms. It might simply be one end of your dining room table. It could be the guest room, as long as no guests come to visit. You might claim a section of your garage, and even build in walls and install a window, shelves, heating, and air conditioning.

If you're serious about your business, you need good work space. You don't necessarily need a separate room, but find a space without too many distractions. Once you've chosen the physical space for your office, consider what will go in it:

■ **A desk or work table.** At the very minimum, you should have a desk or table used only for work. Having to clear your stuff off the dining room table every night quickly gets old. Make certain it's the right height for what you're doing.

■ **A good chair.** Get out of that folding chair and buy yourself something comfortable enough to sit in for hours. Your shoulders and back will thank you.

■ **Good lighting.** Most homes don't have sufficient lighting to work all day, so in addition to overhead and indirect lighting, get a desk light. Don't put your computer monitor directly in front of a window (you'll squint all day), and watch for glare from other windows.

■ **Heaters or air conditioners.** The temperature in your office is more than just a matter of personal comfort (which is very important). If you have equipment in your office, you need a stable temperature. I ruined a computer hard drive because my office was in a room that got very cold at night and condensation formed on the drive.

■ **Storage.** When you run a business from home, you accumulate stuff—a lot of stuff! You need someplace to put it. Purchase an office-type storage cabinet or put shelves up in a closet. Put stuff you need to use frequently within easy reach. Trust me, you'll underestimate the amount of storage space you need.

■ **Electricity.** Surge protector strips have the benefit of increasing the number of your electrical outlets, but be careful not to overload circuits. Buy the kind of surge protectors that can handle "transformers"—those big electrical plugs on many technology devices.

✔ Figure out your phone, fax, and Internet connections

I'm a big believer in a separate business phone line if you're doing business from your home on an ongoing basis. If your cell phone ever drops calls at your house or if call quality is reduced, a traditional land line is helpful for

For tips on setting up an ergonomic computer station, check out OSHA's eTool that outlines the basic design of a safe and comfortable workstation. **www.osha.gov/SLTC/etools/computerworkstations/index.html**

important client calls and teleconferences. And, once your toddler answers a call from your most important client, you'll see the necessity of a separate line for incoming business calls. An extra phone line for business also enables you to have an outgoing business message for that line and a family message on your other line. If you get a high volume of faxes, you may need a dedicated line for that as well.

Of course, you'll need to have Internet access wherever you are. Generally, you'll choose from cable, DSL, or satellite. In addition to evaluating cost, look at the speeds of data transmission and how that will be affected as you add users.

 ## Plan how to meet with customers

If you work out of your home, one of the biggest challenges is often figuring out where and when to meet with customers. If you only meet customers at their place of business, at trade shows, or online, no problem! But if customers are going to come to you, how will you arrange your space so you look professional?

If you're going to meet with others regularly, ideally, you want to set up your work space separately from your family surroundings. If possible, have a separate entrance or at least a path to your office that doesn't go through a messy playroom or kitchen. If you're meeting clients infrequently, or on a regular schedule, you may be able to use your own living or dining room as a meeting space. Just make sure you don't violate any city zoning laws, homeowner's association rules, or lease agreements. Also make sure the rest of the family, if any, know to stay away!

What if you don't want customers in your home but need to meet them somewhere other than their offices? Look for other, "neutral" locations, such as a lunch meeting in a restaurant or a morning meeting at the local coffee house. If you have an ongoing need, find another company from which you can sublet or rent a meeting space or conference room on an hourly basis (such as a small law firm). "Executive suite" services—short-term office rentals—often offer hourly rentals as well.

 ## Decide whether you need a separate business address

When you work from home, you face a dilemma: What address should you give out?

If you use only your home address, are you comfortable putting it on business cards and marketing brochures that you hand to strangers, or put on a website where the world can see it? If you don't put any address on these marketing materials, you might seem less than professional.

One alternative is to get a post office box from the U.S. Postal Service. The problem, however, is that then your business address is only a post office box—or P.O. Box—number. That may make your business seem somewhat insubstantial. Moreover, the U.S. Postal Service usually refuses to accept deliveries from private delivery services such as FedEx or UPS.

Another, often better, alternative is to rent a mailbox from one of the many private mailbox providers (such as "The UPS Store"), also called a "commercial mail receiving agency." A private mailbox gives you a secure place to receive mail, and employees there can sign for and receive your packages. They generally will accept deliveries from private services as well as the U.S. Postal Service. Moreover, they often offer other services such as mail forwarding, calling you if you receive a special delivery, packing and shipping items, and allowing you to call in and check your mail if you're on the road.

One other advantage: With a private mailbox, you can usually use their address, followed by the "#" symbol or the word "number" and your box number, so that you don't have to use the term "P.O. Box" as your address. (For example, PlanningShop's private post box address is 555 Bryant St., #180, Palo Alto, CA 94301). Just be sure to verify your wording with your mailbox service before you print business cards.

Understand home-based office tax deductions

When you work from home, one murky area you'll need to deal with is which business expenses are deductible and which aren't. If you buy a new work table that you use for both your office and for the kids' home-work projects, is that deductible? If you add a space heater to your office in the garage, can you deduct the extra utility expenses? What if you let your kids use your office supplies?

Tax deductions for home offices are daunting and confusing. If you're setting up a home office, you should add these questions to the list when you meet with an accountant (Week Five).

Most normal business expenses that you'd have whether or not you were working from home—postage, office supplies, advertising, wages—are treated the same way as any other business. You can deduct those expenses as part of your regular deductions for the cost of doing business.

Some deductions become more problematic, especially when the expense is—or could be—used for both business and personal purposes, such as telephones, Internet connections, and equipment.

You have an additional tax savings option on your home office if you qualify, and if you choose to take it—the home office deduction. The home office deduction allows you to deduct a portion of your rent or mortgage based on the percent of your apartment or home used exclusively for business. That can be a nice extra tax deduction for you.

Check It Out

The IRS answers questions about the tax implications of running your business from your home. **www.irs.gov/ taxtopics/tc509.html**

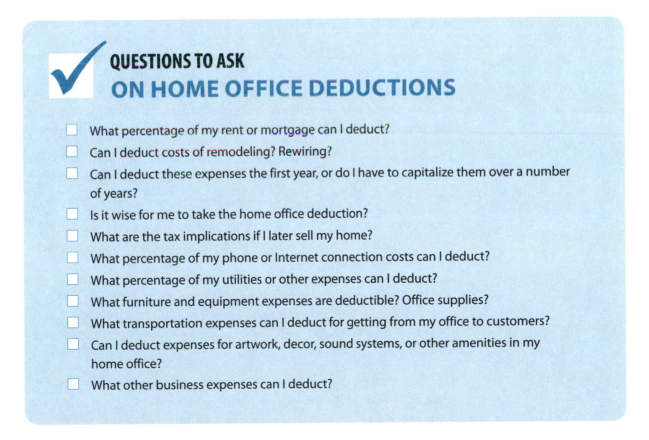

✔ **QUESTIONS TO ASK ON HOME OFFICE DEDUCTIONS**

☐ What percentage of my rent or mortgage can I deduct?

☐ Can I deduct costs of remodeling? Rewiring?

☐ Can I deduct these expenses the first year, or do I have to capitalize them over a number of years?

☐ Is it wise for me to take the home office deduction?

☐ What are the tax implications if I later sell my home?

☐ What percentage of my phone or Internet connection costs can I deduct?

☐ What percentage of my utilities or other expenses can I deduct?

☐ What furniture and equipment expenses are deductible? Office supplies?

☐ What transportation expenses can I deduct for getting from my office to customers?

☐ Can I deduct expenses for artwork, decor, sound systems, or other amenities in my home office?

☐ What other business expenses can I deduct?

However, there are many considerations before you take the home office deduction. You have to meet the IRS's qualifications, and this is one deduction that frequently leads to an audit. Also, there are tax implications if you later sell your home. So you certainly want to discuss the home office deduction—and whether you should take it or skip it—with your accountant or tax advisor. Use the guide "Questions to Ask: On Home Office Deductions" on page 145 to get your conversation started.

 ## Plan ways to separate work life from home life

One of the most difficult tasks for people who work from home is establishing a clear distinction between work and home. If you're not disciplined, you may find yourself distracted by nonbusiness matters. One friend said her house was never cleaner than when she worked from home, since she did housework to avoid taking care of business.

On the other hand, many people who work from home find they never leave "work." They end up working day and night, much to the annoyance of family and friends.

Separating your work life from home life can be especially difficult when you live with others: a spouse, children, or guests who come to visit. Friends and relatives often view home-based entrepreneurs as people who are always available. They don't understand why, in the middle of a work day, you can't run an errand, go to a movie, or pick up kids from school.

The best way to deal with working at home is to be as professional as possible during the time you set aside for business, but allow yourself some of the flexibility you want from working out of your home.

Establish work hours: One of the best ways to protect your valuable personal time yet still have enough time to conduct business is by establishing set work hours.

Structure your week and your workday. Set a work routine that makes you, your family, and others more conscious of your business life. That doesn't mean you have to work from 8 a.m. to 6 p.m.; just establish real working hours.

For instance, you can tell others (and yourself) something like: "I start work right after I take the kids to school; take a half-hour housecleaning break around 10:30; a quick lunch around 1 p.m.; go to the post office, run errands, and drop kids off at classes or soccer from 4 to 6 p.m. Then, if I have to, I catch up on paperwork after 9 p.m. On Tuesdays and Thursdays, I leave work early to go to exercise class."

Make sure that you, your clients, employees, friends, and family know what your work hours are, when and why you can be interrupted, when you'll take days off, and when your busiest time of the day, week, or year is (so they can leave you alone!).

But also make certain you know when your "free" time is and when your workday is over. It's only fair to others—and yourself—that you "leave" the office after hours and go "home."

Be clear with guests about your spare time: Whether your office is in the guest room or the next town, having guests can be a strain on any home-based entrepreneur. Often, guests don't understand how self-employed people structure their workdays or work weeks.

Allow yourself some time to spend with visitors, but be clear about when you'll be with them and the limits on your availability.

Let prospective guests know in advance how much time you'll be able to spend with them, so they'll understand the situation before they arrive. Put this in the most positive light: "I'm delighted I've been able to cancel my meetings for Thursday afternoon to spend with you. Until then, I'm sure you'll enjoy exploring the city on your own." If you need to, make up a list of sights or keep brochures on hand so visitors can find ways to entertain themselves.

Of course, even the best-laid plans may fly out the window when the in-laws arrive!

 # Deal with kids and pets

Many parents find the greatest appeal of a home office is being at home for their children. However, many former work-from-home parents have found, after a year or so of working with crying or demanding children, that an office away from home becomes a vital expense.

Make child care arrangements: Be realistic about the demands that kids place on you. It's not realistic to expect to get work done with kids coming in and out, wanting to be driven places, needing a snack, or demanding that you help settle an argument.

Don't imagine, either, that you can just hand your kids off to a friend or neighbor; tomorrow the neighbors' kids may be in your backyard.

Realistically, you may need to make child care arrangements, depending on your children's ages and the nature of your work. Some businesses are more flexible in terms of deadlines, hours, or phone calls. Others are truly difficult to run when you have a needy two-year-old or teenager.

As a work-at-home parent, you have some added flexibility in child care arrangements that typical office workers don't. If you have school-aged children, you may be able to schedule your work hours from 9:00 a.m. to 3:00 p.m., then spend time with the kids, and return to work at 8:00 p.m., when they've gone to bed. You may be able to share child care responsibilities with a spouse—caring for them during the day, and retreating to your home office at 5:00 p.m. when your spouse returns home from work.

Whatever your arrangement, develop a structured routine for your kids that keeps them busy (and out of your hair) for a set period of time each week so you can get work done. Since you'll naturally want to spend time with your children, set aside specific times. Tell your older children when you'll be available to run errands, make meals, or entertain them.

Pets: If you work at home, a pet is a great companion. A dog or cat makes working at home less lonely. As someone who had a dog in my own home office for years, I can offer some important tips to making the most of a canine colleague.

- **Barking:** Just as you can't have a screaming child in the background, you can't have a barking dog—at least not too often. If your dog barks uncontrollably, put it in another room.

- **Walking:** Dog walking is an excellent way to meet new people, some of whom might be great networking contacts. I got my very first client walking my late dog, Teddy. A gray terrier mix, Teddy introduced himself to a King Charles Spaniel whose owner happened to need a business plan. Presto! My consulting service was launched.

- **Responsibilities:** If you work alone (and have a sense of humor), give your dog a "title" in the company. I made Teddy my marketing director, since over the years I met many additional clients while walking him.

OPTION C:
Set up an "office" in your vehicle

Many people run their businesses not from an office or from home, but from a car, van, or truck. In some industries and lines of work—contractors, sales representatives, real estate agents, landscape designers, to name a few—an efficient and workable mobile office is a necessity.

Since many people do not think of their vehicle as an "office," they don't organize the space appropriately. As a result, their "workplace" becomes unworkable, with important notes shoved in the glove compartment or valuable equipment moving around loose in the back of the truck.

If you know you're going to use your vehicle for business, develop a mobile office plan. There are many commercially available products to outfit cars and trucks for specific purposes, including most kinds of contractors or trades. There are even "desks" for your front seat.

Invest in dependable cell phone accessories for safe on-the-go communications. You'll want a Bluetooth headset so you can keep your hands on the wheel when a call comes in. A belt clip or dash mount keeps your phone nearby and not lost in the clutter. Set up voice dailing if you can, and maybe a solution to record conversations when you can't take notes. And don't forget a car charger to make sure you're never out of touch.

Since your vehicle is your office, you'll also want to ensure that its contents are safe. You probably don't want to store the only copy of valuable documents or records in your vehicle. Where will you keep those instead? Consider where you will park your vehicle overnight; you want to make sure it's safe and secure.

When you get insurance, make certain your policy covers not only the vehicle itself but also your "office" contents or equipment, especially if you regularly carry expensive tools or equipment. And, of course, talk to your accountant or tax advisor about deductions for your mobile office.

Use the worksheet on page 150 to assist you in planning your "office" in your vehicle.

Check It Out
Get Google Maps on your phone to help navigate your mobile office. **www.google. com/mobile/maps**

Check It Out
Using your laptop on the go? For a list of free Wi-Fi locations in your state, visit **www.wififreespot. com**

Check It Out
You'll especially want a fuel-efficient vehicle if you run a mobile business. The U.S. Department of Energy's site (**www.fueleconomy. gov**) provides a wealth of information, from the most fuel-efficient cars and trucks, to a guide on hybrids, to tips for fuel efficiency.

MOBILE OFFICE PLAN

What I will use my mobile office to do: (check those that apply)

☐ Make phone calls	☐ Write up orders	☐ Use computer
☐ Open mail	☐ Carry passengers	☐ Store samples/literature
☐ Store supplies	☐ Haul equipment	☐ Other hauling
☐ Other issues:		

Other Issues: (check those that apply)

Issue	My Solution
☐ Cell phone and accessories	
☐ Storage	
☐ Writing surface	
☐ Office supplies	
☐ Work equipment	
☐ Climate control	
☐ Security	
☐ Safety	
☐ Insurance	
☐ Computer use	
☐ Internet connection	
☐ Parking	
☐ Other issues:	

OPTION D:

Search for shared space: Incubator, accelerators, and coworking spaces

The classic image of the would-be entrepreneur hoping to launch the next Apple or Google is someone working on a fledgling enterprise in a garage or dorm room. But working from home can be awfully lonely, and if Mom, the kids, or hubby keep interrupting, it's hard to create the next big thing.

Today, entrepreneurs have an alternative—spaces dedicated precisely for early stage and novice small business owners. While these launch spaces are exploding in tech-heavy places such as Silicon Valley and New York, coworking, entrepreneur-friendly office spaces are popping up all over America.

The following list outlines loosely the different types of shared working options for new businesses.

- **Incubators.** Prospective early stage and prelaunch companies must apply for a spot in these types of spaces, and typically competition is high. You do not pay rent. In fact, expect to receive money and hands-on guidance as well as space in return for equity in your company. This equity costs dearly in the long run, so make sure you are working with people who have a proven track record of success.

- **Accelerators.** These help nurture high-growth companies after the incubation stage. The best accelerators help high-potential companies grow quickly through introductions to customers, financiers, or key employees. They may charge rent or take equity. True accelerators are highly selective.

- **Coworking spaces.** With these straightforward, turnkey rental spaces, you get a desk—either assigned or drop in—as well as Internet access, use of conference rooms (either included or for an extra fee), and often some kind of coffee service or even a cafe. You do not give up equity and typically no lease is required. They are not very selective.

Check It Out

Does renting a desk in a "coworking" space make sense for you? Find available spaces at ShareDesk (**www.sharedesk.net**).

Would-be entrepreneurs are themselves a lucrative market, and opportunists have moved in to exploit their desire for exciting work environments and their need for short-term, small space. So be careful when considering these spaces. Make sure the costs are fair for what you receive, and don't give ownership in your company away without significant reward.

ACCOMPLISHMENT #2:
Design your work space and production process

My Checklist:

- ☐ **Design your layout**
- ☐ **Design your production process**
- ☐ **Order/install utilities and facility improvements**
- ☐ **Get furniture and equipment**
- ☐ **Order inventory and/or raw materials**

 Design your layout

Once you've found your location—but before you move in—begin to design how you'll use your space.

When thinking through your needs for office and administrative space, ask yourself the following questions:

■ **What are the necessary functions of your business?** Administrative, production, shipping, and the like, and how much space do you need for each?

■ **Do certain functional areas need to be near other functions?** For example, should packing be near shipping or bookkeeping near customer service?

■ **How will you divide the space between different functions?** Will you want permanent partitions, such as walls, or temporary or partial partitions?

■ **How many employees will work in each area of your space?**

OFFICE MOVE-IN CHECKLIST

To Do	Notes
☐ Arrange electrical/gas wiring/piping installation	
☐ Order electric and gas service	
☐ Arrange telephone cabling installation	
☐ Order telephone service	
☐ Arrange Internet and network cabling installation	
☐ Set up space for server/Internet equipment, if needed	
☐ Order Internet service	
☐ Arrange other utility equipment installation (water, etc.)	
☐ Order other utilities	
☐ Order waste disposal service	
☐ Order janitorial service	
☐ Ensure completion of landlord's tenant improvements	
☐ Order and install interior and exterior signage	
☐ Arrange any interior and exterior painting	
☐ Order and install floor coverings	
☐ Order and install any necessary fixtures and equipment	
☐ Other:	
☐	
☐	
☐	
☐	
☐	

- **Will employees work in an open environment?** If so, will you need cubicles or other ways to provide some noise abatement and privacy?

- **Do some employees need private offices?**

- **How much equipment will you have and how large is it?**

- **Do you need conference or meeting rooms?**

- **Do you need a reception/waiting area?**

- **Have you provided space for coffee/kitchen or other break-time/lunchtime needs?**

- **How much space is needed for storage and where is it best located?**

Don't forget to provide adequate space for all the usual business support functions—copying, faxing, mail preparation, bathrooms, and so on.

One way to design your space is to sketch a layout on a design grid, like the one provided for you on page 156. Start with a preliminary layout idea, measure your square footage, and then assign each square on the grid a measurement—1 foot, 10 feet, and so forth. Grab a pencil and start scribbling. You may want to make extra copies of the grid in case you need to start over.

Of course, you could hire an interior decorator or ergonomics specialist to help you with your floor plan, but resist spending more money than you need to now.

 ## Design your production process

One concept that has taken hold in the development of certain products is the "minimal viable product." The idea is to quickly get a product to market, and later make improvements based on the experience of actual customers. Google's product development mantra, for instance, is "Experiment, expedite, iterate." In other words, the company tries a lot of new things, moves quickly rather than getting stuck, and refines and improves along the way.

Clearly you don't want a minimally viable product for a medical device or automobile. But in some categories, such as online services, mobile apps, and personal electronics, consumers are willing—even eager—to pay for version 1.0. Depending on your product, you may want to keep this concept in mind when developing your prototype.

Your production process will vary dramatically, depending on the nature of your product. The process of creating handmade crafts is certainly far different than the process of manufacturing high-tech electronics.

Nevertheless, you still need a "process"—a plan for how you'll handle your product or service from the time an order is placed until it is finally delivered to the customer.

Even if you "produce" a service rather than a tangible product, you'll benefit by considering the process by which you prepare and carry out that service.

Some aspects of designing your production process are:

- **What raw materials or inventory do you need and how will you get them? Where will you store them?**

- **What are the steps for turning those materials into finished goods? What labor is required for each step?**

- **How will you ensure quality control?**

- **How will you ship your products or goods? What shipping providers will you use?**

- **How will you pack your products? What materials will you need for packing? Where will you store your packing materials? Where will you do the packing?**

- **How will you prevent theft or loss?**

- **What kind of electricity, gas, water, or other utilities do you need as part of your process?**

- **What methods can you implement to reduce waste and energy and water consumption?**

Use the worksheet on page 157 to address these key issues.

✔ Order/install utilities and facility improvements

Once you know how you will use your space and have a better understanding of your production process, you can start making your space ready for your business.

Check It Out

For methods and equipment to reduce energy consumption and waste, check the business information at Energy Star. www.energystar.gov

FLOOR PLAN LAYOUT

Use this grid for planning your office or production area layout. Each square is 1/8" x 1/8".
For additional grid space, use graph paper.

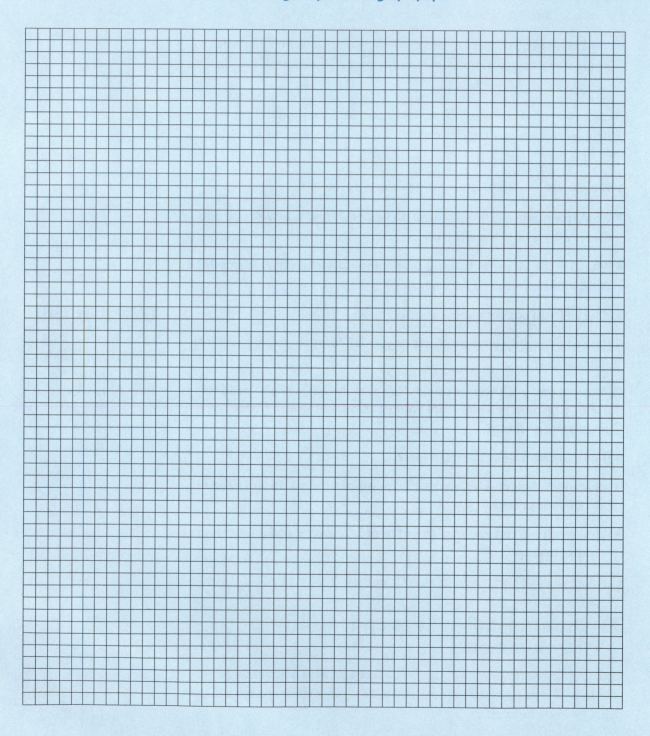

DESIGNING MY PRODUCTION PROCESS

As you outline the steps involved in your production process—whether you produce a product or a service—consider the following items, how long the steps take, and who is responsible.

☐ What supplies do I need?

☐ When do I need them?

☐ How much labor is required?

☐ How will I set standards?

☐ How will I ensure those standards are met consistently?

☐ How will I reduce inefficiencies in the process?

☐ How will I ensure safety?

☐ How will I ensure adequate access to necessary utilities?

☐ How can I reduce waste and conserve energy and water?

☐ How will I dispose of waste?

One of the first things you'll want to take care of is ordering any utilities you need: telephone, electricity, gas, Internet, water, and waste disposal. It may take more than a week for the utility company to be able to install necessary wiring or turn on your service.

You will most likely need to install or adjust the wiring or location of utilities to meet your needs. While utility companies provide this service, you may want to hire private contractors to do the work instead.

Don't forget to look at fixtures in your new space. Is there adequate overhead lighting? And what kind of signage will you need? Signs are particularly important for retail businesses.

It's easiest to make any tenant improvements—new paint, carpet, adding or moving walls, changing fixtures, and the like—before you move in. If you've negotiated for the landlord to pay for any of these tenant improvements, check to make certain that the improvements will be finished in time for you to get your business under way.

Use the "Office Move-in Checklist" on page 153 for planning your move into a new space.

 ## Get furniture and equipment

Few things make you feel like you're finally "in business" as much as having office furniture.

If you're just starting out, getting your stuff off the dining room table and onto your own desk reinforces the seriousness of your enterprise.

When you rent offices, how you furnish your space helps set the tone and "culture" of your company and how you'll be perceived by your staff, clients, and yourself.

RED TAPE ALERT! When buying substantial business assets (furniture, equipment, vehicles), be aware of tax implications. Some assets may be deducted ("expensed") the year you buy them, but the law imposes a maximum amount that can be expensed for any one year. After that—and for nonexpensable items—you must depreciate the asset and spread the tax benefit over as many as 20 years.

WHAT WOULD RHONDA DO?

BUY OR LEASE?

Rhonda's first rule: Purchase less expensive items; lease more costly ones. It generally doesn't make much sense to lease a fax machine or printer; they're less than a few hundred dollars. But if you need a major piece of equipment, don't tie up your cash.

Rhonda's second rule: If you're uncertain about your long-term plans or needs, take short-term leases on your equipment. Even if this means making higher monthly payments in the short run, you want the flexibility of getting out of your lease if your plans change.

Rhonda's third rule: Check the tax implication of leasing versus buying: Some deductions can make leasing actually cost less than buying, while "expensing" purchased equipment may lower income taxes.

And Rhonda's most important rule: Don't get more than you need. Cash in the bank beats a nice conference table any day.

Don't purchase your furniture until you know what space you'll be using. Not only do you want to make certain that your furniture fits your space, but it is possible that you may be offered furniture as part of your lease, especially in an "Executive Suite" or sublet situation.

If you expect to grow or move, look for furniture that is flexible, composed of various modules, and movable.

Remember, "furniture" consists of more than just desks and chairs—you'll need storage cabinets, work tables, floor coverings, lighting, and decorative items. Consider these as you develop your "furniture" budget.

When choosing business equipment, you may find vendors to be a good source of information and advice. For instance, if you're opening a restaurant, vendors of ovens and other kitchen equipment may be able to help you design an efficient kitchen layout.

Some of the best sources of information about industry-specific equipment are industry trade shows. Attending an industry convention or trade show is an outstanding chance to compare products and prices and become more aware of the range of options available.

Start It Free

You can often find office equipment and furniture for free through online classifieds such as Craigslist (**www.craigslist.org**). Click on the "free" category under "for sale" in any city. You'll also find free items at the Freecycle Network (**www.freecycle.org**).

When purchasing equipment, be certain you understand all the ongoing costs of owning it, not just the initial price. Long-term equipment costs include the cost of repairs or service contracts, the price and availability of supplies, the amount of specialized training necessary to operate it, vendor training, and technical support available.

Use the "Furniture Shopping List" on page 162 to compare furniture and keep track of what you've ordered. Then use the worksheet on page 163 to keep track of the equipment you'll need.

Buying versus leasing: As you begin shopping, you'll be faced with deciding whether to purchase your furniture or equipment outright or to lease it instead. All kinds of things can be leased: furniture, equipment, vehicles, computers, telephone systems.

Leasing is tempting: You'll spend less money now. That frees up your capital, an important consideration for a young and likely cash-strapped company. It also may mean that you're able to upgrade or change your equipment sooner than if you make an outright purchase. In a new company, this can be desirable since your business plan is still evolving.

However, in the long run, you'll almost certainly end up paying much more for a piece of equipment or furniture that you've leased rather than bought outright.

Some vendors, especially of expensive equipment, may offer their own financing, whether you're purchasing or leasing. Ask! Supplier-financed leases may be an attractive leasing option, as the vendor may make concessions on either the price of the equipment or the financing costs to capture your business (and will sell you continuing supplies or maintenance). Ask also whether this kind of financing enables you to upgrade to newer equipment during the life of the lease or loan.

Warranties/Service contracts: When shopping for equipment, evaluate the warranties, service contracts, and technical support offered or available as part of the purchase. A good warranty may be worth a substantial amount of money, especially if repairs are very costly. The same is true for free or low-cost technical support if the equipment is difficult to operate.

You may find that the cost of purchasing extended warranties, service contracts, or additional technical support is well worth the peace of mind you get from knowing that you won't be hit with an unexpected expense if something goes wrong.

WARRANTIES AND SERVICE CONTRACTS

☐ Equipment:	
Place Purchased:	
Date Purchased:	
Warranty Terms:	
Expiration Date:	
Contact Info/Phone:	

☐ Equipment:	
Place Purchased:	
Date Purchased:	
Warranty Terms:	
Expiration Date:	
Contact Info/Phone:	

☐ Equipment:	
Place Purchased:	
Date Purchased:	
Warranty Terms:	
Expiration Date:	
Contact Info/Phone:	

☐ Equipment:	
Place Purchased:	
Date Purchased:	
Warranty Terms:	
Expiration Date:	
Contact Info/Phone:	

☐ Equipment:	
Place Purchased:	
Date Purchased:	
Warranty Terms:	
Expiration Date:	
Contact Info/Phone:	

FURNITURE SHOPPING LIST

Furniture	Quantity	Cost per Item	Vendor	Date Ordered	Delivery Date
☐ Desks					
☐ Desk chairs					
☐ Reception desk					
☐ Guest/reception chairs					
☐ Work/equipment tables					
☐ Conference room tables and chairs					
☐ Book and storage shelves/ cabinets					
☐ Filing cabinets					
☐ Lamps/lighting					
☐ Fire safe/security storage					
☐ White boards					
☐ Cubicles/space dividers					
☐ Floor coverings					
☐ Decorative items					
☐ Other:					
☐ Other:					

EQUIPMENT SHOPPING LIST

Equipment (list items)	Quantity	Cost per Item	Vendor	Date Ordered	Delivery Date

If something does break down, how soon can you get the equipment repaired? If a piece of equipment is crucial for your business, every day lost while it's broken is lost income for you.

To help you keep track of your warranties and service contracts, use the worksheet on page 161.

 Order inventory and/or raw materials

The perfect inventory situation for a small business to be in is to achieve just-in-time inventory. That's just what it sounds like: You stock your inventory just in time to sell it. Your inventory is always at or near zero. You've tied up no funds in excess inventory. Neither are you disappointing customers.

However ideal it is, just-in-time inventory is hard to achieve. If you have real-time access to your suppliers' inventory and can get it delivered in less than a day, you're in a good place to do this. But in general, the longer the lead time of your suppliers, the less viable just-in-time inventory management becomes, and the earlier you'll want to order what you need. Be careful, though. Inventory is money sitting around in a different form. Make every item count.

Your suppliers are a vital part of your company's lifeline, especially if yours is a manufacturing or retail business. In effect, your suppliers become your "partners." You depend on them to be able to go forward with your business. So when you select vendors, don't just shop on the

QUESTIONS TO ASK
A POTENTIAL SUPPLIER

- ☐ How long have you been in business?
- ☐ What other customers do you serve in my industry?
- ☐ What is your usual turnaround time on orders? What is the quickest time possible in special circumstances?
- ☐ What payment terms do you offer? How large a credit line will you extend to me?
- ☐ Can you meet special packing or shipping requirements?
- ☐ Do you have minimum order requirements? Are there discounts available?

basis of price: Make certain your suppliers are reliable, can maintain a shipping schedule that works well with your ongoing needs, can respond quickly if you have unusual needs, and can work with you on terms and payment.

Try not to be dependent on only one or two suppliers. If you are, you'll have less flexibility on price, and you'll be vulnerable if they experience problems in their business. If you have very specialized needs, you may be frustrated trying to find the supplies you require. Once again, industry trade shows and associations are a good place to begin.

Remember, however, that if you have highly unusual requirements, you may end up dependent on only one supplier. Instead, try to design your production process so you can use more-standard materials.

Use the worksheet on page 166 to shop around for suppliers.

SUPPLIER COMPARISON CHART

	Supplier One	Supplier Two	Supplier Three
☐ Name of Supplier			
☐ Sales Rep and Contact Info			
☐ Range of Services/ Products Offered			
☐ Direct Costs			
☐ Additional Costs			
☐ Payment Terms			
☐ Order Turn-around-time			
☐ Shipping Costs			
☐ Other Maintenance/ Support			
☐ Other:			
☐ Other:			

ACCOMPLISHMENT # 3:

Research and purchase computers, software, and other technology

My Checklist:

- [ ] **Develop an approach to buying technology**
- [ ] **Choose a phone system**
- [ ] **Choose software**
- [ ] **Choose hardware**
- [ ] **Get online**
- [ ] **Meet your mobile needs**
- [ ] **Find ways to get technical help**

Technology is one part of your business you'll love and hate at the same time. Technology has enabled small companies to compete with large ones and has dramatically lowered the cost of performing many business functions. But dealing with technology can be an immense headache—decisions can be confusing and expensive to make, and difficult and expensive to change.

Whether you love technology or hate it, you've got to deal with it. You don't need to become a geek, but you must learn some of the basics. Just as you couldn't run a business without knowing what "accounts receivable" are, you can't run a company without being comfortable discussing Internet connections or databases.

Before you start shopping for technology, get a good idea of what you'll look for. Outline your critical business needs and then look for solutions that fit those needs. Otherwise, it's easy to get enamored of "gee whiz" technology, even though you don't have a real need for it.

MY PHONE NEEDS

	How Many?	Service Provider?	Special Features?
☐ Voice lines			
☐ Fax/data lines			
☐ Voicemail boxes			
☐ Long-distance service			
☐ Cell phones/ smartphones			
☐ White Pages, Yellow Pages, and online directory listings			
☐ Other:			

☐ Who is your local service provider? Do you have a choice in provider? _____
_____

☐ Will you have phone numbers in remote locations? Where should they ring?_____
_____

☐ How will you receive and direct incoming calls? Will you have a receptionist, an automated system, or an answering service?_____
_____

☐ What types of on-hold features do you need? How can you transfer calls between phone lines?_____
_____

☐ Do you want or need features such as Caller ID, 3-way calling, call forwarding, etc.? How much do they cost?_____
_____

☐ Can you integrate your phone system with your database , other software, or a VoIP application? Can integration better serve your business?
_____
_____

☐ Can you integrate your phone system with other devices, such as cell phones? Can integration better serve your business?
_____
_____

WHAT WOULD RHONDA DO?

TO ORGANIZE TECH "STUFF"

Every time I buy a new piece of hardware or software, it comes with a variety of manuals, cords, installation guides, and more. Once it's out of the box, it's easy to get this stuff really confused with stuff from other equipment. Before long, I don't know which extra cord goes with which machine or which manual goes with which software. So I buy extra-large Ziploc bags and put each product's stuff in a bag of its own. With a permanent marker, I write the name of the software or hardware product and the date I purchased it on the outside of the bag. I then keep all these zipped plastic bags in one big box. I can easily find what I need if I ever have to reinstall something or refer back to the user manual.

 ## Develop an approach to buying technology

With technology changing as rapidly as it does, how do you buy something that fits your budget today yet will continue to meet your needs as your business grows and changes? Should you buy an economy model, realizing you may quickly outgrow it, or should you buy the latest, fully loaded version?

My own rule of thumb has always been to choose products I think will meet my needs and handle technology upgrades for at least two to three years. That rarely means the latest, greatest, fully loaded versions of hardware such as computers, but it also means I skip the low-end model that's about to be discontinued.

Of course, in a new company, every dollar counts. That means you often have to settle for less than you'd ideally desire. Fortunately, many low-cost technology products—printers, copiers, and some computers—offer excellent features that may meet your needs until your business has time to get established.

When comparing your options in choosing technology products, here are some questions to ask yourself:

- **What features do you absolutely need?** If your equipment won't let you do everything you need to do, then you've wasted money, even if you got a bargain on that last laptop on the discount shelf. Consider what functions you need to perform and make sure your technology can handle those well. Having trouble figuring out what you need? Go to CNET (www.cnet.com), ZDnet (www.zdnet.com/topic-reviews), or Epinions (www.epinions.com) for savvy reviews that speak your language.

■ **Are your needs basic or complex?** If your needs are fairly basic, you can start very inexpensively, using low-cost online applications that only require fairly low-powered computing devices. For instance, you can find simple, cloud-based software applications—often for free—to handle tasks such as word processing, bookkeeping, and customer relationship management (CRM). Because you access this software over the Internet, rather than running it on your own machines, you need only the most inexpensive computers.

Complicated or specialized tasks require more-powerful equipment and software. For example, if in your business you will need to create high-end presentations, you will need more-expensive graphics software and more computing power to produce those. If you have a brick-and-mortar retail store, you will need P.O.S. (point-of-sale) systems to keep track of your sales and inventory. If you're in a specific industry, there may be a V.A.R. (value-added reseller) who can help you design and install the appropriate programs and equipment you'll need.

Generally, identify the processes you will need for your specific business, then determine how much computing power those processes will actually require. But whenever possible, look to the cloud (Internet-based applications) for solutions. Cloud-based versions enable you to scale up or down as you add or subtract employees or as your needs change (as they often do in a new business), and you can access cloud applications anytime, anywhere, from any device that has an Internet connection. You will pay a monthly subscription instead of an upfront purchase fee, so you keep more of your cash available for your new company.

It's always a good idea to first decide what kind of software you'll run—on premise or in the cloud—and from that choose hardware that will support it properly.

■ **Does your new technology have to be compatible with other technology?** We live in an increasingly interconnected world where everything has to work with everything else. So be careful buying an unknown brand of hardware or software unless you've checked out that it will work with the other technology you purchase.

MY HARDWARE NEEDS

Use this worksheet to identify hardware you'll need in specific areas of your business.
To outline your needs for software, use the worksheet on pages 172–173.

	Admin/ Production	Accounting	Sales	Other
☐ Computers				
☐ Tablets, smartphones, and other mobile devices				
☐ Printers				
☐ Copiers/fax machines				
☐ Other peripherals (scanners, etc.)				
☐ Internet access devices				
☐ Network/servers				
☐ Data storage devices				
☐ Cables, surge protectors, back-up generators				
☐ Other:				

MY SOFTWARE NEEDS

Things to Consider	Office Suite	Accounting	Customer Management
☐ What key tasks do I need to perform with the software?			
☐ What features would be nice, but are not necessarily mandatory?			
☐ Does the software need to be accessible from remote or mobile locations?			
☐ Which program offers these features at the most reasonable price?			
☐ What is the price?			
☐ How simple is the product to learn and operate?			
☐ How much free technical support is available?			
☐ What will additional technical support cost?			
☐ Can I find employees/consultants who know how to use it? At what price? If not, is training available?			
☐ Will the product integrate with my other software and applications?			
☐ How are the reviews and word-of-mouth about this product?			
☐ Other:			

Inventory Management	Specialty Software	Specialty Software	Specialty Software

One of the many great advantages of cloud-based, or SaaS, applications is that many of these solutions can "talk" to one another and to on-premise software programs, by sharing data. For example, if you use Web-based Salesforce CRM, you can share customer data with an on-premise QuickBooks financial program. When you add new customers to your CRM, their names, contact information, sales transactions, and so forth automatically flow into QuickBooks. You'll want other applications to integrate as well. Your shopping cart for your ecommerce store should integrate with your shipping application. If your shopping cart can also integrate with CRM and accounting, even better! Not only will you enter data only once, saving time and reducing errors, you'll have access to richer data, and you'll be able to share information more efficiently with your team.

- **Do you want single purpose or multifunction equipment?** Many pieces of equipment can now handle multiple functions, such as a fax/printer/copier/scanner all-in-one. But although these can be a good value if you have a fairly minimal need for the various functions offered, keep in mind that such machines don't provide leading-edge capabilities. If you have sophisticated copying demands, for instance, don't buy a combined copier/fax/printer, or you'll just get frustrated.

- **Are replacement supplies readily available, and how much do they cost?** Especially with printers, fax machines, and copiers, "consumables" and servicing actually become much more important issues than the underlying hardware after purchase. It's not unusual for the cost of a printer cartridge—whether ink-jet or laser—to cost more than the printer itself! Certainly, by the time you've owned the printer for six months you will have paid more in consumables than you did for the equipment. And office and discount stores usually carry only supplies for or service the most well-known brands. So if you run out on a day you're under deadline, you could be in trouble if you have to order your supplies direct from the manufacturer. Take all this into consideration before buying.

- **How cool do you want to be?** While you probably don't need the latest and greatest gadgets, you will want to choose a machine for its good design and ease of use, especially if you're a one-person business who works on a computer all day. The bottom line is you want to enjoy using your equipment. So consider design and ergonomics as you shop for technology—just make sure what you choose is compatible with all your other purchases!

COMPARISON CHART: INTERNET HOSTING COMPANIES

Use this worksheet to compare options for Internet Service Providers (ISPs).

	ISP Option One	ISP Option Two	ISP Option Three
☐ Company Name			
☐ Connection Speed			
☐ Hardware Required			
☐ Installation Cost			
☐ Monthy/Ongoing Fees			
☐ Services/Capacity Provided			
☐ Website Hosting Available			
☐ Additional Services Available			
☐ Reviews/Recommendations			
☐ Other Considerations:			

✔ Choose a phone system

Even in this day of high-tech devices, your phone system is a key piece of business communication equipment.

In comparison to many other forms of business communication, phone lines and phone calls are inexpensive. Compare the cost of your monthly phone calls to the cost of printing and mailing even one brochure.

Yet, a typical scenario is the entrepreneur who takes months searching for the right location, spends a bundle on a computer system, and then, at the very last minute, plans a phone strategy. Missed calls and an inefficient phone system are the potential result.

Today, no one would leave home without their cell phone in hand. Gone are the days when people were not reachable because they were away from their desks. In fact, depending on the business you're in, maybe that's the only line you need. Today's smartphones allow you to check your email, surf the Internet, and run applications while on the run yourself. Smartphones are more like tiny computers that make phone calls—and they support an increasingly mobile workforce.

Another telephone technology you should know about is VoIP (for Voice over Internet Protocol). It is a popular alternative to traditional telephone service that sends voice signals over the Internet using the same network that your data flows over. The advantage of VoIP: cost. It may cut your phone bill to a fraction of what it would be with a normal land or cell phone line. The downside can sometimes be reduced reliability and quality of service.

Start It Free

Bring everyone together and save money on travel expenses by holding "virtual" meetings. With FreeConferenceCall (**www.freeconference-call.com**), you get your own dedicated conference call line with which you can make reservationless calls 24/7 with a large number of participants. If you would also like to see your participants, hold a free videoconference for up to 10 people with Google Hangouts (**www.google.com/hangouts**).

WHAT WOULD RHONDA DO?

HOSTED PHONE SYSTEMS

Thanks to the popularity of VoIP, you can get "hosted" phone service for business, in which a third-party vendor handles all aspects of installing, maintaining, and managing your phone system for a low monthly fee. This is an increasingly common choice among small businesses in particular, which typically don't have the in-house technology staff to troubleshoot and maintain complicated phone systems.

As you plan your phone system, keep all this in mind:

- **Develop a telephone plan.** Start by sitting down and planning your phone service, just as you would any other important aspect of your business. How do you use your phones now or anticipate using them? What features must you have? How many lines do you need? How many phone lines should be wireless?

- **Consider special features.** Phone companies offer many enhancements to basic phone services. Investigate ways your phone can be a powerful business tool.

- **Keep it simple.** On the other hand, if your phones are too complicated, they'll be a nuisance to use. Phones come with a variety of features—many of which you'll rarely use. Don't buy "bells and whistles" that will get in the way of using your phone as a phone.

- **Comparison shop.** The features and costs of phone service and equipment vary widely. Shop around for long-distance plans and other services to find the right fit for your business.

- **Think long term.** Will you be expanding, moving, changing your needs? If so, either buy a scalable and changeable system, or buy an inexpensive system that you can replace without a large financial loss.

The worksheet on page 168 will help you plan your phone system.

 ## Choose software

Before you select your computers, think through your software needs—and consider them carefully. Your choice of computers can largely be driven by your software needs. If, for instance, you need powerful software programs, you'll probably need powerful computers. Also, it may be less expensive to buy your computers with programs preloaded than to buy them separately.

Moreover, once you've committed your business to a particular software package, it's often difficult to change, either because you can't export your data easily or because the time and effort needed to learn a new program is a barrier to making a switch.

Your most basic business functions are probably best served by "off-the-shelf," widely available software programs. An integrated office program

> ### WHAT WOULD RHONDA DO?
>
> ## DISASTER RECOVERY AND BUSINESS CONTINUITY
>
> Technology is great, but it can break down, fail to work if there's no power, and can even get stolen (especially laptops, tablets, and smartphones). Being without our technological tools can spell disaster for a business. You should plan at the beginning of your business for *disaster recovery/business continuity*: how you will keep your business running if your hardware and software and data aren't available. Backing up your files is the first, very minimal, action you must take, but there are others. It might make sense to have a consultation with an expert as you set up your technology. Paying a couple of hundred dollars upfront could save you thousands—or even your very business—down the road.

(such as Microsoft Office or Microsoft Works), a basic bookkeeping program (such as QuickBooks or Quicken for very small companies), an Internet browser, an email program, and a calendar or task program will get you started.

Another critical software need is your database. Your bookkeeping program (especially one like QuickBooks) might serve as your database for your customer records and billing. However, you are almost certainly going to need a database to handle customer contact management, and perhaps also to meet special needs such as tracking inventory.

All of these programs are also available in cloud-based versions. By that, I mean these key business functions—payroll, accounting, sales management, document sharing, data backup, and even word processing—are handled somewhere out there in the web-based clouds of cyberspace. These cloud-computing solutions are also known as web-based or online services and SaaS (software as a service).

Advantages of web-based services:

- You pay for what you need now and can add more resources as your company grows
- You always have the latest upgrade, without paying extra
- Predictable costs, usually a low monthly subscription
- More features than you could devise yourself

- No internal tech staff required

- Can access from any computer with an Internet connection

- Many applications integrate; for example, you may be able to link your inventory management software to your sales application

- Information secure and backed up

- Reduces your need for an office computer network

- Relatively easy to move to a more appropriate cloud alternative

- Real-time data and analytics

- Typically, easy to learn and use

Disadvantages:

- Need a fast, reliable Internet connection

- Ongoing monthly cost, even when you don't use it

- Privacy and security concerns, especially if you're not careful

- If the cloud-based company goes out of business, you may lose your data

If you have highly specialized needs, turn to your industry association to find out if software has already been developed for your type of business. Industry-specific software can be considerably more expensive than basic software, so be sure to talk with several users to find out if they're satisfied with the product.

Another approach if you have unusual needs is to have software designed or customized for your own use. However, customized software is more

WHAT WOULD RHONDA DO?

GEEKS TO THE RESCUE

Because technology can be bewildering, small businesses frequently need help. Yet very few have technology expertise on staff—most have to turn to outside consultants to help them buy, set up, troubleshoot, and manage their technology investments. To meet this need, a broad range of tech support businesses have sprung up to offer tech support services to individuals and smaller businesses. Such businesses can be a boon if you lack technical knowledge yourself. However, before hiring a tech consultant, call your local Better Business Bureau, and always check references.

WHAT WOULD RHONDA DO?

START YOUR BUSINESS IN THE CLOUD

At its most basic level, the cloud offers you computing resources—applications, file storage and sharing, and processing power—that you access over the Internet, from a distance. You can use these resources even though they do not reside on hardware (computers or servers) in your business or home. Your use your computer, smartphone, tablet, or indeed any "smart" device, to tap into those resources online. Another term for the cloud computing most small and medium businesses need is SaaS—or "software as a service."

As they became more available, I moved many of my company's critical business functions to the cloud: email, customer relationship management (CRM), email newsletters, and payroll, for example. If I launched my business today, I would choose cloud-based applications right from the get-go. Why? Generally, they save you time, money, and headaches. That's because cloud-based applications are easy to use, you pay for only what you need, and upgrades are always up-to-date and seamless.

expensive to purchase and maintain, and if you have problems, you may not be able to find personnel to assist you.

Use the worksheet on pages 172–173 to identify your software needs and compare products as you shop for them.

 ## Choose hardware

It's easy to get excited when you look at all the electronic gadgets and goodies that are out there. Cool-looking monitors, oversized color printers, and super-sleek computers are all very tempting (until you look at the price tags, of course).

But buying hardware can also be stressful because there are so many choices. There's so much information out there about those choices—much of it written in technobabble—and so much money on the line.

Once again, the thing to do is to plan before you shop. Your needs and your pocketbook should determine your hardware choices. I've seen new companies that start with all the latest hardware before they've even developed a product or found a customer—and that's not the way to spend your money. Instead, buy what you need when you need it.

Almost every business needs the basics: computers, printers, monitors, copiers, and a way to receive faxes. But you don't need to buy it all at once. If you're starting out slow, you can make your copies at the local copy shop. Or send and receive your faxes at a local business center or online. For especially small businesses, you can consider multifunction combination printer/fax/copier/scanner machines. These cost less than buying each machine separately and take up less room. Alternatively, don't scrimp on things you really need. If you're going to do a lot of printing, for example, you will want a laser rather than an ink-jet printer because of the superior quality and speed.

As far as computers go, if you plan to use a number of cloud-based applications, you'll need less computing power. This is good news, as you'll save money. However, you probably don't want to buy the lowest-powered computer you can find. Choose something that can grow with you.

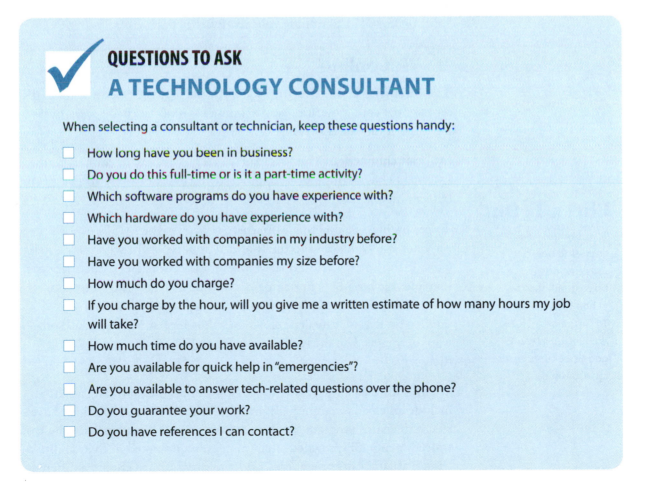

✔ QUESTIONS TO ASK
A TECHNOLOGY CONSULTANT

When selecting a consultant or technician, keep these questions handy:

- [ ] How long have you been in business?
- [ ] Do you do this full-time or is it a part-time activity?
- [ ] Which software programs do you have experience with?
- [ ] Which hardware do you have experience with?
- [ ] Have you worked with companies in my industry before?
- [ ] Have you worked with companies my size before?
- [ ] How much do you charge?
- [ ] If you charge by the hour, will you give me a written estimate of how many hours my job will take?
- [ ] How much time do you have available?
- [ ] Are you available for quick help in "emergencies"?
- [ ] Are you available to answer tech-related questions over the phone?
- [ ] Do you guarantee your work?
- [ ] Do you have references I can contact?

You'll also have to decide whether to purchase desktops or laptops or other mobile devices. Although some people have a desktop for office use and a laptop or tablet for taking work home and for traveling, many people opt to have a laptop computer as their only computer. They keep a full-sized monitor and keyboard on their desk to plug the laptop into (usually through a "docking station") but then also have the mobility they need to take their work home or on the road.

Another thing to consider is how you will do the all-important job of backing up your computer files. There is special backup hardware and software you can buy so you can regularly copy all the contents of your computers to a safe location—either a special disk drive or onto CDs. There are also many fine cloud-based automatic backup services that you access online. These will automatically back up all your files onto a remote computer. You can then retrieve them if anything goes wrong and your computers crash or are otherwise unavailable. Use the worksheet on page 171 to outline your hardware needs.

✔ Get online

The Internet is as much a part of your business as the phone or mail. It's an essential communication and ecommerce tool. Virtually every business uses it on a daily basis.

Internet connection. The first issue you'll face is how to connect to the Internet. The options keep changing, so you'll want to stay abreast of the choices in your area.

To get online, you'll need an Internet Service Provider (ISP). An ISP provides you with access to the Internet, and, typically, with your email. Most ISPs also offer additional services for additional fees. Such services may include hosting your company's website or registering your company's domain name. Other companies can provide additional related services such as website design, database hosting, or writing small software programs. Use the worksheet on page 175 to compare ISPs and their services.

Email. This is an all-pervasive aspect of business life. Virtually all ISPs include an email program with their Internet access, but you don't have to use the email program that comes from your ISP as your only choice. Indeed, many ISP-provided email programs are limited in their ability to handle attachments or graphics, and you may want to choose a different email program. If you travel frequently, you'll need cloud-based email accessible from the Web so you can check messages from any computer with online access.

Most office-suite software comes with an email program. The best-known is Outlook from Microsoft, which comes with Microsoft Office. Microsoft also offers Office 365, with a web-based email program from which you can access your email using any computer connected to the Internet. Outlook. com, along with Yahoo! Mail and Gmail, are also free, web-based email programs. However, you may not want an Outlook, Yahoo!, or Gmail email address as your business email address, as it doesn't give as professional an appearance as having your own name. Still, some of these services offer, for a fee, web-based email with your own domain name.

Domain name: In Week One, you learned how to reserve your own "domain name"—the name by which a site is identified and located on the Web. The domain name of the company that publishes this book, for instance, is PlanningShop.com. The Internet address for that domain name—or URL (universal resource locator)—is www.PlanningShop.com.

Once you have your own domain name, you can use that for your company's website address and for your email (e.g., Rhonda@PlanningShop. com). This obviously looks more professional than having a more generic email address (e.g., somebody@gmail.com).

More importantly, you can use your domain name with virtually any ISP, website hosting company, or email program. This gives you the flexibility to shop around, use the email program that best fits your needs, and change providers if desired.

Ask your ISP, a technical consultant, or a tech-savvy friend how to get set up to use your own domain name with your ISP and email program.

Website: In Week Six, you will set up a company website, with an eye to how you want to market your products or services. During this week, you want to make sure you consider who will host your website as you go about choosing an ISP. After all, you may use the same company that provides you with online access to host your website.

It's not necessary, of course, to have one ISP provide you with both Internet access and website hosting services. However, it is frequently less expensive and less hassle to have one company do both, especially if you have modest requirements for your website.

Check It Out

Running a restaurant? Check out Let's Eat (**www.letseat.at**) for a website builder designed just for restaurants. Photographers can try Zenfolio (**www.zenfolio.com**), SmugMug (**www.smugmug.com**), or PhotoShelter (**www. photoshelter.com**).

However, if you want unique features on your website, you may want to use a company that specializes in hosting business websites. The types of features you might want to include on your site are a blog, online forms for customers and prospects to fill out, a connection to a database of information (such as a catalog), or a shopping cart to enable customers to make purchases. Ask other entrepreneurs for recommendations of website hosting companies that they use.

You might also want to search for website hosting companies that specialize in your industry. These might have "turnkey" solutions for you that can get your website up and running faster than if you had someone design a website for you. They might even provide some kind of joint marketing services. Check with your industry trade association for names of website service providers.

Network: You may want to build your own company internal network—a local area network, or LAN—so all your computers can work together. There are many advantages to having your own network, including the ability to share office equipment, share and store data, provide security, handle Internet access, and maintain your own internal company email.

But having a network is also more complicated than having stand-alone computers. You may need someone who can maintain the network. You'll also need wiring and hubs or routers to connect all the machines, and you may decide that you want a dedicated "server"—a computer whose sole purpose is to handle email, store and/or back up files from other computers, route print jobs to the office printer, and so forth.

Smaller and newer companies can usually get by without a network—often using the Internet itself as their network, sharing files via email or file-storing and sharing programs such as Dropbox (www.dropbox.com) or Box (www.box.com).

If you aren't technologically experienced, hire an experienced company or consultant to set up your company network for you, ideally someone you can turn to on an ongoing basis for assistance. Don't depend on your brother-in-law's cousin who used to install telephones. You'll regret it.

 ## Meet your mobile needs

People no longer run their businesses exclusively from behind their desks or inside a physical store. Assume right from the start of your business that you'll want to access data, to perform certain functions, and to keep operations running smoothly even when you're on the go. You can do this with mobile devices from which you access cloud-based applications for online payroll, time tracking, invoicing, mobile payment processing, inventory management, and so on. You may also hire employees or contractors who travel frequently or work offsite. Choose technology that they will feel comfortable using.

When deciding on cloud-based applications for your mobile needs, remember to research providers thoroughly and ask questions about security and privacy. And always make sure that anyone with access to your precious data uses a password-protected device. Finally, when employees leave, be sure to turn "off" their access to your data.

 ## Find ways to get technical help

Without a doubt, one of the most frustrating aspects of dealing with technology is the lack of capable, affordable help. Unless you have technology-proficient people on your own staff, you will be frustrated trying to find consultants or service businesses to assist you.

If you can find reliable consultants or technicians, use them. Especially when you first get started, use the assistance of a consultant to help you plan and install your equipment and software. Ask for recommendations, especially from other entrepreneurs, of technology consultants they've used. And make sure they speak in nontechnical language that you can understand.

ACCOMPLISHMENT #4:
Consider how you will distribute your products

If you are a manufacturer, you will almost certainly use other parties to bring your product to market—distributors, wholesalers, or retailers. Choosing the right distributor and retailer for your product is vital to your success.

These intermediaries provide a variety of assistance in getting your product or service to customers, including:

- **Their sales efforts and sales team**
- **Their reputation and relationships with customers/retailers**
- **Their expertise in understanding the market**

Check It Out

For a list of associations of distributors in over 100 industries, check the membership list of the National Association of Wholesale Distributors. www.naw.org/about/assoclist.php

- **Their advertising and marketing efforts**
- **Their additional services to you—warehousing, shipping, etc.**
- **Their additional services to customers—shipping, product training or support, installation, etc.**

Distributors: Few decisions directly affect your business and your finances as much as the selection of a distributor. To a large extent, they control whether or not your products have a fair chance to ever reach potential customers. If your distributor can't get your products on retailers' store shelves, you won't be able to make sales.

Your distributor's financial practices—how long they take to pay you, how often, how they report sales, and what percentages they charge—in large part determine your cash flow and profits. And, of course, you want to make certain your distributor is honest and stable.

When just starting out, you may feel lucky to get any distributor to represent your product, because good distributors are in demand by many manufacturers. Nevertheless, be selective!

"Shop" for distributors, and don't choose solely on the basis of how much (what percentage) they'll charge for their services. Compare at least a few distributors. If possible, meet with a representative face-to-face. Always ask for references and check with some of the other manufacturers the distributor represents. Have their other clients been satisfied? Have they encountered problems?

To find a list of potential distributors, contact your industry trade association. Well-respected and known distributors are likely to be active in trade associations, and many associations maintain lists of distributors.

When entering into a distribution agreement, you should absolutely get a legally binding contract, spelling out all the various aspects of your arrangement. Hire an attorney knowledgeable about distribution agreements to review your contract—even if the distributor says it's their "standard" contract. Some of the issues to include in your agreement are covered in the worksheet on page 187.

Sales representatives: In many industries, independent sales representatives serve many of the same functions as distributors (although they are much less likely to do warehousing or shipping of products). These independent sales reps find and call on retailers (or customers) who might want your product. However, in most cases, these independent sales

DISTRIBUTION AGREEMENT

When you enter into a distribution contract, here are some considerations to negotiate.
Be certain to have any and all agreements reviewed by a competent attorney.

	Distributor One	Distributor Two	Distributor Three
☐ Distributor Name and Contact Information			
☐ Is the agreement exclusive or nonexclusive? What is the length of the terms, and how can either party terminate the agreement?			
☐ What percentage do they charge? When and how often do they pay you, and what holdbacks from your payments, if any, do they make?			
☐ What other services do they offer at what fees? What are the total fees you and the distributor are responsible for?			
☐ Who is responsible for nonpayment by their customers?			
☐ What minimum performance guarantees do they offer?			
☐ What marketing efforts do they guarantee? What charges for marketing efforts do you incur or which sales materials are you responsible for?			
☐ How are damaged goods handled/paid for?			

representatives work for many manufacturers at once, and your products become part of the broad list of products they show potential customers.

Working with good independent sales representatives may be an excellent way to secure the services of a talented, well-connected sales force without the cost of hiring an inside sales team. However, good sales representatives are in demand, and you will have to convince them that you are worth taking on as a client.

Moreover, because independent sales representatives handle many manufacturers at once, your products can easily get overlooked in their portfolio. As a result, you need to develop and maintain a strong, ongoing relationship with your independent sales representatives. After all, you want to make certain they continually remember to include your products in their sales presentations to prospective customers.

Once again, the best place to find a list of potential sales representatives is through an industry trade association.

Retailers: Your choice of retailers, too, is critical. The retailer needs to be able to attract a sufficient number of customers, promote and merchandise your products, and then pay you in a timely fashion.

Don't be entranced by big or well-known retailers. My first client was a sportswear manufacturer who was thrilled when he landed a major department store to carry his line. Over time, however, he discovered this store had costly requirements about how he had to package and ship his merchandise, and then it made payments very late. And many large retailers are notoriously tough negotiators when it comes to price.

You may think that the deal you finally closed with that well-known big-box retailer is a dream come true, but once you discover how thin your profit margin will be, coupled with the retailer's strict requirements on everything from how you label your boxes to which shipping company you use, you may end up feeling that all the effort and expense of fulfilling this huge order just isn't worth it.

If you are selling directly to retailers (instead of using a distributor to reach them) be sure you understand all the terms of your arrangement. Who pays shipping? Will returns be permitted? Under what circumstances? What discount will you give them? How long will they have to make payments? Use the worksheet on page 189 to keep track of each retailer's specifics.

RETAILER COMPARISON CHART

	Retailer One	Retailer Two	Retailer Three
☐ Retailer Name and Contact Information			
☐ What discount schedule/price will they pay you?			
☐ Are sales final or can unsold merchandise be returned?			
☐ What are their packaging/shipping requirements, if any?			
☐ Who is responsible for damaged goods?			
☐ What are their payment terms/schedule?			
☐ What promotions, advertising, or other sales efforts will they make?			
☐ What "co-op" advertising or other promotions will you have to participate in?			
☐ What charge-backs or other fees do they take?			
☐ What is their reputation with other wholesalers?			
☐ Other:			

Design procedures for handling administrative tasks

Once your business is up and running, you'll quickly find yourself dealing with a wide variety of ongoing administrative tasks. If you don't prepare to deal with these, inevitably you'll soon feel overwhelmed and things will start falling through the cracks.

You can prevent this by establishing some positive time management habits right from the start of your business and by setting up procedures to help you keep track of all the many tasks and administrative details you have to manage.

Of course, in a new business you don't yet know all of the administrative issues you'll have to deal with. Don't worry, your administrative procedures will certainly evolve and change over time.

Nevertheless, every business—whether large or small—has to deal with many of the same administrative functions: making sure bills are paid, invoices are sent out, and things that should get done actually get done.

These can be broken down by general area of responsibility/function:

General office management:

- **Answering the phones**
- **Responding to emails**
- **Handling incoming mail and packages**
- **Preparing outgoing mail**
- **Answering customer inquiries**
- **Ordering supplies**
- **Scheduling**
- **Project management**
- **Managing the "to do" list**

Bookkeeping/accounting:

- **Paying bills**
- **Sending invoices**
- **Collecting on outstanding invoices**
- **Reconciling bank statements**

- **Transferring funds from accounts**
- **Preparing forecasts and financial statements**
- **Meeting tax deadlines and completing tax forms**

Order fulfillment:

- **Order taking**
- **Packing**
- **Shipping**
- **Tracking shipments**
- **Handling customer complaints**
- **Ensuring sufficient supplies and inventory levels**

One way to approach these issues is to begin an "Operations Manual" detailing how you handle the tasks you perform repeatedly. As you deal with an administrative task, jot down the steps you've used to complete it. That gives you the beginning of a procedures manual, so you won't have to reinvent the process each time. Also, it will make training employees much easier.

Another useful approach is to create "templates" of all the forms you'll use over and over again, such as invoices, statements, proposals, product/service descriptions, and the like. You can often find standard templates as part of your software programs (such as invoices, statements, and packing slips in QuickBooks) or from your industry trade association.

You can even prepare standard answers to email or phone inquiries. It's OK to use the same form over and over or to repeat yourself from one customer or client to the next. After all, you don't have to be very creative in handling these tasks.

Here are a few ways to make the most of your time and reduce administrative hassles:

- **Maintain a calendar and keep it visible:** You can use a paper calendar on your desk or on the wall, but you may find some of the features of calendar software programs (such as pop-up reminders) helpful. A good calendar feature is included in Outlook, included in Microsoft Office. Be careful, however, that you don't forget your appointments when the computer is turned off. You can also download an Outlook or other calendar app for your smartphone.

- **Make a "To Do" list:** Keep it somewhere where you can see it all the time. Look at it frequently and revise it daily. Check off tasks as you complete them—that gives you a sense of accomplishment.

- **Prioritize:** Often the things that are most important to your business don't have deadlines. Make sure those vital tasks are on your "to do" list and keep them on the top of the list. Don't let the pressing but unimportant details of your business keep you from attending to the truly critical.

- **Set time aside:** Make "appointments" with yourself to do important tasks, and don't allow interruptions. Make certain you schedule time for sending out your invoices.

- **Reduce shopping time:** Keep a list of things you need so you reduce repeat trips. Make certain you have enough of supplies you use regularly. Order online and have supplies delivered.

- **Eliminate errands:** Keep a list of errands and do a number of them at one time. Schedule your errands for the end of the business day, rather than prime time. Use delivery (and pickup) service for frequently used services (such as copy companies and shipping).

- **Use your "Vital Statistics" list:** In Week Three (page 93) you started developing a list of key company data. You're likely to be asked this information on many forms or dealing with suppliers or government agencies. Have it handy so you don't have to go digging through files.

- **Make color-coded files:** Use files of different colors—or at least different colored labels—so you can quickly find the kind of information you need on your desk or in your file drawers. You might want to use blue files for client project-related documents, green files for financial information, yellow files for suppliers, or whatever works for your company. Mark your files by year, so you can easily archive older files.

- **Keep frequently used files handy:** Get a desk with at least one file drawer so you can use the files you need regularly without having to get up and go to a filing cabinet.

- **Become an email power user:** Take time to learn a few key tasks in your email program, particularly setting up folders and filters. Create your address book or email "groups" for those you'll email regularly.

■ **Handle mail once:** The ideal way to manage paper is to handle incoming mail only once. In other words, as soon as you read it, deal with it. If you don't need it, throw it out. If it should be filed, file immediately. If you have to take action, do so. Of course, this isn't always possible, but get in the habit of deciding what to do with stuff as you get it.

Outsourcing administrative tasks

One of the things that has freed up entrepreneurs and small business owners to be more creative is the trend toward "outsourcing." When you outsource, you delegate—for a fee, of course—some aspect of your business to be done by people or organizations outside of your four walls. Of course, small businesses outsource all the time. Chances are good, for example, that you don't have an on-staff accountant or lawyer, but instead use the services of outside professionals on an as-needed basis. Likewise, you probably don't keep a janitorial staff, but outsource that to a cleaning service.

With the Internet and related technology, outsourcing has been taken to a new level. You can outsource your receptionist: calls from your office can be routed transparently to a call center in another state, where someone answers your phone with your company name, tracks you down on your cell phone if needed, and takes messages for you that can be delivered to your cell phone via text messaging. Or you can outsource your warehousing and shipping by having all orders for products transmitted electronically to a business that fulfills all your orders remotely, and updates your internal databases when an order is shipped so that a customer can be billed.

Then there are cloud-based, or SaaS, applications. Rather than having to buy hardware and software to do a certain task—let's say, payroll —and then hire someone to install, use, and manage that system, you can outsource the entire thing. A number of SaaS providers offer payroll services on-demand: you log onto their website, and securely enter payroll information into an easy-to-use interface. The service generates all the forms, reminds you when to make payments and how much, keeps track of payroll taxes and benefits, and generally acts as your bookkeeper—for much less than it would cost to buy the software and have a bookkeeper work on your premises. You can outsource just about every business function there is this way—if it's not a core part of your business, there's someone out there with a technological tools and the know-how to do it for you.

ACCOMPLISHMENT #6:
Deal with insurance

One of the most frustrating expenses you'll incur when running a business is the money you spend on insurance. After all, you can't "see" what you're getting. If this is your first business, you'll be absolutely overwhelmed by the different types of insurance you'll need or want.

Figuring out your insurance coverage will be daunting. Guaranteed! So you'll need a good insurance agent, or two or three! Ideally, you'll find an agent who understands business insurance for companies of your size and industry. It's best if they're a "broker" who can offer you policies from a number of different companies rather than just representing one insurance company's products.

If you don't know any insurance agents, ask for referrals from other business owners or from service providers. You'll want someone whose advice you can trust because you are likely going to rely on their recommendations for the type and amount of coverage you should have.

Also, check with your industry trade association. Many trade associations offer lower-cost insurance specifically for the needs of companies such as yours. But still be cautious: Just because a policy comes from a trade association doesn't necessarily mean it's best for you.

When you sit down with an insurance agent, consider three aspects:

- **Incentive:** insurance you want because it's desired by your workers (including yourself) such as medical, dental, life insurance, retirement

- **Protection:** insurance in case something unexpected happens: liability, accident, fire, theft, business interruption

- **Legal necessity:** insurance others require—perhaps your landlord, such as fire or liability, or required by state law, such as workers' compensation if you have employees; because the Affordable Health Care Act requires companies with 50 employees or more to provide workers with health insurance, most likely you will not have to provide this coverage when just launching your business

Check It Out

For 18 questions Rhonda recommends that you ask insurance companies or agents, go to **www. planningshop.com/hire/ insurancequestions**

Health insurance is the kind of insurance most desired by your employees. To keep costs manageable, you may want to look for health insurance policies provided by:

- **HMO—Health Maintenance Organization**: HMOs cost less than other plans since the number of health care provider choices is limited.

- **PPO—Preferred Provider Organization:** for a wider range of choices of doctors and hospitals that agree to set prices for services. Make certain there's a long—and good—list of choices for you and your employees.

- **POS—Point of Service plan:** A POS plan is the middle-of-the-road option in managed plans, falling between HMOs and PPOs in terms of premium costs and provider flexibility.

Traditional indemnity plans are nonnetwork or "fee-for-service" plans. They have the highest premiums and offer employees the most freedom to select providers and hospitals.

When looking for health insurance, here are some of the things you'll want to find out:

- **Do you have to, or want to, provide the same benefits for *all* employees**—or all of a certain class of employees (such as full-time employees)? This is likely the case, as a result of either state law or insurance company policy. That means you will get the same kind of coverage for yourself and make the same amount of financial contribution as your employees.

- **How much of a contribution do you want to make to employees' coverage?** What percent of coverage or what dollar figure?

- **Do you want to pay all or part of dependents' coverage?**

- **How long of a "sabbatical" do you want to offer**—in case employees take a leave of absence from the company or medical leave?

"Cafeteria" plans allow employees to choose among benefits. Employees receive a certain dollar figure credit from you, their employer. They can then each choose the benefits that are best for their individual situation. This gives your employees more flexibility and is particularly good when you have a diverse workforce. However, there may be some financial costs in setting up or administering these cafeteria plans. Check with your accountant, attorney, or insurance agent.

Check It Out

The National Association of Insurance Commissioners has links on its website to each state Insurance office website. www.naic.org/state_web_map.htm

Some kinds of insurance coverage—often health benefits—require you to have been in business a period of time before coverage can begin.

Always ask about the strength and honesty of your insurance provider—the company itself as well as the agent. You want to make sure the company is financially strong. After all, you need them to cover their policies in case there's a major disaster such as an earthquake or flood.

Deciding what types and how much insurance to carry is always a juggling act. You want to have enough coverage in case of problems, but the costs can be discouraging, especially for a young company.

Use the worksheet on page 197 to help you plan and compare your insurance needs.

COMPARISON CHART: INSURANCE COVERAGE

	Option One	Option Two	Option Three
☐ Health			
☐ Dental			
☐ Vision			
☐ Life/Disability			
☐ Workers' Compensation			
☐ Fire			
☐ Loss/Theft			
☐ Business Interruption			
☐ Malpractice (errors & omissions)			
☐ Vehicles			
☐ Unemployment			
☐ Offsite equipment			
☐ Offsite employees			
☐ Other:			
☐ Other:			

Health Options Pros and Cons

PROS	CONS
HMO	**HMO**
Most affordable premiums	Most limited provider choice
Minimal co-pays and deductibles	Minimal or no out-of-network coverage
Free or cheap preventive care	Need referral from primary physician
PPO	**PPO**
Affordable premiums	Higher premiums than HMOs
More in-network providers than HMOs	May be difficult to find providers in some locations
Can go out of network	Expensive to go out-of-network
POS	**POS**
More affordable than indemnity plans	Higher premiums than HMOs
Minimal costs staying in-network	Need referrals from primary physician
Some coverage for out-of-network	Costly to go out-of-network
Indemnity	**Indemnity**
Greatest choice of providers	Most expensive
No referrals required	May have most paperwork for policyholder
May be only/best option in some communities	High co-pays and deductibles

week 5

week 5

Main accomplishments:

#1   Deal with money matters

#2   Consider financing options

Make appointments with:

◼   Accountant

◼   Banker

Deal with Money Issues

MONEY, MONEY, MONEY. This week is all about dealing with the financial side of your business, from setting up your accounts to opening up a bank account to figuring out how you're going to finance your new company.

We each bring our own personal issues to the topic of money. Almost all of us are uncomfortable talking about it. Money, after all, is one of the few things left in modern life we don't discuss openly with even our closest friends or family members.

In a business context, this discomfort often extends to a reluctance to deal with budgets, bookkeeping, and accounting. Most of us are intimidated by numbers. (Who, after all, really liked math class?) More often, we just find it unpleasant to think about cash flow and profit margins and, especially, debt.

Well, it's time to deal with it. You *must* learn to deal with money and numbers in a matter-of-fact, businesslike fashion. You have to look at your financial reports without imagining they're a report card of your character, discuss a raise with an employee without feeling you're under attack, and tell a client the price of your services without flinching.

ACCOMPLISHMENT #1:
Deal with money matters

My Checklist:

- ☐ **Meet with an accountant**
- ☐ **Learn the lingo**
- ☐ **Take stock of your personal financial situation**
- ☐ **Clean up your credit**
- ☐ **Set up your books**
- ☐ **Establish your prices**
- ☐ **Open a bank account**
- ☐ **Consider accepting credit cards**
- ☐ **Prepare simple financial forecasts**
- ☐ **Learn about taxes**

Money is at the heart of every business, and understanding money—how to raise it, account for it, and manage it—is critical to business success.

Managing money is particularly important. It's not enough to just make a profit; it is certainly possible to be profitable and still not have the cash on hand to pay your bills. That's why understanding and planning cash flow are important. Likewise, it's possible to grow a healthy business while you're not yet profitable—by planning the right kind of financing.

Setting up financial procedures right from the start of your business will help you avoid problems as you grow.

 Meet with an accountant

As you get your business under way, you'll need the assistance of a good, small business accountant to help you in most aspects of managing your money. An accountant who understands small business issues can help you set up your accounting procedures and books, can explain any financial or tax issues you'll face, and can help you in tax planning. You'll avoid a lot of problems by getting things set up the correct way right from the start. And you'll almost certainly lower your taxes too!

Believe me, a good accountant can save you more than you pay them.

Some accounting firms can also provide you with bookkeeping or bill-paying services or recommend a reputable outside bookkeeper. If your business will require lots of invoices, bills, or bookkeeping, you may want to ask about these options, especially if you don't have the funds to hire an in-house bookkeeper.

Read through this entire section before you meet with your accountant, so that you have a more thorough understanding of the issues you need to discuss.

Use the guide "Questions to Ask an Accountant" on page 204 when you meet with your accountant for the first time.

 ## Learn the lingo

Once you're in business, you'll encounter some money-related terms repeatedly. Don't be afraid to ask someone what they mean. No one expects you to understand it all.

But to make you seem less like a novice, here's a list of some frequently used money buzzwords. Soon you'll sound like you've been discussing money for decades:

"Red ink" or "in the red." On accounting ledgers, negative numbers used to be written in red ink. So the expressions "red ink" or "in the red" refer to showing a loss.

"In the black." Positive numbers, on the other hand, were written in black ink. So if your accounts finish "in the black," you've come out with a profit.

The "bottom line." At the top of your financial statements, you list your income. You then deduct your expenses. The number you're left with on the last line of your profit and loss statement is how much money you've made—or lost. That's your company's "bottom line."

Overhead, or fixed expenses, or your "nut." These terms refer to the expenses you have each month, even if you don't make a sale. Fixed expenses include items such as rent, utilities, insurance, phone service, and administrative salaries. Your "nut" is the total amount of these fixed expenses.

QUESTIONS TO ASK
AN ACCOUNTANT

☐ What kinds of taxes will I have to pay? What are my tax deadlines?

☐ How can I reduce my taxes? Which expenses are deductible, are nondeductible, or have to be depreciated?

☐ What kind of bookkeeping system should I set up? How can I set up systems to reduce the possibility of theft or embezzlement?

☐ How should I pay myself—salary or draw?—and what are the tax implications?

☐ Should I use the cash or accrual form of bookkeeping?

☐ Do I need to keep track of inventory? If so, what method do I use?

☐ How do I handle payroll taxes?

☐ Do I have to collect sales tax? When? From whom?

☐ What are the implications of doing business in more than one state?

☐ What kind of retirement program can I set up and how much can I contribute each year? What kind of retirement programs can I set up for my employees?

☐ What other accounting and tax considerations are there for my type of business?

Your "burn rate." This is how much money you go through each month. This can be different than your fixed expenses, depending on what you spend on variable expenses, such as marketing, temporary help, buying new equipment, and so on.

Variable expenses. These are the costs that change depending on how many sales you make. In other words, if you run a sporting goods store, your rent is fixed no matter how many golf clubs you sell, but the amount you spend on marketing may change.

Cost of goods sold (COGS). This refers to what it costs you to purchase inventory to sell to others or to purchase materials to manufacture your products.

General and administrative expenses (G&A) or operating expenses: The amount you spend to operate your business other than COGS or sales costs. This includes all overhead expenses (such as rent, utilities), salaries, marketing, and so on.

Revenue: Total amount of money received from sales.

Income: The amount of money received from any source. You can, for example, bring money into your business from loans or as a result of investments.

Profit: Money you have left after deducting your costs. There's gross profit or net profit.

Gross profit: The amount of money left after deducting the cost of goods sold but *before* deducting general and administrative expenses.

Net profit: The amount of money you receive after deducting the cost of goods sold, sales costs, and operating expenses.

Net loss: The amount of money you're in the red if, *after* deducting all expenses from all revenue, you have lost money instead of having made money. (Let's not even think about that for now…)

Take stock of your personal financial situation

When you start a business, you may hope to use OPM—"other people's money"—to build your company. Be warned: You're going to have to rely on your own money and your own credit to be the primary source of funding—at least until you start making sales!

So as you begin to deal with your new company's finances, take stock of your personal financial situation and monetary assets. This will help you plan your expenditures and prepare you to meet with an accountant.

Of course, many of the most important assets for starting a business are not financial—assets such as ambition, perseverance, willingness to work hard, intelligence, creativity, and so on.

But it certainly helps to also have some financial assets—such as savings in the bank, liquid investments, home equity, or a spouse's income.

Use the worksheet on page 206 to note your existing financial assets and the specifics of each.

Also, take note of current or upcoming financial obligations that will reduce your financial assets. This gives you a clearer picture of your overall financial situation.

TAKING STOCK: WHAT ARE MY EXISTING ASSETS?

	Specifics (amount, type, etc.)	How Readily Available
Financial Assets:		
☐ Savings		
☐ Income from other sources		
☐ Spouse's income		
☐ Credit lines/Credit cards		
☐ Stocks & other liquid assets		
☐ Home equity		
☐ Retirement funds		
Tangible Assets:		
☐ Equipment		
☐ Furniture		
☐ Space/Location		
Business/Professional Assets:		
☐ Marketable skills		
☐ Specialized knowledge		
☐ Business experience		
☐ Certifications/Credentials		
☐ Licenses, Memberships		
☐ Ability to make sales		
☐ Good customers/client relationships		
Personal Assets:		
☐ Education/Training		
☐ Intelligence		
☐ Excellent communication skills		
☐ Outstanding work habits		
☐ Business or financial connections		
☐ Rich relatives or friends		
☐ Supportive family or friends		
☐ Ambition & passion		
☐ Other:		
☐ Other:		

Right from the start, keep track of the money you invest in your new company. There are important reasons for this. One, you want to be certain you can take every tax deduction you're entitled to, and without records it can be a lot more difficult. Two, you want an accurate record of all expenses and sources of income. And finally, you may want to treat some of this money as loans you are making to your business rather than as an investment. Ask about the tax implications of doing so when you meet with your accountant this week.

 ## Clean up your credit

According to a study by the Small Business Administration, personal credit cards are the number one source of financing for small companies. Expect to use your personal credit—or give personal guarantees—for many business-related purchases or credit needs.

So you're going to want to make certain you clean up your personal credit record and give yourself as much credit as possible.

This doesn't mean it's impossible to start a business if you have bad credit—not at all. But the better your credit record looks, the easier time you'll have getting financing from suppliers, landlords, and lending sources such as banks. Even investors may check your credit report.

- **Get a credit report:** Your credit history (payments on things such as credit cards, car purchases, mortgages, student loans) gets reported and recorded. Under the Fair Credit Reporting Act, you are entitled to a free copy of your credit report once a year from each of the three main credit reporting agencies: Equifax (www.equifax.com), Experian (www.experian.com), and Trans Union (www.transunion.com). Not all credit-granting or credit-checking companies use all three, so you may want to get copies from each of them.

- **Learn your credit score:** As a result of these reports, you will be assigned a credit "score." The primary credit scoring agency is a private company, Fair Isaac (FICO). Most major financial institutions—particularly banks and mortgage lenders—use your FICO to determine how good your credit is and whether they will lend to you. So you certainly want to check your FICO score. You can do that online.

- **Make certain everything is accurate:** Read over your credit reports in detail. If you find any inaccuracies, contact the credit bureaus and

Check It Out

You can purchase a combined report of all three agencies plus your credit score, from either Fair Isaac (**www.myfico.com**) or ConsumerInfo (**www.consumerinfo.com**).

the lender to correct any incorrect or outdated information. They are required to investigate within 30 days, but this doesn't mean your credit report will get cleaned up within that time, so get on top of this as fast as possible.

■ **Pay your bills on time:** You want to start creating a clean credit history as soon as you can. The best way to do this is to pay your bills on time *every month*. If necessary, just pay the minimum amounts required, even if you have to maintain higher balances. Remember, you'll need credit a year from now, so if you start paying your bills on time today, in 12 months you'll have a much stronger credit report regardless of what it looks like now.

■ **Don't increase your debt:** If your credit is really bad, cut up your credit cards and pay for everything in cash. Don't cancel your accounts—even old accounts. It's generally better to have more credit available to you than you actually use. And don't think that cutting up your cards means you don't have to pay the outstanding balances!

■ **Increase your credit limits:** If your credit is good, and you handle credit well, ask for an increase in your credit limits. Now that you're in business, it may come in handy to have more funds available, especially if you need to purchase materials to fill an order or travel for business.

■ **Reduce your interest rates:** You may have fairly high interest rates on some of your credit cards, especially if you've had them for some time. Call the companies and ask them to reduce your rates to be more competitive with current rates.

■ **Make a list of your credit cards:** You'll find it very handy to have a master list of all your credit cards, credit limits, interest rates, and balances. That way, when you need to use a credit card, you'll know which one to choose. Since you may not be able to get business credit for a while, designate certain credit cards to use only for business and keep those records separate.

Use the worksheet on page 209 to make a list of your credit cards and their current balances.

MY CREDIT CARDS

Use this space to track credit card offers, credit cards you already have, credit card debt you need to pay off, or other useful information about your credit cards.

	Name of Card Issuer	Card Number	Credit Limit	Interest Rate	Other Fees	Current Balance
☐						
☐						
☐						
☐						
☐						
☐						
☐						
☐						
☐						
☐						
☐						
☐						
☐						
☐						
☐						

✔ Set up your books

I'm not sure where the term "books" first came to be used for a company's accounts, but that's the basis of the term "bookkeeping." Perhaps it's because the record of a company's financials transactions were written down in a journal or book.

In fact, many small businesses still keep their books in an actual book. I did. My first set of company "books" was a simple lined ledger. On one set of pages, I wrote down my income as I received it—that gave me a picture of my total income for the year. On other pages I wrote down each time I billed a client and their payments—that gave me a record for each client. On another set of pages, I wrote down each time I spent money or paid a bill for my business—that gave me a picture of my total expenses for the year.

This was hardly the most efficient way to keep accounts, but at least I could see how much money I had made, how much each client owed me, and, at the end of the year, how much to deduct when preparing taxes. Of course, it was tedious to have to figure out how much I spent on different categories of expenses (equipment, travel, meals, office supplies, etc.) and I couldn't do any kind of "data mining" to later market or follow-up with clients. But it worked much better than nothing!

Today, simple and inexpensive computer programs enable you to keep track of your company's accounts quickly, and give you a lot more power in analyzing your expenses, following up on customers, and preparing your taxes.

Bookkeeping software: If yours is a very small business, you may be able to handle all your bookkeeping needs with a simple "checkbook" money-management program, such as Quicken, made by Intuit. This is designed primarily for personal record-keeping, but many small businesses use Quicken and find that it's quite sufficient.

However, it's likely that you'll need a more powerful bookkeeping program, such as QuickBooks. QuickBooks, also made by Intuit, has become the standard for small business accounting, and your accountant or bookkeeper is likely to be very familiar with it. Because it's the standard, it's easy to find forms (such as blank checks) from third-party providers. It's fairly easy to learn and use, and it's not very expensive. It's what we use in our office.

Start It Free

Track income and expenses, upload information from your bank accounts and credit cards, create reports, send invoices, and more with the free accounting program Wave (**www. wave.com**). Freshbooks (**www.freshbooks.com**), an invoicing application with a free version, enables you to easily track time, create invoices, and organize expenses.

There are other small business bookkeeping programs, such as MYOB (www.myob.com) or Sage (http://na.sage.com/sage-na/products-solutions/by-small-business), to name just two. Both companies offer online versions and on-premise versions of their accounting programs. You may also be able to find industry-specific bookkeeping programs; check with your industry association. However, be careful of getting programs that do not integrate well with other standard programs (such as Microsoft Excel).

Accounting method: One thing you'll need to determine is whether to keep your accounts on a "cash" or on an "accrual" basis. Your accountant will advise you.

- **Cash basis:** You enter expenses and income as they actually are paid or received. This is by far the easier method of accounting. Most small companies can keep their accounts on a cash basis.

- **Accrual basis:** You enter expenses and income as they are incurred—whether or not they are paid or received. This is more complicated, but the IRS requires certain businesses (especially those with inventory) and larger companies to keep their accounts on an accrual basis.

In other words, let's say you sign an agreement to purchase $5,000 worth of inventory in January, but you don't pay the bill until March. On a cash basis, that purchase would show up on your books in March; on an accrual basis, you'd enter that purchase as an expense in January. Of course, which method you use has significant tax implications requiring you to talk to an accountant.

✔ Establish your prices

Figuring out how to price your products or services is certainly one of the most perplexing questions for first-time entrepreneurs or those who are new to an industry.

Here's an old joke: A store owner purchases pencils for ten cents apiece and then sells them for a nickel. Noticing this bizarre behavior, his partner asks, "How do you expect us to stay in business that way?" The man replies, "Volume!"

Surprisingly, many novice entrepreneurs choose a relatively similar business strategy. They imagine all that's necessary for success is to price their

Check It Out

Compare features of Quicken and the different versions of Quickbooks, including an online version, at **www.quicken.intuit.com** and **www.quickbooks.intuit.com**

products or services less than the competition. Low prices, they assume, will generate sufficient sales to more than make up for smaller profits.

Competing on price alone is risky. Some discount outlets do build thriving businesses on low prices, but this strategy almost always means narrow profit margins, which in turn means less cash floating around your company. With a small financial cushion, you're vulnerable with every slight increase in costs. The landlord raises your rent 5%? That may be your entire year's profit. And you're at risk from competitors: If you become a serious threat and they have deeper cash reserves, they can just undercut your prices and wait until you're squeezed out of the market.

Moreover, customers attracted solely by price are fickle. If they shopped around a lot before choosing you, they're probably going to shop around continually. And as soon as someone has a lower price, you're history!

Of course, when you're just starting out in business, you may want to set your prices lower (even much lower) than the competition. This gives you a chance to build a customer base and get some experience. Especially if you're in a service industry, you're going to be learning a lot while working for your first customers, so it's only fair to charge them less.

In Week Two, you did some research on the prices competitors are charging (see page 64), and that should help you get an idea of the market as you establish your own prices.

Professional service fees

Setting fees is more of an art than a science when what you're selling is expertise. After all, if you're smarter than the lawyer down the street but he has more experience, should you charge less or more? What if you work faster? Why does one management consultant charge $50 an hour and another $250? Is the second really five times better than the first?

Clearly, setting professional fees is inexact. Nevertheless, there are generally accepted practices and ranges. The two primary ways of pricing services are on an "hourly" basis or on a "project" basis.

■ **Hourly:** Most professional services can be charged on an hourly fee. This rewards you appropriately when you are performing long, complicated tasks for a client. However, you may find yourself shortchanged when what you are selling is your existing knowledge or expertise, and it doesn't take long to convey that to your client.

- **Project:** On a "project" or task basis, you establish a set or minimum fee for an entire project. Clients often like to pay on a project basis because they like knowing what they will be charged before they commit. Project fees reward you when your knowledge enables you to finish projects quickly but penalize you if you've badly misjudged the amount of time a given project will take.

One way to establish fees is to determine typical fees charged by others for similar services. Contact an industry association, ideally located in your geographic area, to get a sense of typical fee structures and ranges.

WHAT WOULD RHONDA DO?

MONEY MANAGEMENT TIPS

- **Review your books regularly.** When you're running your business, you may not take the time to sit down and look at your financials. But you can't manage your money without having the facts. At least once a month, preferably once a week, look at your figures: accounts payable and receivable, expenses, cash flow, and so on.

- **Send them your bill!** I'm always surprised by how many businesspeople, especially consultants and professional service providers, delay sending out their invoices. You may feel uncomfortable asking someone for money, afraid of being challenged on how much you've billed, or just too busy working. But the longer you wait to send out your invoices, the greater the chance you won't get paid.

- **Watch your inventory.** If you produce goods, you'll always be tempted to produce more because you get savings based on volume. But inventory can go "bad"—become outdated, unsaleable, or time- or weather-worn. Inventory doesn't just apply to finished goods for resale. You may have "inventory" in the form of marketing materials. Keep an eye on your actual use and make your purchases not only on the basis of price but also on whether you can get small quantities only when you actually need them.

- **Manage your growth.** You want your business to get bigger, but if you grow too fast you may not be able to sustain it. Growth costs money—you incur many expenses before you see additional income. Plan your growth so you have the financial resources to pay for it.

- **Save.** Every business has income fluctuations. The best way to have cash when you need it is to put some away when you've got it.

In the final analysis, the appropriate fee is always the same: whatever the market will bear. Only time will help you sort that out.

Prices for goods and other services

If you are a retailer or a reseller of products or services produced by others, it's often relatively easy to figure out how much to charge. Most industries have generally accepted markups over the cost of goods (for example, 100% in department stores, 200% for jewelry).

Understanding normal practice in your industry is a good place to start when figuring how much you want to charge. Suppliers themselves will often let you know what the normal markup is on their goods (but be careful—there are some laws limiting suppliers from setting the final prices of their goods). Of course, you may want to price your goods more aggressively, especially in the earliest days of your business.

If you are the manufacturer or producer of goods or services sold by others, the reseller will set the final price to the end-user. They, in turn, are going to set their prices based, on large part, by what you charge them. If your costs to the reseller are too high, then they won't be able to make money and won't purchase from you. It's critical for you to know what your competitors are charging those same resellers.

Of course, you have to cover your costs and make a profit. And that's typically how manufacturers and others set prices. This is "bottom-up" planning: Figure your costs for raw materials, labor, overhead, shipping, returns, and so forth, and then set a reasonable figure for profit.

Some brilliant businesspeople have built great companies by knowing how to maintain ultralow prices or convince customers to pay premium prices. Most of us, however, need to stick to the normal range.

Open a bank account

A good relationship with a bank can be a big help to a growing company. Many people just select the bank located close to them, or the one with the lowest fees. But that doesn't mean it's the right bank for you, especially as you grow your business. Ideally, you want a bank that will work with you and your company as you grow, that will provide some understanding of your situation and allow some flexibility in dealing with you.

"Interview" a number of banks and meet their business account representatives. Develop a relationship with a good business bank while your business is still small. But expect that relationship to pay off—in terms of credit—as you get larger.

Take some time to shop for a bank for your business. The worksheet on page 216 can help you compare banks and banking services.

 ## Consider accepting credit cards

Credit cards! We like using them and so do our customers. But getting approved to accept credit cards—be a "credit card merchant"—isn't necessarily easy, especially for a new business. You will have to go through a credit check and submit financial documents, and even with excellent credit, you may still not get approved.

The first thing to do is to check with your bank to see if they can help you become a credit card merchant. They may be a bit more expensive than other credit card processors, but you may be more likely to be approved by your own bank. Be careful to avoid scam artists—your email is likely to be filled with spam offering you the chance to "accept credit cards." Beware—you're going to give them a lot of personal financial information. Only deal with a reputable company.

Accepting credit cards benefits you as well as your customers:

- **You receive payment right away.** If you bill your customers yourself, they may take 30 days or more to pay.

- **The credit card company, instead of you, generally assumes the risk of nonpaying customers.**

- **You have less paperwork since you don't have to send invoices or statements.**

- **It increases the number of customers who do business with you.**

These benefits come at a cost, however. Consider some of the fees:

- **"Discount" fee.** The credit card issuer (typically a bank) takes a small percentage (2–4%) of every charge. This is the basic cost of administering the credit and assuming the risk, as well as marketing.

- **Transaction charge.** This is a small set amount (25 cents to 50 cents) on each transaction regardless of amount.

- **Monthly minimums you must meet.**

COMPARISON CHART: BANKS

	Bank Option One	Bank Option Two	Bank Option Three
☐ Bank name			
☐ Location/phone number			
☐ Name of bank rep. handling business accounts			
☐ Accounts offered and fees charged			
☐ Loan or credit lines available			
☐ Special business services offered			
☐ Your overall impression of this bank and its services			
☐ Other notes:			

- **Setup fees.**

- **Equipment purchase or leasing.**

- **Chargebacks.** This is the amount the issuer will charge any time a customer refuses payment on a charge of yours stating dissatisfaction with the product.

For instance, if the bank's discount was 2%, the transaction fee $0.30 and the monthly minimum $20, each $100 transaction would cost you $2.30. If you conducted ten $100 transactions in a month, the bank would make $23.00, but if you only made five transactions, the credit card issuer would only have made $11.50 ($2.30 times five), and you'd be charged another $8.50 to meet your minimum.

The manner in which you accept credit cards affects your costs. If a customer presents the card to you in person, and you can physically see and swipe the card, you'll be charged less than if you accept phone, fax, mail, or online orders. The reasoning behind this is that there is less fraud committed when a customer has to physically present the card.

Deciding which provider to use depends on how you'll deal with credit cards. If you'll have few point-of-sale (POS) credit card charges, look for a low monthly minimum, even if the discount or transaction fee is somewhat higher. If you expect large transactions, shop for a low discount rate.

If you're not ever going to see or "swipe" cards, you theoretically shouldn't have to pay for the credit card equipment. However, that's in theory. Many companies make you lease the equipment anyway, but don't accept that without asking.

Once you decide to accept credit cards, be careful to follow the issuer's rules. Credit card companies typically have strict rules prohibiting merchants from applying extra charges for accepting credit cards.

One less expensive alternative is using an online credit card payment service such as PayPal (www.paypal.com). A big advantage is there are no setup fees, monthly minimums, or equipment rentals. PayPal charges a modest fee per transaction. For some premium flavors of PayPal you also pay a monthly fee. You can use PayPal to accept payments from PayPal members, or from anyone via credit or debit cards.

Check It Out

Intuit Merchant Services (http://payments.intuit.com) offers a few methods of credit card processing—point-of-sale, online, and mobile—all of which can integrate with the accounting program QuickBooks.

To accept payments with minimum fuss, consider mobile payment processing. With mobile payment services, you run credit or debit cards through your smartphone or tablet wherever you are. This type of acceptance is a boon for mobile small businesses—plumbers, electricians, lawn services, and so forth—and those who sell at locations such as crafts fairs or farmers markets. Increasingly, brick-and-mortar businesses and professional service companies are tearing out their POS systems and also accepting mobile payments.

Three established mobile payment services are GoPayment from Intuit (www.gopayment.com), Square (www.squareup.com), and PayPal Here (www.paypalhere.com).

To begin, simply go to the website and sign up. You'll receive a small device to swipe cards that plugs into your phone or tablet. Download the accompanying app, and start swiping cards and processing payments. These mobile applications also work with a cash drawer and printers, so you can still provide paper receipts to customers. (You can also email receipts.) GoPayment and PayPal Here may run a credit check before approving you.

Intuit's GoPayment gives business owners the greatest integration with QuickBooks and other back-office systems, reducing double entry and giving you greater business intelligence than other options. Square has built-in loyalty tools, enabling small businesses to offer free or discounted services to regular or new customers. "Square Wallet," an app for consumers, promotes nearby Square-accepting businesses, which helps market local companies. PayPal Here also has its own consumer wallet. And PayPal Here gives merchants a debit card, and money is available on that card right after a transaction. You can use it to make purchases or to withdraw cash from an ATM.

Of course, costs matter, and the most affordable solution depends on how many transactions you typically do, and at what dollar amounts. Fees for these three services range from 2.7% to 2.75% for swiped transactions to 3.5% to 3.75% plus transaction fees for "unswiped" charges.

Read the fine print. Some swiped cards incur higher fees, and extra charges may apply if you go above certain transaction amounts.

Prepare simple financial forecasts

People in business usually fall into one of two categories—those who are fascinated with numbers, and those who are frightened by them. If you're in the second category, you're probably intimidated by the very prospect of having to fill in the financial forms in this section.

Take heart. Numbers are neither magical, mysterious, nor menacing. They merely reflect decisions you have already made in your business planning process. Every decision leads to a number, but numbers themselves are not decisions. You cannot pull a number out of thin air because the financial forms call for a specific figure on a specific line.

If yours is a very small business, you may only need to prepare a simple budget: a forecast of your estimated sales and a list of how much you plan to spend on the various components of your business. Most other businesses will benefit from preparing at least simple financial forms—especially cash flow projections to help you determine or adjust your spending. And if you seek outside financing, you'll need a range of financial documents to give to potential lenders or investors.

Besides helping you figure out your spending, there's another reason to draw up financial forecasts—it helps you set goals. Writing down specific numbers for your anticipated sales gives you a target to work toward.

One key to good financial planning is to create your financial projections at the same time you plan your business. If you choose to locate your business in one town versus another, there's a cost associated with that. If you exhibit at a trade show, there's a cost with that, too.

Budgeting strategies

Successful financial projections are achieved by budgeting from the "bottom up," not the "top down."

"Top down" numbers are enticing to work with because they always come out looking good, but they're not realistic. Here's how they work: you look at the big picture—the total market size, growth rate, average sales price, and average profit margins. You make what seem to be reasonable assumptions, something like achieving a 10% market penetration, or improving margins by 2%. Then you fill in your financial statements to make the totals come out to the big numbers projected.

For example, let's say you've invented a new golf club, and you project achieving 1% market penetration within 3 years. If total annual sales of golf clubs is $2 billion, then you'll achieve $20 million in annual sales. With a profit margin of 15%, your net profit will be $3 million.

Sounds good, doesn't it? "Top down" projections result in some very impressive numbers—the kind that make you and perhaps some potential investors excited. They're just not very realistic.

Instead, the best financials are developed from the "bottom up." You do the real business-building legwork: examine different distribution channels, source manufacturers and suppliers, develop a staffing chart, outline your marketing program, and design operations. You plug in numbers from these realistic projections of how much things will cost, and then you determine how much income you need to sustain that cost.

So, let's say you're that same golf club manufacturer, and you build your financials from the "bottom up"; here's how it would work:

You first compare distribution channels, and then choose one. Let's say you decide to sell through specialty golf retailers and country clubs. This channel has associated costs and impact on income. You'll need to budget for a sales force to sell to those shops, exhibit at the annual sporting good trade shows, and advertise in *Golf Retailer* magazine. But you will only receive 40–45% of the final sales price of the club, since the retailer takes half and the salesperson receives a commission.

Now you're starting to get real numbers to plug in to each of the lines of your financial forms. You've got numbers for advertising, staffing, and income.

All this planning takes work, but there's help. The best place to start is by speaking with others in your industry, attending trade shows, and contacting your industry association.

Cash flow

If the three most important things in real estate are "location, location, location," the first three rules of business are "cash, cash, cash."

It's necessary, of course, to be profitable, but "profit" is a number that shows up on your accounts at the end of the year; cash is money you have in the bank. In a small company, it's cash that determines whether you can pay your bills.

No matter what your business is, you're going to have a lag between outgo and income. If you're a consultant, you have to pay for your phone, computer, marketing materials, and rent before you get your first client. Once you've got them, you're not going to see complete payment for at least 30–60 days after you finish a project.

Things are much worse if you're a manufacturer. You've got to pay for raw material, equipment, and employees many months before you'll see final payment.

The following methods help improve your cash flow:

- **Sell sooner.** Through pre-sales, early season sales, and gift cards, you can sell your product or service before you actually fulfill the order.

- **Get paid faster.** Make it as easy as possible for customers to pay you. Accept credit cards and mobile payments, and always send out your invoices out as soon as possible.

- **Reduce costs and waste.** Reduce costs by forecasting what you need and purchasing carefully. If you don't really need it, don't buy it. Whether it's extra inventory, shipping materials, utilities, or trips in your van, if it's unnecessary, you're spending money for something you didn't use.

- **Defer payments.** Negotiate payments terms, ask for payment installments, or pay bills with a credit card. If you run an ecommerce site, arrange for a vendor to directly fulfill your customer orders—you hold little or no inventory, and receive cash before you make the expenditure.

So draw up a cash flow projection. Even if you don't write up a budget or income statement, it's a good idea to sketch out when you expect money to come in and when you need money to go out.

Use the financial worksheets on pages 222–225 to develop the range of financial forecasts for your business. Be certain to do the "Cash Flow Projection" worksheet on pages 226–227 to forecast your cash needs. You can find electronic versions of these worksheets at www.PlanningShop.com.

Learn about taxes

Nobody likes paying taxes, but if you're in business, you're going to have to pay them. In fact, the more successful you are, the more taxes you'll probably pay.

SALES PROJECTIONS

	Monthly 1st Year	Total 1st Year	Monthly 2nd Year	Total 2nd Year	Monthly 3rd Year	Total 3rd Year
Product Line 1						
Unit volume						
Price						
Gross sales						
(Commissions)						
(Returns and allowances)						
Net Sales						
(Cost of goods sold)						
GROSS PROFIT						
Product Line 2						
Unit volume						
Price						
Gross sales						
(Commissions)						
(Returns and allowances)						
Net Sales						
(Cost of goods sold)						
GROSS PROFIT						
TOTALS FOR ALL PRODUCT LINES						
Total Unit volume						
Total gross sales						
(Total commissions)						
(Total returns and allowances)						
Total Net Sales						
(Total cost of goods sold)						
TOTAL GROSS PROFIT						

NOTE: *An extended, computerized version of this worksheet is available in PlanningShop's Business Plan Financials package, available from www.PlanningShop.com.*

MARKETING BUDGET

	Monthly 1st Year	Total 1st Year	Monthly 2nd Year	Total 2nd Year	Monthly 3rd Year	Total 3rd Year
Professional Assistance						
Marketing/PR consultants						
Advertising agencies						
Direct mail specialists						
SEO specialists						
Graphic/Web design						
Brochures/Leaflets/Flyers						
Signs/Billboards						
Merchandising Displays						
Sampling/Premiums						
Media Advertising						
Print (newspaper, etc.)						
Television and radio						
Online						
Other media						
Phone Directories						
Advertising Specialties						
Direct Mail						
Website						
Development/programming						
Maintenance and hosting						
Trade Shows						
Fees and setup						
Travel/shipping						
Exhibits/signs						
Public Relations/Materials						
Informal Marketing/Networking						
Membership/meetings						
Entertainment						
Other						
GRAND TOTAL COSTS						

NOTE: *An extended, computerized version of this worksheet is available in PlanningShop's Business Plan Financials package, available from www.PlanningShop.com.*

PROFIT & LOSS PROJECTION

Year:	January	February	March	April	May
INCOME					
Gross Sales					
(Commissions)					
(Returns & Allowances)					
Net Sales					
(Cost of Goods)					
GROSS PROFIT					
EXPENSES - General & Administrative					
Salaries and wages					
Employee benefits					
Payroll taxes					
Professional services					
Marketing and advertising					
Rent					
Equipment rental					
Maintenance					
Depreciation					
Insurance					
Telecommunications					
Utilities					
Office supplies					
Postage and shipping					
Travel					
Entertainment					
Interest on loans					
Other:					
Other:					
TOTAL EXPENSES					
Net income before taxes					
Provision for taxes on income					
NET PROFIT					

NOTE: *A computerized version of this worksheet is available in PlanningShop's Business Plan Financials package, available from www.PlanningShop.com.*

June	July	August	September	October	November	December	TOTAL

CASH FLOW PROJECTION

Year:	January	February	March	April	May
CASH RECEIPTS					
Income from Sales					
Cash sales					
Collections					
Total Cash from Sales					
Income from Financing					
Interest income					
Loan proceeds					
Total Cash from Financing					
Other cash receipts					
TOTAL CASH RECEIPTS					
CASH DISBURSEMENTS					
Inventory					
Operating expenses					
Commissions/returns & allowances					
Capital purchases					
Loan payments					
Income tax payments					
Investor dividend payments					
Owner's draw					
TOTAL CASH DISBURSEMENTS					
NET CASH FLOW					
Opening cash balance					
Cash receipts					
Cash disbursements					
ENDING CASH BALANCE					

June	July	August	September	October	November	December	TOTAL

Understanding key tax concerns is critical for most businesses. You will make some decisions—or alter them—based on tax implications.

Some business expenses are fully deductible, others are only partially deductible, others have to be depreciated over a number of years, and others are not deductible at all. You should have at least a fair understanding of those issues as you make choices in your business.

If you purchase a very expensive piece of equipment, for instance, expecting to deduct the total cost of that from your income, you may be rudely surprised that the expense has to be spread out over as many as five to 10, even 20 years.

Tax codes are complicated and always changing. Certain tax laws apply to incorporated businesses and not unincorporated ones, or vice versa, and business tax laws differ from regulations for individuals. And of course, every U.S. state has its own tax laws as well!

So, plan on spending some time with your accountant just talking about taxes. Ask him or her to help you understand which taxes you're liable for, when your taxes are due (e.g., quarterly income taxes), and how various transactions and expenses are taxed (meals and entertainment expenses, for instance, cannot typically be fully deducted while other marketing expenses usually can be). Have your accountant help you plan how to reduce your tax liability.

Many businesspeople find it helpful to set up separate savings accounts just for income taxes. With each check they receive, they set aside a certain percentage in this separate tax account, so when income tax time arrives they have the money necessary to pay their bill.

As a business, you often have responsibility for collecting and then paying taxes owed by others. For instance, if you are a retailer, you must charge and collect the sales tax on items you sell to consumers. Set up records to keep track of those taxes that you've collected—and pay them by the dates due.

You may want to—or sometimes be required to—set up separate accounts to keep the taxes you collect distinct from your other funds. Governments, whether federal, state, or city, really frown on your keeping their money.

You may be surprised by the variety of taxes you face. There are income taxes, sales taxes, payroll taxes, property taxes, personal property taxes,

MY TAX DEADLINES

Tax	Amount	Where to Send/File	Dates Due
☐ Income tax: federal, state, county, perhaps local (e.g. New York City)			
☐ Payroll and other employment-related taxes (Social Security, Medicare, workers' compensation, unemployment, etc.)			
☐ Sales tax			
☐ Personal property tax and use taxes			
☐ Property tax			
☐ Special taxes (hotel, food, transportation, etc.)			
☐ Import/export, custom taxes and duties			
☐ Transfer taxes			
☐ Capital gains taxes			
☐ Inventory taxes			
☐ Other:			

WHAT WOULD RHONDA DO?

MANAGING PAYROLL

Soon after I hired my first full-time employee, I started using a payroll service. Determining payroll deductions and depositing payroll taxes with the proper authorities can be time-consuming and exacting. Moreover, the penalties for being late or getting things wrong can be substantial. It's much easier—and safer—to hire a professional service to take care of the administrative details of payroll for you.

A payroll service charges a modest amount, based on the number of your employees, and how many states they are located in, but you're likely to easily save at least this amount in terms of your own administrative staff time, bookkeeper's or accountant's help, and any penalties you may incur for late or inaccurate payments.

Check It Out

You can pay your employees with an online SaaS payroll service like Intuit Online Payroll (**http://online.payroll.intuit.com**) or ADP's Small Business Online Payroll Service (**www.smallbusiness.adp.com**). Both handle payroll electronically and each offers a mobile app so you can even run your payroll from your smartphone.

inventory taxes, special use taxes, general business taxes, and others. Some taxes incur substantial penalties for late or under payments, so be certain to keep track of when taxes are due and give yourself enough time to prepare them.

Sales tax

Sales taxes were discussed in Week Three—see page 96 to review what sales taxes you'll need to collect. Then talk to your accountant this week about any questions you have about sales taxes.

The worksheet on page 229 can help you keep track of your tax obligations and due dates.

ACCOMPLISHMENT # 2:
Consider financing

My Checklist:

☐ **Determine whose money you want**

☐ **Develop a business plan**

Ask an entrepreneur starting or expanding a business to name their biggest problem, and you'll probably hear: "Where do I get the money?"

What may come as a shock is how long it will take for your business to reach a level of income where it can pay its own way. If you're dependent on your business income to support yourself or your family, you may want to consider looking for outside funding.

Just be warned: Raising money is not easy and it's not fast. It's unlikely you'll be able to get financing within a six-week time frame, especially if you're seeking investors. And looking for outside money may distract you from going after the most important source of funds—making sales!

One basic difference you must know before looking for money is the difference between "debt" and "equity" financing.

- **Debt:** This is usually a loan, line of credit, or equipment financing. The money must be paid back whether or not the business flourishes. You often begin making payments on the debt soon after receiving the loan ("debt service") so you have an additional monthly expense. You give up no ownership of the company, however.

- **Equity:** This is usually referred to as getting an "investment." With equity financing, you give an investor a piece of the ownership of the company and a share of future profits and, often, a say in decision-making. But if the company fails you do not have to pay anyone back.

There are also a few forms of financing that combine the two, such as "convertible debt" in which a loan can be turned into stock. If you or your investors or lenders want to explore some of these options, consult an attorney or accountant.

 ## Determine whose money you want

Not all money is equal. When you first start looking for financing, you may be tempted to take any money you can find. Be careful. The various sources of money seek different rates of return on their loans or investments, have varying levels of sophistication and comfort with risk, and provide you with significantly different advantages and disadvantages.

Remember, you'll have an ongoing relationship with your money source. You'll save yourself a lot of time and grief if you seek money only from sources that are right for you.

✔ **QUESTIONS TO ASK**
POTENTIAL INVESTORS

☐ Why are you investing in this business?

☐ What aspect of this business is most appealing to you?

☐ What other businesses have you invested in before?

☐ May I call some entrepreneurs you've invested with before?

☐ How soon do you expect to see a return on this investment?

☐ How would it affect you if you were to lose the money you're investing?

☐ If you felt I was not capable of building this company to the stage you'd like, what would you do?

☐ How do you see decisions being made? By whom?

☐ What role do you want, if any, in the company (e.g., board membership, etc.)?

☐ Do you understand all the risks in making this investment?

The main funding sources for starting or expanding a business are:

Your own assets. Forget the old saying about using "other people's money." It's better to start or grow a business with your *own* money. If you have sufficient assets, particularly savings or other income that doesn't require you to take on additional debt, you're in the best financial position. You don't go into debt, and you don't give up equity. If your savings are owned jointly with a spouse or partner, be certain to get their acceptance and understanding of your plans.

Sales/Income. The very best way to fund a business is from sales revenues. If you can grow your company based on money received from customers, then you don't take on debt and you don't give up equity. This is not as impossible as it sounds, especially if you are starting a low-cost business. The key is to try to line up clients before you actually set up shop, and to grow only as big as your revenues permit. Your growth may be slower, and it doesn't seem as sexy as getting a huge investment, but you'll sleep better at night.

Credit cards. Experts will tell you credit cards are a terrible way to finance a business—they cost a lot (high interest rates) and put your personal credit at risk. The experts are right—if you have other alternatives. The truth is most people use credit cards at one time or another to pay business expenses, particularly in the start-up phase. And credit cards can be a useful way to handle short-term cash flow problems; if you realistically expect income soon, credit cards may be an easier or better alternative than other loans or taking on an investor.

But be careful! Credit cards are generally an expensive form of financing (exceptions are low introductory rates). You can incur very high charges if you are even a day or two late on your payments. Credit card debt easily gets out of hand, and you have to pay the money back.

If you haven't already, fill out the worksheet "My Credit Cards" on page 209 to keep track of the credit cards you have.

Friends and family. Want to lose a friend? Borrow money from them or have them invest in your business. Getting family or friends involved in your business is dangerous, but there are exceptions. If the person understands your business, truly comprehends the risks, and is someone with whom you can communicate well, the situation may work. Always have loan or investment papers drawn up with the terms of the repayment or investment absolutely clear.

Banks. Realistically, banks loan money only to companies that have been in business for at least one or two years and have been successful. As your company grows, you'll likely want a line of credit from a bank to help you manage your cash flow. If you do get a bank loan for a new business, you'll almost certainly have to give a personal guarantee and have to put up personal assets as collateral. The Small Business Administration provides loan guarantees to banks to encourage them to make small business loans.

Check It Out

To find out more about loans through the SBA, go to **www.sba.gov**. For information about the Canadian government's loan program, go to **www.ic.gc.ca/eic/site/csbfp-pfpec.nsf/eng/Home**.

RED TAPE ALERT!

A no-interest loan from a friend or family member may face what's called "imputed interest" by the IRS. The lender may not be receiving any interest from you, but the IRS will tax them as if they were. If the IRS views the loan as a gift, the lender is subject to federal gift tax rules and will have to pay taxes on the money if it is more than the maximum allowed by law. The lender must charge an interest rate that reflects a fair market value. Talk to your accountant if you're getting money from friends or family members.

COMPARISON CHART: INVESTORS

	Investor One	Investor Two
☐ Investor's name		
☐ Contact info (email, phone, address, fax)		
☐ What type of investor is this? (venture capitalist, angel, family, other)		
☐ What industries do they invest in?		
☐ What stage of companies do they invest in? (seed, start-up, second round, etc.)		
☐ What range of amount of investment do they make?		
☐ What geographic areas do they invest in?		
☐ What are their other criteria for investment?		
☐ What other companies have they invested in?		
☐ Whom do I know who can help me reach this investor?		
☐ How do they prefer to be contacted?		

Investor Three	Investor Four	Investor Five

In Canada, the Canada Small Business Financing Program (CSBFP) provides guarantees to lenders who make loans to qualified small businesses. But keep in mind, the government doesn't give out business loans—it just assumes a percentage of the risk on behalf of the lender.

Strategic partners. There may be other businesses that want you to succeed, and they may be willing to help you get under way. Perhaps they are a supplier, customer, or business serving the same market. In some cases, they may directly invest in your business or give you loans. Perhaps they would let you use their offices or equipment or otherwise help offset some of your expenses in return for the benefits you bring them.

Venture capitalists. Venture capitalists are professional investors using institutional money. They generally only invest in companies needing substantial sums of money to grow very large very quickly, and will serve very large markets. They do provide early–stage investments as well as financing for companies that are growing. They are particularly active in technology-related businesses. VCs have high expectations of return on their investment but are willing to take substantial risks. VCs take an active role in managing the companies they invest in, often even replacing or removing the founders from management.

"Angels." Angel is the term applied to private individuals who invest their own money in new companies. Because it is their own money, they often invest in a wider range of kinds of companies, and seek more-diverse types of returns on their investment, than professional investors such as venture capitalists. They usually invest a smaller

HOW LONG WILL IT TAKE?

Finding an angel investor takes time. The time you spend looking for investment funds is time spent away from running your business. Factor this into your planning and consider delegating some, or possibly all, of the fund-raising work to one of your partners or a trusted advisor.

Find angels and set up meetings	Meet with angels	Negotiate terms	Due diligence/ Draft final documents	Total time
1–4 months	3–6 months	1–3 months	1–3 months	6–16 months

QUESTIONS TO ASK
BEFORE YOU SEEK FINANCING

- ☐ Are you willing to give up some amount of ownership of your company?
- ☐ Are you willing to incur debt that you must repay?
- ☐ Are you willing to risk property or other assets?
- ☐ How much control of the oversight of your company are you willing to relinquish?
- ☐ What other help do you want from a funder besides money?
- ☐ How fast do you want to grow?
- ☐ How big do you want your company to be?
- ☐ What do you see as the long-term relationship between you and your funding source?

amount of money than professional sources. Angels are generally much more accessible and more appropriate for small companies. A number of "angel networks" or organizations have sprung up in large cities.

Crowdfunding. Once again, the Internet has democratized another area—this time, raising funds for start-ups. The concept is called crowdfunding and, as the name implies, it's the ability to raise money from a "crowd"—strangers who believe in your idea and are willing to put some of their money into your new business. While venture capitalists typically invest millions, and angels invest hundreds of thousands of dollars, individuals can "invest" small amounts of money to help you get funded. As with other forms of funding, you'll have to be prepared. As "investors" get more sophisticated, they'll want more than just a great video to motivate them to part with their money. They'll want to see that you have a team that can execute, plus a reasonable business plan. And that they'll have a good chance of making their money back—or that at least you'll use the money as intended. Simply because the amounts of cash exchanging hands is smaller, that doesn't mean you won't face some of the same scrutiny you would from established investors.

Use the comparison chart on pages 234–235 to help you decide whose money you want. Consider your various financing sources, and answer the questions to find the one that suits you and your business best.

Check It Out

New crowdfunding sites pop up regularly. Some of the more established ones are Kickstarter (**www.kickstarter.com**), IndieGoGo (**www.indiegogo.com**), AngelList (**http://angel.co**), and Crowdfunder (**www.crowdfunder.com**).

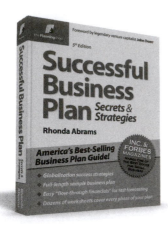

 ## Develop a business plan

If you're going to seek funds from outside investors or lenders, you'll need a business plan. This is a document that outlines your entire business strategy, financing, competition, staffing, future developments, and the steps necessary to achieve your results. It's different from an operating plan, which is designed primarily to help company management organize day-to-day activities. And it's different from this guide, which is designed to get you up-and-running!

Successful Business Plan: Secrets & Strategies leads you step-by-step through the process of developing and writing a business plan and looking for funding. It's available in bookstores throughout the U.S., or from PlanningShop, www.PlanningShop.com.

week 6

week 6

Main accomplishments:

#1 Develop a marketing plan

#2 Set up a simple website

#3 Begin online marketing

#4 Start making sales

#5 Hold your grand opening

#6 Look toward the future

Make appointments with:

- Potential customers
- Key referral sources

Open Your Doors!

GET READY TO OPEN YOUR DOORS! This is the week when you're finally ready to start making sales. After all, the most important component in running a business—at least a successful one—is the ability to attract and keep customers.

In earlier weeks, you've set up your business, taken care of red tape, found a location, dealt with money matters, and got your operations up-and-running. This week you'll design your marketing plan and sales strategy, centered on a clear message for your company. Then you'll go out and call on potential clients or customers—or open your doors so they can call on you. You might even hold a grand opening. Congratulations!

ACCOMPLISHMENT #1:
Develop a marketing plan

My Checklist:

☐ **Clarify your company's message**

☐ **Come up with your elevator pitch**

☐ **Decide on your marketing vehicles**

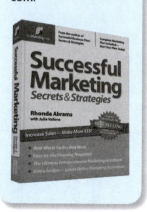

You need to have customers to stay in business: It's the most basic business truth. Since reaching customers costs money, and money is always limited, your marketing strategy must be carefully and thoughtfully designed. That's why you need an overall marketing plan.

First, let's define the terms "marketing" and "sales" and how they differ.

Marketing increases customer awareness and delivers your message. It includes activities such as advertising, social media marketing, creating brochures and collateral materials, and doing public relations.

Marketing also includes what's called "networking"—meeting potential customers and referral sources through informal activities, such as joining organizations, attending industry events, or taking people to lunch. In smaller companies, networking may be the major marketing activity.

Sales, on the other hand, is the direct action taken to secure customer orders. The term "sales" encompasses telemarketing, sales calls, special promotions, and direct-mail solicitations.

In each of these activities—whether it's a direct sales call, an advertising campaign, or a Rotary luncheon—you want to convey a consistent, clear message about your business, and more importantly, what your product or service does for your customer: its features and benefits.

 Clarify your company's message

Every business sends a message through its marketing. Your message is based on the strategic position your company stakes out for itself, such as "low-price leader" or "one-day service." Your message could also specify a particular market niche: "specialists in estate planning" or "software for residential architects."

Most marketing strategists agree that people buy benefits, not features. Customers are more concerned about how a purchase will affect their lives than about how the company achieves those results. No matter how cool you think your new improved business process is, your marketing message should concentrate on the benefits customers receive.

The four Ps of marketing

What messages do you send customers to motivate them to purchase your product or service? Traditional marketing experts emphasize the elements known as "the Four Ps" in influencing customers to buy:

1. **Product.** The tangible product or service itself.

2. **Price.** The cost advantage.

3. **Place.** The location's convenience and decor.

4. **Promotion.** The amount and nature of the marketing activities.

These elements leave a lot out of the marketing picture, however—especially as customers look for products or services not just to fill an immediate need but to enhance their overall sense of well-being.

What customers want: Rhonda's five Fs

A better way to sum up what customers want is through the Five Fs:

1. **Functions.** How does the product or service meet customers' concrete needs?

2. **Finances.** How will the purchase affect customers' overall financial situation? Finances include not just the price of the product or service, but also potential savings and increased productivity.

3. **Freedom.** How convenient is it to purchase and use the product or service? How will customers gain more time and reduce worry in other aspects of their lives?

4. **Feelings.** How does the product or service make customers feel about themselves, and how does it affect and relate to their self-image? Do they like and respect the salesperson and the company?

Check It Out

"Solopreneurs": Read Rhonda's five tips for learning to sell yourself. www.planningshop.com/sellyourself

5. **Future.** How will customers deal with the product or service and company over time? Will support and service be available? How will the product or service affect their lives in the coming years, and will they have an increased sense of security about the future?

Customers, of course, would like to receive benefits in *all* these areas, and you should be aware of how your product or service fulfills the entire range of their needs. But your primary message must concentrate on one or two of these benefits that can effectively motivate your customers.

When you don't understand what customers want, it's tough to effectively sell your product or service.

Come up with your Elevator Pitch

When someone asks, "What does your company do?" you need a brief, clear answer that quickly sums up the nature of your business. This has to be short!

Here's the test for whether a marketing statement is brief enough: Could you explain your business if you ran into a potential client on an elevator ride in a three-story building? That's why it's called the "elevator pitch." If it takes you more than three floors to describe your company, you're saying too much.

The message must not only be short; it must be clear. Unless you're in a highly technical field, your neighbor or your grandmother should be able to understand your services well enough to describe them to someone else. If people you meet can't quickly grasp what you do, they'll never be able to do business with you or send business your way.

Every successful business has its strengths—its place in the market. So how do you get your message across?

Your elevator pitch should touch—very briefly—on the products or services you sell, what market you serve, and your competitive advantage.

If you're in an easy-to-understand business, your elevator pitch theoretically could be very short: "I sell real estate." But that doesn't distinguish you from all the other Realtors out there. A more memorable elevator pitch sets you apart: "I sell homes in the Lakewood district, specializing in first-time buyers."

MY ELEVATOR PITCH

Use this worksheet to develop your elevator pitch. Remember to keep it short; focus on what customers get, not what you do; and make it easy to remember.

My Company…

Is named:
Does:
Serves this market:
Makes money by:
Is like these other companies:
Will succeed because:
Aims to achieve:

When you can cut straight to the heart of the matter with your elevator pitch, customers immediately understand your benefits. It's like the Vietnamese restaurant I used to go to; I never knew the real name, but always referred to it by the big sign out front: "Fresh, Cheap, Good."

The worksheet on page 245 helps you develop your elevator pitch. After you've written a draft or two, time yourself saying it out loud. Can you deliver it in three floors or fewer? If not, you've said too much.

✔ Decide on marketing vehicles

Once you've clarified what you want to tell customers, you have to get that message out there. How will you reach your customers?

The methods you choose are called your "marketing vehicles." You have a variety of marketing vehicles to choose from. The best methods for you depend on your marketing budget, target market, product or service, and marketing message.

Create a marketing budget

The most important part of your marketing program is that you can afford it. Every marketing vehicle costs money, so carefully plan how you intend to spend your marketing dollars. Often the best marketing vehicles are not the most obvious or the most expensive. A large ad in a specialty publication may prove far more effective and less expensive than a small one in a general newspaper.

If you spend a ton of money on a huge advertising campaign but it leaves you without the money to pay the rent or make payroll, you're going to be in hot water. So, make sure you can afford the choices you make. In devising your overall marketing program, be sure you look for:

- **Fit.** Your marketing vehicles must reach your actual target customer and be appropriate to your image.

- **Mix.** Use more than one method so customers get exposure to you from a number of sources.

- **Repetition.** It takes many exposures before a customer becomes aware of a message.

- **Affordability.** Do these vehicles fit within your budget?

MY PRINTING NEEDS

Use this worksheet to project how many professionally printed materials you will need.

	Color or B&W	Quantity	Printer	Cost per Unit	Total Cost
☐ Business cards					
☐ Brochures					
☐ Pamphlets					
☐ Fliers					
☐ Publicity photo					
☐ Advertising specialties (mugs, pens, etc.)					
☐ Signage					
☐ Vehicle signs					
☐ Uniforms, t-shirts, etc.					
☐ Other:					

The worksheets on the following pages help you choose between a variety of marketing vehicles. Several worksheets focus on specific marketing vehicles, such as social media marketing, printed materials, trade shows, and public relations.

The "Marketing Vehicles Comparison Chart" on pages 250–251 helps turn your message into a comprehensive marketing program using the following techniques for getting your message to the right people:

Printed marketing material

Every company needs "stuff" to hand out. Whether you call them brochures, sales collateral, or "leave behinds," you must have printed materials. The most important piece of printed material is your business card. Get those done right away. Use the worksheet "My Printing Needs" on page 247 to plan and budget for your printed materials.

Customer-based marketing

The best business is repeat business. So remind past customers you exist. Keep a mailing list, send postcards or email newletters when you have special offers, or send a note or holiday greeting. In general, contact past customers no less than twice a year and no more than every month. Specialty items, such as pens, mugs, or calendars, are another good way to remind customers you exist. And most importantly, ask customers for referrals!

Trade shows

Trade shows are a great way to meet potential new customers and for them to meet you. A face-to-face meeting makes doing business with you a lot more inviting, and the trade show setting makes it easy for them to ask you questions about your company.

Trade shows can be expensive—the cost of being an exhibitor, preparing your booth, printing marketing materials, and, of course, bringing enough personnel to staff the booth. But a trade show is often the best place to reach your target market.

Before choosing to exhibit, however, find out as much as you can from the show's organizers about who will be attending. Talk to exhibitors from previous years' shows and ask how successful they were. Use the worksheet on page 249, "Trade Shows and Industry Events," to keep a list of potential trade shows to attend.

TRADE SHOWS AND INDUSTRY EVENTS

Use this worksheet to track trade shows or events that you are considering. List the costs to attend and to exhibit, and note specific details about the type of people who attend.

Name of show/event: _____

Sponsor: _____   Date: _____

Location: _____   Costs: _____

_____   Attendees: _____

Deadlines: _____

Notes: _____

Name of show/event: _____

Sponsor: _____   Date: _____

Location: _____   Costs: _____

_____   Attendees: _____

Deadlines: _____

Notes: _____

Name of show/event: _____

Sponsor: _____   Date: _____

Location: _____   Costs: _____

_____   Attendees: _____

Deadlines: _____

Notes: _____

Name of show/event: _____

Sponsor: _____   Date: _____

Location: _____   Costs: _____

_____   Attendees: _____

Deadlines: _____

Notes: _____

MARKETING VEHICLES COMPARISON CHART

QUESTIONS	DIRECT MAIL brochures, fliers, coupons	SIGNAGE vehicles, building, billboards	PRINT MEDIA newspapers, magazines, phonebook	BROADCAST MEDIA television, radio
☐ What market do they reach?				
☐ How big is their reach?				
☐ What percentage of their market is my target market?				
☐ What is the Cost per Thousand (CPM) reached?				
☐ What frequency will I need to be effective?				
☐ What is the reasonable immediate response I can expect?				
☐ How expensive is the ad to prepare?				
☐ What are this vehicle's advantages?				
☐ What are this vehicle's disadvantages?				
☐ Other:				

ONLINE website, SEO, SEM, ads, email newsletters, daily deals, mobile marketing	TRADE SHOWS, NETWORKING	PUBLIC RELATIONS, PUBLICITY	SOCIAL NETWORKING blogs, Facebook, Twitter, YouTube, LinkedIn, Pinterest, etc.	OTHER In-store marketing, sampling

Public relations/publicity

The best publicity is often "free" publicity. Getting a story about your business in the local newspaper or on TV can be more powerful than a paid advertisement. But that's not to say that such coverage won't cost you: While you don't pay for the stories directly, it will take time and effort to get the media's attention and, in the end, you may have to hire a public relations specialist.

If you want to get a story about your business in the newspaper, in a magazine, on the radio, or on TV, the typical way is to send a press release. Of course, it takes a lot more than just sending out a press release to get coverage, but writing up a press release is a necessary—though not sufficient—way to get media coverage.

When designing your press release, remember that most people in the media are overworked. The more you're able to make your story "easy" for them—in the sense that the details are all there—the better your chances of getting publicity.

Most important, of course, you've got to have something the readers, listeners, or viewers of a media outlet will find interesting. Sure, you think it's important you're opening a dry cleaning business, but why should the newspaper care? Is yours the first dry cleaning business in the city? Do you provide a genuinely unique process for cleaning clothes?

What you need is a "hook." A hook is an aspect of your story that "hooks" readers in—the thing that makes your news compelling. Some stories, of course, are naturally compelling: a closely contested election, a hot sports contest, a really cool new consumer product. But let's face it: Most of us don't have stories that are naturally gripping.

Instead, we must find an angle for reporters, showing our story is timely, amusing, or informative. One way is to tie your story to outside events that generate their own publicity, such as holidays, local celebrations, sporting events, or new legislation. Reporters always need timely tie-ins.

Here are other tips to help your press release be successful:

- **Be creative.** Reporters are tired of seeing the same old stories. The offbeat and unusual grabs attention. Sometimes just a little "twist" on a story is enough. For instance, in advance of Earth Day, you might send

Start It Free

Write a release promoting your new business and post it for distribution free using PRLog (**www.prlog.org**) or prFocus (**www.prfocus.com**).

RED TAPE ALERT!

Beware! Not all marketing expenses are treated the same by the IRS. While taking an ad out in a newspaper is 100% deductible, taking a client out to lunch is not. Although business entertainment is often *the* major marketing expense for smaller companies, most meal and entertainment expenses are only 50% deductible.

For example, if you spend $60 on lunch for you and your customer, you can claim only $30 as a deductible expense. Meals are also only 50% deductible when you're traveling, even on a totally business-related trip. There are a very few exceptions to the 50% rule, such as when you're providing food for a company employee retreat or picnic. But far more often, the IRS takes a careful and dim view of entertainment expenses. Be able to verify that business was actually discussed and you had a legitimate business purpose.

out a release about how your new dry cleaning process is environmentally friendly. If you're an accountant, you might want to send out a list of the "Ten Worst Tax Deductions" instead of the Ten Best.

- **Be visual.** Television, in particular, needs visually stimulating stories, but offering a good photo opportunity will help you make it into the newspaper, too. Find ways to make your story visual: like the pet store that holds an Easter parade with pets in Easter bonnets. In your images, avoid "BOPSA": Bunch of People Sitting Around.

- **Work with others.** Leverage the power of other organizations to gain visibility; consider unlikely coalitions, not just similar interest groups.

- **Come up with statistics.** Media outlets love numbers. If you can provide objective, trustworthy information related to your industry or market, you've got a better chance of having the story covered. Include colorful graphic representations of the statistics if possible.

- **Be available.** No one can cover or quote you if they can't reach you. Include all your phone numbers and contact information in your press release. And don't send out a press release and then leave on vacation.

- **Follow-up.** Reporters get hundreds of press releases a week. They're not necessarily going to read yours. Make a follow-up phone call.

GETTING PUBLICITY

Use this worksheet to list newsworthy ideas related to you and your business that can generate free publicity for your company.

☐ **Timely stories:** Tie your activities to events such as holidays, local celebrations, or new legislation.

☐ **Creative angles:** The unusual, amusing, or extraordinary always gets attention. If you can, involve celebrities.

☐ **Joint publicity opportunities:** Consider unlikely coalitions, not just similar interest groups.

☐ **Visual stories:** Television, in particular, needs visually stimulating stories.

☐ **Issues on which you're the "expert":** Provide trustworthy, objective information, preferably with statistics.

MEDIA CONTACTS

*Keep a list of potential media contacts: reporters, editors, columnists,
and bloggers who cover issues relating to your company.*

Name: _____

Title: _____

Media outlet: _____

Areas of interest: _____

Contact info: _____

_____

Name: _____

Title: _____

Media outlet: _____

Areas of interest: _____

Contact info: _____

_____

Name: _____

Title: _____

Media outlet: _____

Areas of interest: _____

Contact info: _____

_____

Name: _____

Title: _____

Media outlet: _____

Areas of interest: _____

Contact info: _____

_____

Name: _____

Title: _____

Media outlet: _____

Areas of interest: _____

Contact info: _____

_____

Name: _____

Title: _____

Media outlet: _____

Areas of interest: _____

Contact info: _____

_____

Name: _____

Title: _____

Media outlet: _____

Areas of interest: _____

Contact info: _____

_____

Name: _____

Title: _____

Media outlet: _____

Areas of interest: _____

Contact info: _____

_____

- **Respect deadlines.** Don't call reporters when they're "on deadline," typically late afternoon for daily journalists. Mid-morning is usually the best time.

- **Do your homework.** Get to know which media outlets (TV, radio, newspapers, websites, and trade publications) cover your industry or the type of story you're likely to have.

- **Develop a database of appropriate journalists, and keep in touch with them.** If possible, get to know them personally. Reporters need reliable sources they can turn to quickly.

Finally, keep trying—over and over! The companies that often get the most coverage are those that regularly and repeatedly send press releases. A one-time press release is far less likely to get you coverage than an ongoing public relations campaign.

Use the worksheets on pages 254 and 255 to keep a list of publicity opportunities and media contacts.

Advertising

Advertising works. It gets your company's name and message to a large number of people with relatively little effort on your part. But it costs money. Don't buy ads based merely on the number of people they'll reach; make sure the ad reaches the *right* people: the customers you want.

A badly designed and poorly written ad may be worse than no ad at all, so spend the time and money to develop a good one.

One of the most frequent mistakes people make when designing ads is to omit necessary details, such as the company's location, hours of operation, phone number, website, or social media profiles and pages. Usually the reason is that the person writing the ad takes basic information for granted. After all, you already know what city you're in or what your area code is, so you forget that it's not obvious to the reader.

Essential details:

1. **The name of your company!**

2. **The nature of your product or service.** Unless you own Macy's or Microsoft, don't assume readers automatically know what your business sells. Even if you send your ad only to existing customers, many

people remember a business by what it sells—not its name (e.g., "The drycleaners at Main and Second Streets," "that cute clothing store downtown").

3. **Where you're located.** Include the city and state (even your country if doing business internationally or online). This is critical if you're in retail, but even if your customers don't come to your store or office, including a location helps customers relate to your business.

4. **Hours and days you're open or hours and days of the sale.**

5. **Website address.**

6. **Phone number with area code.** If you're not going to be available to answer calls, record a message with vital information. Include the country code if you do business internationally.

7. **Email address.**

8. **Special terms or limitations, if any.** In other words, are the discounts not applicable to certain types of items or services, or does the offer expire after a certain date?

9. **Social media sites.** If you use Facebook, Twitter, Instagram, or Pinterest, for example, to market your company, be sure to include your information so potential customers can find and follow you.

Those are the basics. Once you've got those covered, what can you do to make your ads more effective in getting sales?

1. **Create an eye-catching headline.** The first thing you have to do is get attention. This doesn't have to be incredibly clever—"Fifty percent off" gets my attention.

2. **Tell the benefits.** Let potential customers immediately know why they should be interested in doing business with you. This can be something as simple as "Lowest Price for your Auto Insurance."

3. **Provide lots of information.** Ads chock-full of specific products are often surprisingly effective, as long as they're not too cluttered.

4. **Have a pleasing design.** This doesn't have to be the most creative or unique design, but be certain to have appropriate "white space" and don't use more than one or two typefaces.

5. **Include a call to action.** Customers often respond to a direct appeal for action, such as "Hurry—Supplies are limited," or "Call today to book your appointment!"

Finally—before you go to print, have two other people read your ad. Also keep in mind that professionals estimate it takes an average of *nine* exposures to an ad before it registers in a viewer's mind. So be prepared to run your ad repeatedly!

Promotional products

Look around your desk. How many advertisements do you have sitting at your fingertips? None? Maybe one—a clipping from the newspaper about something you're thinking of buying this week? Otherwise, most of us don't keep ads framed above our desks.

Look again. You probably have quite a few ads, yet you just don't think of them that way. Many of the ads you're likely to have are in the form of calendars, pens, pencils, magnets, mugs, notepads, mouse pads, and various gadgets—all imprinted with a company name.

These represent some of the most powerful, affordable, and overlooked forms of marketing: "specialty advertising" or "promotional products."

One of the great advantages of this kind of marketing is that your customers see your name repeatedly. Studies show it takes multiple exposures to an ad before a person notices it. How many radio advertisements can you afford? Compare that to the cost of calendars or pens. If someone wants a pizza, and they have a magnet with the name and phone number of your pizza restaurant on their refrigerator, your chances of their calling you—rather than your competition—increase greatly.

Promotional products can also make other forms of advertising more effective. Offering a free gift in your online ads for new customers or sending a small item in your direct mail piece can make customers pay more attention.

Interestingly, the largest percentage of promotional items sold are what the advertising specialty industry calls "wearables": t-shirts, caps, windbreakers, and the like. Many of these are given not to customers, but to employees, as a reward for reaching certain goals (such as safety), to promote an internal company campaign or message, or most importantly, to reinforce the company's image and logo.

Check It Out

From pens, to clothing, to water bottles, and more, you can have your company name and logo imprinted on just about anything at Concepts in Advertising (**www.imprintedeverythings.com**).

To get the most of your specialty ads, keep this in mind:

1. **Target your market.** Is your audience male or female? Do they spend most of their time in the office, home, or car? Choose items your target customers will use and see repeatedly.

2. **Choose items that are useful, different, or interesting.** A lot of people get the same thing over and over.

3. **Choose a gift related to your business and appropriate for your customers.** A keychain may work for a mechanic; an accountant might want to give calculators or *big* erasers.

4. **Simple messages are better.** You don't have a lot of space.

5. **Don't just look for price.** Customers often will keep higher quality, more thoughtful items longer, increasing the effectiveness of your promotional product.

Networking

Networking is a vital part of a company's marketing program, especially smaller companies. Join professional or industry associations and become active. Participate in community groups. Bring business cards with you when you attend events, whether they're Chamber of Commerce meetings or assemblies at your child's school.

"Guerrilla marketing"

Finding inexpensive and unique ways to reach potential customers has become commonly referred to as "guerrilla marketing" since the term was popularized in the 1980s.

The term reflects the concept of guerrilla warfare—using methods that are surprising, indirect, and cheap. Guerrilla marketing, however, doesn't need to be clever or outrageous to do the job. As long as the campaign carefully targets the right people and has *some* flair, it's likely to be successful. Here are some real-life examples:

■ When my first book, *Successful Business Plan,* debuted, I had thousands of paper napkins printed with a humorous description of a "Business Plan on a Napkin." I attended the huge American booksellers' trade show and put stacks of these napkins on the coffee carts around the convention center hall and convention hotel bars.

Check It Out

Inc.com offers tips on how to make your online advertising and marketing more effective. www.inc.com/guides/marketing

- Les Schwab, a tire dealership in the Pacific Northwest, has run a highly successful "Free Beef in February" campaign since the 1960s. That's right—beef. Each year, the company gives away over $1 million of it to customers, who literally eat it up.

- My niece, Adeena, while handling the public relations for a company, ordered Chinese fortune cookies with clever sayings inside mentioning the business she represented. She then researched which Chinese restaurants were near the offices of the newspapers and magazines she hoped would write about her company, and gave them the cookies—free—to use whenever someone from those publications ordered Chinese food delivered.

- A bank near my office gives free Vidalia onions away once a year to anyone who comes in. It's such a fond, and odd, local tradition that the bank gets lots of local press coverage each year.

- My hairdresser just moved to a new location, with few pedestrians. The biggest source of walk-in customers comes from the popular dry cleaners across the street. He gave the owners of the dry cleaners free haircuts in return for putting discount coupons on their counter.

- Weekly, a Houston restaurant donates appetizers to a nearby motel for the hotel's afternoon guest reception. In return, at no charge, the restaurant posts ads in each room.

As with guerrilla warfare, the problem with most guerrilla marketing campaigns is that they use a scattershot approach, hitting everything within reach. That means spending lots of time and money on things that never bring actual customers. And small businesses can't afford that.

So while you might want to adopt some guerrilla marketing *techniques*, don't forget that you still need an overall, disciplined marketing *plan*.

Customer loyalty programs

In my wallet, I have:

- **Two airlines' frequent flyer cards**
- **A punch card from a beauty supply store**
- **A coffee house frequent buyer card**
- **A frequent parker card for the airport parking lot**
- **A punch card from a car wash**
- **Three hotel chains' membership reward cards**

All these cards are evidence of my participation in these companies' customer loyalty programs. Programs like these have exploded over the last few decades, as companies have realized the importance of retaining their customers, not just attracting new ones.

The key to creating a successful loyalty program is being aware of what you want to achieve. Some goals for a loyalty program are:

- **Customer retention.** Even if customers spend no more than they would have without a program, how much are you willing to do to keep them in your store rather than a competitor's?

- **Maintain spending habits.** Perhaps more important than retaining a customer may be inducing them to keep their current level of spending. So you may want to reward customers for purchasing a certain number of products or spending a particular dollar amount with you each week/month/year.

- **Rewarding customers.** As airlines have learned, frequent user programs can often be most effective by giving rewards to their best customers. Making customers feel appreciated can be a powerful tool for maintaining their spending and loyalty.

- **Information gathering.** One benefit of loyalty programs is finding out what your customers—individually as well as collectively—want. Grocery store loyalty programs use this as a way of selectively marketing products based on customers' buying habits.

- **Increasing sales.** The hope is that customers will actually spend more if they feel loyal to you.

What kinds of loyalty programs tend to be effective?

- **Buy-ahead discount.** When I purchase a prepaid card for $20 at my nearby coffee store, I get one free drink at the time of purchase. My neighbor gets a 10% discount when she prepurchases a series of exercise classes. The benefit is immediately apparent to the customer, and you get money in the bank now. A certain percentage of prepaid cards will be lost or never used, increasing your profit margins.

- **Free reward after reaching purchase level.** The long-term airport parking lot gives me one free day after I stay 35; I get one free car wash after buying 10. Besides feeling encouraged to keep coming back, I carry these cards with me—which serves as a constant ad for the business.

- **Upgrades/special treatment.** Giving extras to your loyal customers may cost relatively little but mean a lot. Some examples: an upgrade at a hotel, free dessert at a restaurant, free alterations at a clothing store.

- **Surprise rewards.** Periodically, I receive a coupon for a big discount or $10 or $25 off any purchase from companies where we do a lot of business—office supply stores, copy shops, and so on. It's like getting an unexpected gift from a friend.

- **Membership/clubs.** You can offer discounts or rewards to people who agree to sign up to be a member of your club or to be associated with you. These include "supermarket clubs," where customers get discounts and special offers in return for enabling the supermarket to track their purchases and continue to market to them. These work well with customers who are regularly targeted by competitors' marketing campaigns.

- **Discounts after purchase.** Discounts given as a reward after purchase serve to encourage additional purchases and to thank customers. An example would be a discount coupon for the next purchase placed in an order shipped from a clothing company.

What kind of loyalty programs do I find *less* effective?

- **"Percent off" discount after reaching purchase level.** Unless the discounts are substantial, these tend to feel more like a promotion for the business rather than a reward. These are different from a specific dollar amount off or a specific reward free.

- **End-of-year rebates.** Waiting 12 months defers gratification too long. The customers who are likely to be motivated by such programs are those who are most cost sensitive, not necessarily your most profitable.

No program, though, can overcome bad service and bad products. A few years ago, I switched airlines even though I had premier status, because I had tired of the continually rude treatment, not to mention all of the canceled flights. Treating customers like they're platinum keeps you in the gold.

Forming a virtual company

You may find that you're failing to land prospective clients because they think your company is too small or that you can't serve the scope of their needs. One way to add size, depth, and strength to your company without adding even a single employee is to form a "virtual company."

For instance, in a brochure for a consulting company I use, in the section "The Team," it lists an impressive group of people, each with top credentials and expertise. Looking closely, I can see that only two of these consultants are actually employed by the company. Instead, the two company founders have an *alliance* with a group of experts.

This isn't being deceptive. Below the name of each "team member" is clearly printed the name of their own individual businesses. Nevertheless, by listing these experts together as a team, the consulting company creates a positive impression; I have a full range of top specialists at my disposal.

Creating a "virtual" company—or a marketing alliance—enables you to:

- **Do joint marketing.** It's less expensive—and more effective—to combine marketing lists and create combined marketing materials. You can also reach a larger pool of potential clients.

- **Offer clients a broader range of services.** Sure, you may believe that you can serve all of your clients' needs, but the client may not feel the same way. Many clients prefer to hire specialists rather than generalists. By offering clients a team of specialists, you're more likely to get—and keep—their business.

- **Reduce clients' apprehension.** Many clients are reluctant to hire new businesses, or one-person or very small companies. They're fearful that they could be stranded if something happens to the one key person.

- **Present a more impressive image.** Together with your partners, you're going to have a longer list of former clients, as well as a broader range of experience, awards, and other references, than you would have on your own.

One of the biggest barriers to putting together a virtual company is recognizing that it's not always best to go it alone. You may have to give part of a client's business to someone else. Are you willing to get a small piece of a big pie rather than all of a very small pie—or no pie at all?

Keep in mind that virtual companies are not legal entities. There are no rules—one member of the alliance can bill the client and then subcontract with the other members, or each individual member can bill separately. The key is to stay flexible so you can meet the client's needs.

When you're looking to put together a "virtual company," seek out partners that fit your own style of communication and that maintain the same level of quality. And, as always, only do business with those you trust and respect.

Remember, you can't be everything to all clients, and you can't do everything yourself. As the old saying goes, "The whole is greater than the sum of its parts."

ACCOMPLISHMENT #2:
Set up a simple website

Your website is a key part of your marketing program. Your customers and potential customers will turn to it to get information about you and your company. The first step in building a successful website is to be clear on what you want it to achieve—and make sure those goals are realistic. Many entrepreneurs suffer from the "if you build it, they will come" syndrome, imagining that if they put up a website, they'll get a flood of new customers. That's not a realistic goal.

Websites can take many forms and serve a multitude of purposes. In fact, most sites combine a number of functions, such as informing the public about the company *and* selling products or providing customer service. From a marketing point of view, however, you'll want to concentrate on how your website attracts, retains, and motivates customers to do business with you.

Websites can be categorized generally along the following lines:

- **Brochure sites.** Like a print brochure, a good brochure website includes an overview of a company's products or services, basic information about the company (such as location and hours of operation), and background on the company's history and the people who run it. Brochure sites serve as the face of a company for anyone interested in learning more. Brochure sites are *not* generally used for ecommerce, though some such sites provide links to purchase products or services.

- **Ecommerce sites.** The primary purpose of ecommerce sites is to sell products and services directly to customers. Although this type of site may well include information about a company and its products or services, its primary function is to promote and process sales.

- **Content sites.** These are websites with the primary function to provide information, advice, or entertainment to users. The content of such sites

Check It Out

If you run a service business, make it easy for clients to book appointments with you by accepting online bookings through a service such as Schedulicity (**www. schedulicity.com**).

MY WEBSITE CHECKLIST

Check off the elements you plan to include on your website, noting what each section will say:

Website Information/Features	Details/Description
☐ Home page	
☐ Overview of products/services	
☐ About the company	
☐ The team: founders/key employees	
☐ Contact info	
☐ Relevant content/info/advice	
☐ Pictures/videos	
☐ Client list	
☐ Testimonials/awards	
☐ Samples/demos	
☐ Catalog	
☐ Newsletter signup	
☐ Links to company social media sites	
☐ User-generated content	
☐ Media/press coverage	
☐ Customer service info and/or forms	
☐ FAQs (Frequently Asked Questions)	
☐ Job opportunities	
☐ Site map/search box	
☐ Investor information:	
☐ Other:	

may be created especially for the sites, adapted from other media (such as magazines), or brought together (*aggregated*) from other sources (such as websites, blogs, and videos). In most cases, these sites are supported by advertising and are free to users. In other cases, companies offer content related to their products or services as a way to draw in and retain visitors.

- **Lead generation sites.** One of the primary purposes of such sites is collecting leads for salespeople to call upon. Such sites often require that visitors provide contact info if they're to access the site's content, videos, and/or downloads. The company then uses this contact info to follow up with users.

- **Portal sites.** The basic function of these sites is to attract users who share a common interest, then send them to related sites and show them relevant advertisements. For example, a portal site for a vacation spot such as Hawaii might have nothing more than ads from people who own condos and beach homes in Hawaii that they want to rent out.

- **Social networking sites.** These sites are designed to let users develop communities, interact with one another, create connections, make referrals, and have fun. Some of the best known are Twitter, Facebook, Pinterest, Instagram, and LinkedIn. Remember to add icons on your website that link out to your company's social media pages.

- **Customer service sites.** Customers often need support for the products and services they purchase. These sites provide it. Offering everything from technical advice to shipping information, such sites—whether they're devoted exclusively to customer service or represent a portion of an existing site devoted to the topic—enable companies to reduce costs and increase customer satisfaction.

When deciding what you're going to use your website for, keep in mind not only the initial cost of the site's design and development, but the ongoing maintenance. If your site will require frequent updates and changes, you'll want to make sure the site is designed in such a way that you can easily make those changes yourself.

Remember, most companies can succeed very well with a simple website that describes the company's services and products, basic details, and answers to most-asked questions.

Use the worksheet on page 265 to plan the functions and information you want on your website.

Check It Out

A number of companies offer a range of website hosting services and do-it-yourself website design templates. Two of these companies are Intuit (**www.intuit.com/websitebuilding-software**) and Squarespace (**www.squarespace.com**).

Website design and hosting:

In putting up your website, you basically have two options:

1. **Do it yourself.** Many website hosting providers offer tools to help you design your own business website, and then they will host that site for you. This can be a fairly inexpensive way to get your website up-and-running. But be warned—even though this is getting easier all the time, it may still be frustrating, especially if you have complicated requirements or you are not tech-savvy. But if you're willing to spend some time learning the necessary skills, developing your own site may be a viable option.

2. **Get someone else to do it for you.** There are a wealth of website designers and hosting companies out there for you to choose from. But the very fact that there are so many—and the costs are so varied—makes it difficult to know which one to choose. So ask around and get recommendations from others. Certainly check with your industry or professional association; you'll probably find some developers who specialize in just your type of business. Also, ask other entrepreneurs in your community for recommendations. But don't think that hiring someone else to develop your site lets you off the hook for planning it—you'll still need to decide on exactly what you want and need, then communicate that clearly to your developer. Spend some time looking at other sites related to your industry, and then make a list of what you like and don't like. Let this help guide your planning sessions with your developer.

A general word of caution: Don't spend a ton of money on your website until you've been in business for a while. Most new companies find that they have to adjust the nature of their products or services as they encounter the realities of the market. So, don't lock yourself in to an expensive website that is likely to need changing within a year.

ACCOMPLISHMENT #3:
Begin online marketing

SEO and SEM

"Build your website, and they will come," right? Not necessarily. For starters, how will people know you even have a website and that it contains something they're interested in? Sure, you'll do everything possible

---

Start It Free

You can get your website up quickly without paying a cent using one of many free website builders. Three to consider are Weebly (**www.weebly.com**), Wix (**www.wix.com**), and Moonfruit (**www.moonfruit.com**).

offline to direct people to your website—put its address on your business cards, brochures, ads, and so on—but the people in the best position to visit your website immediately are already online. So how do you get them to notice you? One of the best ways is by making sure your site is easy to find via search engines—Google, Yahoo!, and Bing, for example.

For the vast majority of online users, search engines serve as the main gateway to information on the Web. This means that if your website is highly visible in the results that appear when someone types in a keyword or phrase associated with your type of business, there's a decent chance that person will click on over to your website. There are two primary ways to ensure that your website is highly visible on search engines.

Search engine optimization (SEO) is the process of trying to design your website and the words on it so that it appears naturally in the top results when someone types a keyword into a search engine. With SEO, you don't pay search engines to have your site appear high on results pages. SEO is often referred to as organic search.

SEO is an art and a science, based on secret algorithms from the search engines. It's unlikely that you will master it on your own to make your site consistently appear at the top of unpaid search results. Nevertheless, you should understand at least the basics of SEO to ensure that your site shows up, over time.

The first thing you need to do is figure out which words your target customers will most likely use when searching for the types of products or services (or content) you offer. Once you've determined that, repeat those keywords throughout your site—in your content, headlines, page names, and more.

Imagine, for instance, that you own a company that creates and sells educational software parents use to help teach their kids math. There are lots of terms you'd expect searchers to use when looking for products like yours—and these are the terms you'd use when developing your site's content, regardless of whether you were considering SEO: terms such as "software," "educational software," "math software," and even "kids software."

These, though, are all rather broad terms—that is, lots of companies sell math software or educational software. This means your site is unlikely to show up high in natural search results based on those keywords because millions (yes, millions) of other sites are also using them. Instead, you'd be

Check It Out

Do a search for "Google SEO Starter Guide" to find a link to a helpful PDF file full of basic information on SEO.

better off focusing on keywords that are more specific to your products—so in the case of that educational software company, something like "kids math software" used over and over would yield better results.

And since these keywords need to be peppered throughout your site if a search engine is to list it high in its results, you need to have SEO in mind right from the start as you develop and update your site.

Search engine marketing (SEM) refers to the process of paying search engine companies to ensure that your website (or specific pages of it) appears in users' search results, typically either at the top or in a column that appears beside other, nonpaid results. This is also referred to as search engine advertising, paid placement, paid search, or sponsored listings.

Here's how SEM works: Advertisers choose the keywords that they think searchers will most likely use when looking for products, services, and content similar to theirs. Then, when the customer enters into a search engine one of the keywords that advertiser has purchased, a small ad appears either above or near the list of naturally generated search results. Most such ads consist of just simple text, often indistinguishable from the actual search results except for their placement on the page or a faint background color. These ads are quite small—usually just a headline, followed by 10 words or so, plus an inviting link to a website or a page within a website.

SEM has proven to be an extremely effective advertising medium for two primary reasons:

- **Highly qualified prospects.** Searchers are often highly qualified prospects—especially for the most narrowly defined terms. For instance, if someone types in the term "bike repair San Francisco," there's a good chance they or someone they know is in Northern California with an immediate need to get their bicycle fixed.

- **Effectiveness of pay per click (PPC).** Another reason that SEM is so popular is that advertisers pay only when a searcher clicks on their ads (called a click-through). Advertisers do not pay simply for having their ad displayed—and this fact distinguishes PPC advertising from virtually every other type. If you run an ad for your bike repair shop in the newspaper or the Yellow Pages, for example, you'll pay the same amount for that ad no matter how many people actually see it. You may get zero response, but you'll still have to pay. With PPC, you pay only for each click-through to your site that a prospect makes.

Check It Out

You'll need to choose relevant keywords for your business for both SEO and SEM. A good place to start is with Google's free keyword tool (**https://adwords. google.com/o/ KeywordTool**).

Check It Out

Google's Adwords (**www.google.com/ adwords**) and Microsoft's Bing Ads (**www.bingads. microsoft.com**) are two providers of search engine marketing.

Ways of Calculating SEO and SEM Success

The three most common ways in which online advertising is purchased are CPM, CPC, and CPA.

CPM (Cost Per Thousand) is where advertisers pay for exposure of their message to a specific audience. CPM costs are priced per thousand impressions. The M in the acronym is the Roman numeral for 1,000.

CPC (Cost Per Click) is also known as Pay Per Click (PPC). Advertisers pay only when users click on their listings and are redirected to their websites.

CPA (Cost Per Action; Cost Per Acquisition) Advertisers pay for actual results, based on those who complete a transaction, such as making a purchase or signing up for a service.

As with every other aspect of your marketing plan, you should carefully evaluate the return on investment (ROI) of your SEO and SEM marketing efforts. Fortunately, this is one area of marketing where ROI is extremely easy to measure.

Web analytics quantifies website traffic and every action taken in your SEM activities and by your website visitors. It can tell you how many times your ad was shown to searchers (called impressions), how many times it was clicked through, what Web pages users visited once they clicked through, how long searchers stayed on your site, whether they took certain actions (such as making a purchase) after they had clicked through to your site, and more.

Social Media Marketing

Facebook. Twitter. LinkedIn. YouTube. Blogger. Pinterest. The digital world is a connected world, and is forever expanding. A huge number of people are constantly attached to the Web, their phones, and each other. And as any good marketer will tell you, any time millions of people are connected, a marketing opportunity exists.

Where once social media sites like those named above were designed merely to enable individuals to share their interests and opinions, they're now also vehicles for promoting products and services. Many opportunities abound—whether you pay for ads in social media sites or you actively use social media efforts to make your business more visible and create connections to your target market.

Start It Free

Google Analytics (www.google.com/analytics) is an easy-to-use tool that analyzes your website traffic—how many people are visiting your site—and gives you an impressive array of information about them, such as what pages they are viewing, how long they view them, at what point they abandon your site, and so forth. It's extremely versatile and offers a broad array of reports to help you make changes in your site to improve your results.

One of the first things you need to determine is which social media platforms best suit your target market. Are you trying to reach consumers or businesses? Does a mass-market site (Facebook, Twitter, YouTube), or a special interest site (such as Chowhound for food), or a professional networking site (like LinkedIn) suit your offerings? Before launching a social media campaign on a given site, be certain that its audience is truly interested in your offerings.

Once you've identified the most appropriate social media sites, the key to your marketing campaign's success will be providing content that appeals to your target audience. Social media can be a powerful tool for getting a message out fast. If you can capture the attention of an audience with something clever, controversial, or timely, you may be able to generate a powerful viral marketing campaign.

Like anything else in your business, social media marketing requires both a strategy and time to execute successfully.

Use social media sites to:

- **Spread the word and create buzz about your products or services**
- **Advertise with campaigns designed to target your specific audience**
- **Create your own group or community to get feedback from customers**
- **Build referral sources and networking connections**
- **Engage more deeply with prospects and customers**
- **Enhance your credibility by contributing meaningful content**

Blogs

Blogs, short for "Web logs," are frequently updated online journals that can contain text, audio, video, graphics, and photos. From a marketing perspective, blogs work well for businesses in which expertise is valued— for consultants, technology service providers, professional service businesses, and so on.

Whether you create your own blog or regularly contribute to a popular blog in your field, your blogging efforts can greatly enhance your visibility and credibility. If you offer readers something of value (beyond a sales message), it's likely you'll attract people looking for your services or products.

Start It Free

You can set up a blog quicky, easily and for $0 on Blogger (www.blogger.com) or Wordpress (www.wordpress.com). Wordpress has the added benefit of potentially sending traffic your way. After you post a blog, it will appear in the "Freshly Pressed" section of the site. There, if it catches the eye of interested readers, you'll get some clicks on your post.

Effective use of blogs can:

- **Build name and brand recognition**
- **Establish you as an expert**
- **Attract customers and clients**
- **Create links to your website**
- **Generate buzz around a new product**
- **Tap into a committed market**

Check It Out

How do you find blogs that reach your target market? Check blog directories or blog search engines:
www.Blogarama.com
blogs.botw.org
www.Blogsearchengine.com
www.bloggeries.com
www.Technorati.com
www.aripaparo.com/archive/000632.html

Other online social media marketing tactics

Creating your own podcast—a radio or TV program that gets downloaded to computers and mobile devices—might be a good option if you have compelling content on the most popular podcast topics: technology, politics, and business. What about a video? While YouTube is the best known of the video-sharing sites, many others are out there, and some of them focus on "how-to" videos, possibly providing a perfect opportunity to showcase your expertise.

Choosing a social media marketing strategy

With so many interactive online marketing tools to consider, how do you choose the right one for you?

- **Make sure your target market actually participates in these online activities.** Closely follow the LinkedIn groups or Facebook pages, read the blogs, listen to the podcasts, and participate in the community before you decide to spend a great deal of time and money on any particular site.

WHAT WOULD RHONDA DO?

CONSIDER YOUR SOCIAL MEDIA EFFORTS AN INVESTMENT

It can be difficult to measure ROI (return on investment) of your time and expenditure on sites such as Facebook, Twitter, Instagram, and Google+. But using social media increases your visibility—and attracts customers in the long run. Just be sure to keep an eye on how much time you spend on these sites.

■ **Determine whether you have the time for "unpaid" social media.** Are you willing to develop and maintain an active online presence? If you lack the time, then pay for ads—they can be persistent even when you can't.

■ **Understand that online activities can come with pitfalls.** Most notably, dissatisfied customers may make unfavorable comments—not all of them even fair or honest—about your products, services, or customer service.

■ **Keep experimenting.** Because the Internet is a fast-moving medium, you can quickly adapt marketing strategies to find the approaches that work best for you. And new social networks develop continually. Use the worksheet on page 99 to outline your social media marketing strategy.

Daily Deals

The prospect of getting a bargain has driven the phenomenal success of daily deal sites such as Groupon, Living Social, and hundreds of others. For some companies, these offers are invaluable business builders. Other companies, which have lost money and attracted only bargain-hunting customers, have rued the day they ever signed up.

A deal site sends an email daily to those who've registered. People interested in your discounted product or service purchase your deal. You typically pay nothing to be included, but the deal site gets a hefty piece of the sale: 30% to 50%. And typically, you must offer at least a 50% discount. So if your business creates custom photo books using images your customers upload to your site, here's what a money breakdown might look like: You offer your $40 leather-bound photo book for $20. With each sale, you get $10; the site gets $10. Those who never redeem the coupon add to your profit margin: Businesses report 5% to 40% nonredemption rates.

Deals are best offered to launch a new business or get your name out there, for slow or off-season periods to drive new traffic, and to move excess or last season's inventory.

If you're considering offering a daily deal, keep these 10 strategies in mind:

1. Offer services, rather than products. It's generally far less costly since you won't have the cost of goods.

2. To help build a committed customer base, create offers for which customers must come back repeatedly ("your third visit free"; "four manicures for $99"; and the like).

3. Try not to cannibalize existing customers. Craft deals that are more likely to appeal to new customers.

4. Experiment with different offers and several sites to determine what works for you. A more-targeted site may be a better fit and less costly than a general, national one.

5. Include your own fine print. Limit redemption to "only one per customer," "not to be combined with other discounts," and other restrictions that make sense, to protect you.

6. Avoid sites that require you to deal with them exclusively. Some sites affect your ability to offer deals on other sites; limit your involvement with those.

7. Understand the fees and terms. Make sure you know about all other fees. Some sites charge credit-card processing fees; others may pay you slowly or in long-drawn-out installments.

8. Build your marketing list. Look for sites that give you a list of those who've bought the deal. Some sites give you only an identification number. Others will give you names and email addresses—enabling you to keep marketing to those prospects.

9. Do everything you can to ask for and capture contact information from new customers so you can continue to market beyond the deal or coupon.

10. Negotiate with deal sites. And negotiate hard. There are lots of daily deal sites. Most important, know what works best for you and for your business. Don't let salespeople pressure you.

Keep your expectations realistic. And remember, these sites are more a marketing tactic than a way to make quick sales. They are a good example of loss leaders—offering a product or service at or below cost so as to bring people through your doors.

Mobile marketing

Mobile devices have transformed the way customers deal with local businesses. How long has it been since you used your smartphone to find a business? To reserve a table at a restaurant? To get directions? Likely, not long. Most of us use mobile devices to shop. That's a lot of people looking for businesses on their mobile devices. Depending on the type of start-up you launch—mobile marketing is especially well-suited to local businesses that deal with consumers—you'll want to take advantage of mobile marketing.

You don't have to develop a gee-whiz app or use every mobile method available in order to reach the increasing number of people searching for businesses like yours on their mobile devices. You do, however, need a mobile version of your website.

Most of the following mobile marketing techniques are easy, and often free:

■ **Get found.** "Claim" your business for free on sites such as Yelp, Bing Places for Business, Yahoo! Local, Google Places for Business, and Foursquare. When someone in your area looks for a business like yours, you'll show up in the search results.

■ **Offer coupons and deals.** Like adding your listing, this is also free and easy to do. You simply add a coupon to the sites listed above. You can also use business-oriented applications especially designed to present coupons to customers, based on location, such as Yowza (getyowza.com), CouponSherpa (couponsherpa.com), or DealChicken (deal-chicken.com), as well as daily deal sites like Groupon or LivingSocial.

■ **Build relationships with customers.** Do this through social media sites such as Facebook or Twitter. More-powerful customer connection programs, like RewardMe, enable customers to receive rewards for coming back to you repeatedly.

■ **Display your location, hours, and main products or services.** Make sure your home page has the most critical information in highly readable type—large fonts and dark print on a light or white background—that doesn't require typing or moving away from the home page.

Review Sites

Positive reviews on sites such as Yelp, Angie's List, TripAdvisor, Zagat, Google Places for Business, and the like, can be powerful marketing tools for your business. Customers often use—and rely on—sites like these before making reservations, booking appointments, or purchasing products. Although you have no control over what reviewers post about you, you can claim your business page on these sites and add information about your company.

Use the following tips to manage your online reviews:

- **Encourage satisfied customers to post reviews.**

- **Monitor your reviews at least weekly.**

- **If a site allows "owner's response," respond to negative reviews with clear, nonargumentative explanations and thank positive reviewers.**

- **Prevent negative reviews: Train your employees on excellent customer service.**

- **If available, "claim" your page; add business info, pictures, and coupons.**

- **Don't try to "game" the system; concentrate on building a great business.**

Email Newsletters

A financial planning consultant sends an email newsletter containing 10 investment tips to her customers. A retail store sends an announcement of an upcoming sale via email. A dentist's patient gets a notice in his inbox alerting him that it's time for a checkup. All of these represent ways businesses can stay in touch with customers and prospects via email newsletters.

In an email newsletter, you can include information and tips your customers can use, short articles, business updates, special announcements, or coupons and special offers. For most businesses, avoid filling your newsletter solely with sales information about your products and services—instead, provide recipients with some benefit for opening your email. That way, they're more likely to read the next one you send. If, however, your business strictly sells products, then "news" of discounts, sales, and new products may be all the benefit your customers look for.

Of course, people are deluged with email, and as with any kind of marketing piece, there's the possibility that your communication may well just get tossed—after all, it's easy to hit that Delete button. But if an email communication comes from a recognized and trusted source and offers something of interest to the recipient, there's a good chance it will be opened—and perhaps even viewed as something valuable.

Check It Out

Many companies provide easy-to-use, turnkey online email newsletter services to help you create and send email newsletters in a snap. Here's a short list of some: AWeber (**www.aweber.com**), Constant Contact (**www.constant-contact.com**), Emma (**www.myemma.com**), and Vertical Response (**www.verticalresponse.com**).

Email marketing is:

- **Effective.** Customers and prospects look at their email continually.

- **Affordable.** Email is significantly less expensive than print communication.

- **Quick.** Messages can be prepared and sent virtually immediately.

- **Easy.** A variety of email communication services make it a snap to stay in touch via email.

But a word of caution about all email marketing: Be careful not to abuse it. Send email only to those who've signed up to receive email from you or have had some dealings with you (including giving you their business card), or you may be breaking the law. Limit the frequency of your messages; generally once or twice a month is enough for an email newsletter. Try to use a compelling "Subject" line to increase the chance that people will open and read your mail. And make sure your mailings are meaningful, are valuable, and don't contain offensive content or language. If not, recipients will soon block your email, and if enough people do that, email filters will block your messages to many larger servers.

Online Advertising

You'll find them on just about any commercial website you visit. They're either lurking at the side of the page or incorporated right into the design. Some are static; others blink or flash messages at you; and some float across the page. Then there are those that pop up in front you, obscuring the website you're trying to view until you can figure out how to get rid of them.

Even if you find most online ads bothersome, it's a good bet that there are others you're happy to see. For instance, if you're looking for environmentally sensitive products—solar-powered heating, energy-efficient lights, recycled building materials, and so on—and you come across a website listing suppliers of such products, you'll be thrilled. You won't care that these companies paid to be listed; you're just glad to find all of these resources in one location.

What's important is that you design your online ads to attract (not annoy) your target customers and then place them where potential customers are most likely to see them.

Start It Free

At this point in your business, your contact list of customers and prospects may be short. Email newsletter service MailChimp (**www.mailchimp.com**) offers a "forever free" account that allows users with smaller lists to create and send out email newsletters at no cost. As your business grows, you can upgrade to a paid subscription account without any disruption to your newsletter marketing campaigns.

Some major types of online website advertising opportunities are:

Portal sites/directories. Portals and directories serve as online hubs—usually grouped around a common theme, topic, product, or location—where users come to look for information, products, and services. As such, portals can provide effective (and affordable) places to advertise your product or service—especially if you have a clearly defined target market and are using a portal or directory site that generates a lot of traffic. For example, DeliciousItaly.com is a portal for visitors interested in travel, food, and culture centered on Italy.

Website ads. Banner ads typically include graphics or photos as well as text, and are placed adjacent to the content of the webpage itself. Interested viewers can then click through to the advertiser's website.

Another form of website advertising is interstitial ads—that is, ads that appear between (or before) other content and websites. With this type of ad, viewers become a captive audience. After they type in a website address, an ad appears before the actual site they want to visit opens.

Sponsorships. With a sponsorship, an advertiser pays to support a website, portion of a website, content within a website, or the organization behind the website. In return, the website gives the advertiser visibility and recognition. Often, this visibility takes the form of a static banner ad; however, it can also mean displaying the sponsor's name, logo, or tagline in immediate proximity to content.

Online classifieds. Some of the most effective ads are pure text (or, perhaps, text augmented with a few pictures). These are the equivalent of online "classified" ads.

The best known is Craigslist (www.craigslist.org). While most people look for jobs or used goods on Craigslist, many businesses also use the site to advertise their new products or their business or professional services. Advertising on Craigslist takes time (you have to continually update your ad to stay visible), but, in most cases, it's free.

Affiliate auction. Online auction sites, such as eBay, are more than just places for individuals to auction off used goods to the highest bidders. Representing huge online marketplaces, such sites have created myriad marketing opportunities for entrepreneurs.

Sure, online auction sites are designed for ecommerce—that is, the direct selling of products—but that doesn't mean you can't also use them as marketing tools. Since you can set up "stores" on these sites or list products as "Buy It Now" without conducting an auction, you can use auction sites as an advertising medium—just as you would online classified sites.

All you need to do is register, pay the fees, and upload some descriptions and photos to get your products—and your business—in front of a marketplace that consists of millions of eyeballs.

Affiliate programs. Affiliate advertising offers incentives for others to place your ads on their sites in exchange for a piece of the action—usually in the form of a sales commission on customers who come through their site. For instance, let's say you were selling your brand of tennis accessories. Other websites—such as those for tennis magazines, tennis clubs, or sporting good retailers—could agree to place your ad (including a link back to your website) on their webpages. Then, if one of their site visitors clicks the ad, goes to your site, and makes a purchase, the originating site gets a commission on the final sale.

ACCOMPLISHMENT #4:
Start making sales!

If your marketing plan has been successful, you'll soon have potential customers interested. Now you have to make the actual sale!

Getting your first customer

While the Starship Enterprise may go "where no one has gone before," most customers only follow where others lead. Customers prefer to patronize companies that already have other customers. What a dilemma! You have to have customers to get customers.

Don't despair; there are a number of tricks to snare that first client or customer.

The simplest method is to just give your product or service away. This isn't as stupid as it sounds. Technology companies often give potential customers "beta" or test versions of their software. They use this as a way both to improve their product and to expose future buyers to what they make. And Post-It Notes never caught on until 3M gave away thousands of samples. You, too, can allow potential customers to sample your products or services or to serve as "beta" testers.

Another approach is to charge your early clients far less than they would pay elsewhere (and less than you'll charge later). This enables you to start building a reputation and perhaps creates some word-of-mouth advertising. Lots of companies use "introductory pricing" for their products or services to start to build market share. Use community and social networking sites to help get the word out.

You might also find your first customer by asking your competitors for excess work they can't handle. Yes, I said "competitors." One of the biggest mistakes I made when I started was that I avoided talking to others in my field. I figured they would view me as a threat, and the less they knew about me, the better. I was wrong. It turned out my "competitors" were great sources for new business and industry information. Competitors may be interested in subcontracting or referring work to you.

If you can do so legally, or if you're on good terms with your former employer, see if there are customers you can take from your last job. Some of the most successful small businesses are those that serve customers that bigger businesses no longer wish to handle.

Successful sales techniques

If you're in business, sooner or later you have to make sales. Some entrepreneurs view the prospect of a sales call with the same sense of fear and loathing as having to face an IRS audit.

Take heart: Sales is a craft, not an art. It can be learned. Here are a few keys to successful sales:

- **Listen.** No sales skill is more important than the ability to listen. A great salesperson hears what the customer wants—their concerns and priorities. When calling on a customer, it's tempting to immediately launch in to a sales pitch, especially if you're nervous. But by listening, you can better understand how your product or service meets the customer's needs and desires. If a woman shopping for a car says she likes to drive fast, tell her about performance instead of cup holders. If a man is concerned about safety, focus on the airbags and antilock brakes. Don't just tell the customer what you think they'll be interested in or stick to your standard sales patter.

- **Ask questions.** You can't listen to a customer unless you get them talking. Ask relevant questions to draw them out: "What do you like in your current car?" "What don't you like?" "What features are the most important?" Don't just ask questions to qualify them as a hot prospect, such as, "Are you ready to buy a car today?"

- **Tell them what they get, not what you do.** You work with your product or service every day, so it's natural to focus on details of your work. But customers don't want to know the ins and outs of your business; they want to know how you meet their needs.

- **Appreciate the benefits of your product or service.** Genuine enthusiasm is contagious. If you truly believe you're offering the customer something worthwhile, you'll be a more effective salesperson. On the other hand, if you don't believe in your product, you shouldn't be selling it.

- **Don't oversell.** It's tempting to land a sale by telling the customer anything they want to hear, but that's almost certain to lead to customers' being dissatisfied or disappointed. An acquaintance of mine who owns a successful chain of moderately priced hotels told me that his strategy is to "promise customers a Chevy, then deliver a Cadillac." By underpromising and overdelivering, he has built an exceptionally loyal customer base and generates terrific word-of-mouth marketing.

- **Be honest.** Lying is not only unethical and possibly illegal; it's a surefire way to lose customers and potential customers. You may even find yourself facing a lawsuit.

- **Compare, don't criticize, your competition.** Yes, I know, your product or service is *so* much better than your competitor's, and they're really not very nice people either. But disparaging your competition makes you appear malicious. Instead, factually—and positively—compare your benefits and value to those of your competitor.

- **Build relationships.** One of Rhonda's Rules is "people do business with other people." We all prefer to do business with people we like and trust. Consider the "lifetime value" of a customer, not just a one-time sale. Often, you might want to make a little less profit to begin an ongoing customer relationship. Get to know your customers; find out about their businesses or families. One way small businesses can compete with the big guys is by building strong customer relationships.

Your sales pitch

By listening to customers, you find out which issues are important to them in making a purchasing decision At some point, though, you will need to make the pitch—actually ask a "prospect," a prospective customer, to buy your product or service.

MY SOCIAL MEDIA STRATEGY

Use this worksheet to plan your social media marketing strategy. Remember that social media can take up an inordinate amount of your time. Budget your hours wisely.

Social Media Site	My Target Audience on This Site	Type of Content I'll Post	Visuals I'll Add	Widgets and Third-Party Applications I'll Use
☐ Facebook				
☐ Twitter				
☐ LinkedIn				
☐ Pinterest				
☐ Instagram				
☐ YouTube				
☐ Google+				
☐ Other social media site				
☐ Other social media site				
☐ Blogs to follow				
☐ Blogs to write				
☐ Podcasts				
☐ Other:				

My Goals for This Site	Who Will Maintain the Site, Number of Hours Weekly	Will I Use Paid Advertising?	Resoures Required (for writing, posting, pictures, etc.)

A sales pitch can come in many forms, but it has three distinct stages:

- **Your pitch**
- **The customer's concerns and objections**
- **Your rejoinder, or reply, to those concerns and objections**

After you've been in business for a while, you'll know the objections or concerns that keep most prospects from making the decision to buy. Work on those, so you sound confident in responding to them should they arise in the course of a sales call.

It's generally best to anticipate objections and respond to them before they're even raised. This way, you can address whatever shortcomings or problems the prospect may be thinking about but doesn't want to mention out loud.

Use the worksheet "My Sales Pitch" on page 287 to outline the points you'll make to prospective customers and how you'll handle their reservations and objections.

Feeling at ease making presentations

"I'd rather have a root canal!" my friend replied when I asked if she'd rather go to the dentist or give a speech. She's not alone. Most people list speaking in public as one of their greatest fears. But in many types of businesses, you'll have to make presentations—often sales presentations—with the attention focused on you.

Whether you're introducing yourself to 15 other entrepreneurs at a Chamber of Commerce meeting, or describing your product to 300 potential customers at a trade conference, being comfortable in front of people is a competitive advantage. When you're at ease, listeners pay more attention to your message.

The single biggest aid to increasing your comfort level when eyes are turned in your direction is to accept yourself just as you are. We all have aspects of ourselves we wish we could change. For one person it's weight, for someone else it's a receding hairline, for another it's a slight stutter that kicks in only when they're nervous. It's important to remember that *everyone* worries about their little "flaws"—it's part of being human. But it's our imperfections that make each of us distinctive, unique, and real. Learn to accept and even cherish that which makes you different, and you'll go a long way toward being a more confident speaker.

WHAT WOULD RHONDA DO?

AT A BUSINESS LUNCH

Many people take prospective customers to lunch (or breakfast or dinner) to try to make a sale. But how, exactly, can you make the most of that opportunity with a prospect? Most inexperienced lunchers believe the main purpose of a business lunch is either to: (1) conduct business, or (2) eat lunch, and they're unsure how to mix the two.

Don't worry! Business lunches aren't about either business or lunch; they're about building relationships. Here are the keys to a successful business lunch:

- **Listen.** Listen to what the other person cares about, what makes him or her tick. Many of us, when we're nervous, tend to talk a lot. Instead, let your guest do the talking. Ask questions. You don't want to conduct an interview, but you'd be surprised how smart people think you are if you ask questions and listen to their replies.

- **Go for no reason.** Don't make the business lunch seem like a sales call. Instead, ask for an informal get-together: "I'm starting a new business, and perhaps I can take you to lunch and pick your brain for some advice." Or, "I'm often in your area, how about having lunch some time?" Once you've taken the time to get to know your guest, setting up a sales call in the future will be easier.

- **Order slow food.** Preferably, have the other person suggest a place to eat. If you have a limited budget, you choose a nice, midpriced restaurant. Forget McDonald's. Don't be in a rush. Order "slow food," not "fast food." You want as much time with your guest as possible.

- **Don't order messy food.** Pass on the spaghetti, and be careful about piling chili on the burger. Forget the "three-martini" business lunch. It's wisest not to drink any alcoholic beverage at lunch, and only do so if your companion orders one first. No matter what your companion does, stick to an absolute one-drink limit. This, after all, is still business.

- **Turn off your cell phone.** Stay focused on your companion—you've taken the time to arrange a lunch meeting, so don't waste it away on phone calls with others. It sends the message that you aren't really interested in them. Your goal is to listen and learn from your guest.

- **Bring your credit card or sufficient cash.** If you did the inviting, pick up the tab, even if your guest says, "I can put this on my company's credit card." But don't have a scene arguing over the check. You can just say, "You can get the next one." Some companies have policies that don't permit employees to be treated; in that case, split the tab.

Good luck and bon appétit!

Nevertheless, learning to accept yourself as you are is probably a long-term project, and it's not much help if you've got a sales presentation to give next Thursday. So here are a few tips to help you get over the jitters when standing in front of people:

- **Prepare.** If you're making an important sales call, learn everything you can about the prospect's company, needs, worries, market, experience with other suppliers, and the like, so that you're not "flying blind." Your audience will be impressed that you've taken the time to learn about them and their needs. The same tip applies if you're making a presentation to a large group, perhaps your industry association—the more you know about who they are, the more credible you'll sound to them and feel about yourself. You've heard it before: Knowledge is power—and it can make you *feel* powerful, too!

- **Practice.** Run through your pitch or presentation in front of friends or family. Have them ask questions, so you can practice coming up with answers on the fly. Even if your presentation doesn't justify developing a formal script, you'll want to have an outline on hand to make sure you cover all the important points. Also, rehearse the key phrases, explanations, examples, statistics, anecdotes, and so on, that you'll want to draw upon, so they'll roll off your tongue with ease.

- **Wear something that gives you confidence.** Whether it's a new outfit or your favorite tie, you'll feel more relaxed if you think your clothes are appropriate and make you look good. New clothes can give you a sense of pride, but I know businesspeople who have one great suit or dress they've had for years and always wear for initial meetings or presentations. Make sure your clothes are clean and neat; you can hardly be relaxed if you think everyone's staring at the spot on your shirt.

- **Wear or carry something that makes you feel terrific.** There's great power in knowing that you're wearing the special watch your favorite uncle gave you, or the "lucky" shoes that have seen you through other anxiety-generating events. These "tokens" are more than superstition; they remind you you're someone special.

- **Concentrate on what you're good at.** Remind yourself of the special talents or knowledge you bring, and let your confidence grow from those. You'll look and act more assured.

MY SALES PITCH

Use this worksheet to develop your sales pitch. Under "My Pitch," list the key strengths that distinguish you from your competition. Then, anticipate objections prospective customers might raise under "Their Objections." Finally, prepare "My Rejoinder" that counters the objection and convinces your prospect to buy.

My Pitch	Their Objections	My Rejoinder

- **Stop looking in the mirror.** It's normal to check yourself before you meet with people, but there's a limit. If you've made certain your hair is neat, makeup fixed, and fly zipped, don't take "just one more look."

- **Bring visuals.** If you're nervous when people look at you, bring lots of visual materials to distract attention. While the audience is staring at your colorful charts, they won't be looking at your face. Completely petrified before you have to make a presentation in front of a group? OK, then prepare a PowerPoint presentation, so most of the time you're in a dark room.

- **Pay attention to others.** You'll make yourself more appealing by paying attention to your audience. Interact with them, ask questions, make eye contact, smile. Think complimentary thoughts even if you don't speak them out loud ("What a nice group," "She seems friendly"). When you think well of others, you give off a welcoming glow.

You may never get used to standing up in front of others, but it doesn't have to feel as bad as dental surgery. Just organize your thoughts, put on a nice outfit, smile, and you'll get rave reviews.

One-page sales sheet

When a prospective customer asks for information about one of your products or services, you'll find it useful—and easy—to hand them a one-page product or service sales sheet. You'll find many uses for such a sales sheet: trade shows, leave-behinds for sales appointments, packing inserts, and material to send in response to phone or email requests.

To give you an idea of what a one-page sales sheet looks like, take a look at one we frequently use (on page 292). Here's how to make your own:

1. **First, write up your text.** Keep in mind one of Rhonda's Rules: "People don't read." So keep your copy short, snappy, and to the point. Start with a one-paragraph description of your product or service. Provide the basics: what it is, what it does, and why your customer should buy it.

    Focus on your product's benefits, not just its features. In other words, think of your product/service from your readers' point of view—you may be thrilled that you just bought a brand-new high-end photocopier for your print shop, but what does that mean for me, your customer? Better quality? Cheaper copies? Faster service?

Use bullet points to list key features and benefits. Use powerful, descriptive—but true—adjectives.

2. **Next, you need a photo of your product.** Or a graphic. Or anything visual. In this case, a picture really is worth a thousand words. If your product or service isn't particularly photogenic, use a chart or graph that illustrates benefits or cost savings.

3. **If it's appropriate, include the price of your product.** In some cases, your prices may vary by customer or season, so you'll want to maintain separate price lists.

4. **Finally, you'll want a call to action.** Tell people where and how they can order your product or get further information.

Now, it's time to take all this copy and put it on the page. Here are secrets professional designers use to make print materials look polished:

1. **Divide your page into columns.** Short spans of text are easier to read and more visually appealing than long lines. Divide your letter-sized sheet into columns.

2. **Leave "white space."** Text and graphics "pop" when they have some breathing room. At the very least, make sure you have about one half-inch margin on all four sides of your sheet and leave one quarter-inch space between columns and other graphics. It's better to eliminate some text than cram in too much.

3. **Use a maximum of two typefaces.** Your computer is loaded with wonderful, fun fonts; save most for your kids' school projects. For text, use a serif font (with those tiny lines—or feet—at the ends of letters; the text you are reading now is set in a serif font) and for headlines and captions, use a sans serif font (without the decorative lines, such as the font we used for the first sentence in this paragraph). Times Roman is a good serif choice and Arial is a popular sans serif font. Serif fonts are easier to read; sans serif fonts look cleaner and more modern.

4. **Use color and boldface type sparingly.** While you may want to make a few key words or phrases jump off the page by using colors or fat type, if you try to make everything pop out, nothing will.

There! You'll have a sophisticated, effective one-page sales sheet you can proudly distribute to potential customers.

Responding to prospective customers

Your phone rings. It's a prospective customer wanting information about your services, requesting a bid or proposal. That's a good thing, right?

Well, yes and no. Obviously, it's great to have potential customers knocking on your door. But not all prospects will convert to paying customers—no matter how good your sales skills, how competitive your prices, or how outstanding the quality of your products or services. The sad truth is you can waste a lot of precious time and money answering inquiries and preparing bids or proposals for prospects who are not ready to buy or who are just plain "looky loos."

Figuring out how much time and energy to spend on prospective customers is a delicate and difficult balancing act. You need to devote enough time to make a sale to a genuine prospect, but you don't want to waste too much time on those who won't ever buy.

Realistically, you have to be responsive to all potential customers. But there are ways to limit the amount of time, money, and effort you spend on dead-end shoppers. Here's how:

1. **Have general information prepared and available, such as your one-page sales sheet.** Most prospects will try to figure out whether a company is a good fit for them before taking up too much of their—or your—time. Let's say you sell and install floor tiles. Do you specialize in commercial or residential? Do you only serve a specific geographic area? Do you install countertops as well as floors? That kind of information enables prospects to weed themselves out before calling you. Be sure to provide this information on your website.

2. **Ask questions of the prospect.** Professional salespeople refer to this as "qualifying" the prospect. By asking a few simple, nonintrusive questions, you can get a much better sense of how serious the prospect is. Some questions to ask:

   - **What's the scope of the project?**
   - **What's the time frame for the work to be started and completed?**
   - **How soon will you be making a decision on a vendor?**
   - **How many bids are you getting?**

Check It Out

Two sources of sales lead list available for purchase are Dun & Bradstreet, (**www.dnb.com**), and InfoUSA (**www.infousa.com**).

- **What other alternatives (not competitors) are you considering? (In the floor tile example, for instance, the question might be phrased as "What other types of floor coverings are you looking at?")**
- **What are the most important considerations in your decision— price, quality, convenience?**

Questions such as those give you a much better sense of whether a prospect is ready to make a decision, whether they're likely to find you a good choice, and how much time to spend with them.

3. **Don't get starstruck.** It's easy to get excited if you're approached by a large or well-known company or customer. Don't lose your judgment. Such customers often take up more of your time, take longer to make decisions, and expect highly competitive bids. Sure, it would be nice to have the biggest company in town or the star of the major league baseball team on your customer list, but is it worth it if you don't make a profit?

4. **Give prospects a reason to make a decision sooner rather than later.** It's human nature to put off making choices until the last minute, but that often puts your business in a crunch. If you can, come up with realistic, positive ways to encourage customers to make a decision quickly—"I've got an opening in my calendar in two weeks but then I'm booked for a few more weeks" or, "I can get a discount on materials this month only."

5. **Be cautious of prospects who want *too* much information.** Some prospects use proposals as a way of getting free consulting services. This is true of both small customers and Fortune 500 companies.

6. **Don't count your chickens before they hatch.** It's easy to get excited about a prospect, especially if it's a big one. So, keep your sales pipeline full, and remember, a deal is not a deal until the check clears.

Finding sales leads

Before you can make a sale, you need someone to sell to. How are you going to find potential customers?

Sure, if a prospective customer walks in your door or calls, it's relatively easy to make a sale. It's much harder to find those who haven't called but have the potential to become customers—in other words, sales leads.

PlanningShop™

Successful
Marketing SECRETS & STRATEGIES

Designed to Sell

- Complete Marketing Plan: step-by-step templates guide readers through each step
- Dozens of interactive worksheets, charts, and sidebars make the information easy to read
- Highly graphical design attracts browsers from the minute they pick up the book
- Two-color printing throughout—information pops right off the page

About the Author

- Sold more than one million business books
- Syndicated column: USAToday.com & 100 newspapers nationwide

Marketing Plan

- National publicity campaign
- Email blast to 25,000+
- Direct mail campaigns
- In-store promotions
- Trade shows

Successful Marketing: Secrets & Strategies

By Rhonda Abrams and Julie Vallone

500 pages; 2-color

ISBN: 978-1-933895-05-5

List Price: $34.95

Published by
PlanningShop
Palo Alto, California

Distributed by
Ingram Publisher Services, Inc.

COMPANION GUIDE TO BEST-SELLING SUCCESSFUL BUSINESS PLAN: SECRETS & STRATEGIES

What is the #1 Issue on Business Owner's Minds? Marketing!!

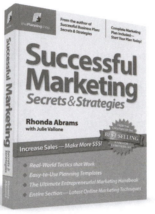

Finally! The complete, ultimate guide to marketing. Three years in development, *Successful Marketing: Secrets & Strategies* provides entrepreneurs with everything they need to know to create a successful marketing plan, increase sales, and make more money. It's all in here—from postcards and flyers to traditional advertising to the latest in online marketing techniques!

This comprehensive book covers all the marketing essentials: theoretical fundamentals, strategies, and tactics. Everything an entrepreneur or business owner wants to know and needs to know about how to market their businesses successfully is included:

- Advertising
- Online Marketing
- Brand Identity
- Direct Mail
- Public Relations
- Person-to-Person Marketing
- Viral Marketing
- Email Communications
- Social Media Marketing
- Search Engine Marketing
- Trade Shows
- In-Store Marketing
- Sampling
- Loyalty Programs
- Print Collateral

This thorough book includes a step-by-step guide to creating a **Complete Marketing Plan**. Dozens of worksheets help readers develop their company name, logo, taglines, print, radio and TV advertisements, PR pitches, websites, brochures, media kits, out-of-the box marketing campaigns, and much more.

It also includes a **Special Online Marketing Section** devoted to the latest techniques. From creating a website, to understanding search engine optimization and marketing to email communication and social media marketing, this section helps readers use the web to increase awareness and sales.

Successful Marketing: Secrets & Strategies has a number of **Exclusive Features** including: the first ever Affordability Scale, which shows the true costs of marketing tactics, and Cost Calculators throughout each section help readers decide what's worth it and what's not.

Destined to Become the Definitive Marketing Guide!

Books and tools for entrepreneurs!

Your sales leads are a natural outgrowth of defining your target market (see Week Two). The better you've defined your target, the easier it will be for you to home in on your most likely prospects. If you manufacture plumbing fixtures, for instance, you'll be far more effective in finding sales leads if you know whether your primary target is new construction or remodels, residential or commercial, contractors or consumers.

So where can you find good leads for your company?

- **Entrepreneurs' groups.** Most new and smaller companies get their first sales leads by joining organizations. There are numerous kinds of local entrepreneur groups: Chambers of Commerce, women's or minority groups' business organizations, leads or referral clubs, and so on. Typically, these groups set aside time at meetings for members to network, or even give direct sales pitches. Most entrepreneurs' organizations make available members' directories, and you may use that list for leads. Some groups hold "table top" mini-trade shows. To make your membership effective, attend regularly, or even volunteer to serve on committees.

- **Trade associations.** These groups are similar to entrepreneurs' organizations, but they are formed around one particular industry. You'll find local chapters of many national trade associations in most large or midsize cities. It's a mistake to view others in your industry solely as "competitors." They can be a good source of referrals, as well as provide information and advice. In addition to joining an association in your own industry, consider joining associations of industries that you sell to or serve. Often, as a member of an association, you are given a list of other members that you can then use as a source of sales leads. Some trade associations sell their membership lists, but typically only other members are given access to this valuable resource.

- **Trade shows.** Trade shows reach a large number of targeted prospects in a short period of time. But one additional benefit of exhibiting at a trade show is that you are often given (or are allowed to purchase) a list of attendees. These lists can be incredibly valuable in giving you a source of highly targeted sales leads.

- **Newspapers.** One of the very best sources of information about your community, and thus potential customers, is your local newspaper. A real estate agent in Miami I know relies on the obituaries for leads: He solicits surviving family members of people who've died (without spouses) to see if they want to sell the deceased's home. Yes, I know it sounds ghoulish, but it works for him.

Check It Out

To find a comprehensive list of trade asociations, visit **www.planningshop. com/associations**

You don't have to be so morbid; try checking other parts of the paper such as:

- **Public notices or advertisements about new businesses or business name changes**
- **Stories about new or expanding businesses**
- **Business sections of daily newspapers or business journals for listings of companies, such as largest employers**
- **Wedding or birth announcements**
- **Help wanted ads**
- **General advertisements and classified listings**

- **Networking organizations.** Some business groups form solely so that their members can do business with one another and develop referral sources. Most such organizations—though not all—are not-for-profit associations of businesspeople. Generally, members come from diverse industries, and meetings tend to focus on finding ways to help members secure customers and referrals. There may also be an educational portion to the meetings, but most often one or a few members will discuss their businesses. You may have a chance to be the featured speaker at a meeting, or you might be able to showcase your business on their website or newsletter. Look for business networking groups in your community; they often meet at breakfast or lunchtime. Their goal is to help members increase their income. The downside: There may be a number of members from your industry, and many of the members may not necessarily be good prospects for your business.

Check It Out

Among the numerous networking groups you'll find at Meetup (**www.meetup.com**) is one dedicated to developing leads (**www.leads-group. meetup.com**).

- **Leads groups.** Leads groups are a subset of networking organizations. As the name suggests, these are organizations formed to help members develop sales leads. They tend to maintain very specific group structures and formats, usually allowing only one or two members from each industry so that leads don't become diluted. Generally, at meetings, members give brief statements about what they do and what they need. If you get a customer lead that would be of interest to the group member who represents a particular industry, you're expected to refer that person to your leads group member. Some of these organizations are for-profit enterprises and may, in fact, be part of a franchised operation. One example is LeTip International, a for-profit business with hundreds of chapters throughout the U.S. and Canada.

- **Nonbusiness groups.** Networking isn't always about business. You'll find plenty of social networks based on a wide range of communities and shared interests. These include nonprofit and community organizations, service associations, religious organizations, environmental organizations, sports and hobby groups, social clubs, school and alumni groups, and on and on. While these groups are not specifically designed to help you build your business, your active involvement in them could lead to many local clients, as well as to referrals throughout your community. However, you'll want to take a far less aggressive approach to networking within these groups because people don't generally join them to do business. Build trust first, wait till your business comes up in conversation, and present your card only if someone asks for it.

- **Phone books.** Don't forget the good old-fashioned Yellow Pages. If you've identified particular types of businesses as potential customers, you can find a local list just by letting your fingers do the walking. Of course, unsolicited telephone calls aren't the most productive way to get new business!

- **Public records.** Many for-profit companies compile and sell lists of public records that might be used for sales leads. These include new business licenses or incorporations, building permits, wedding licenses, and birth certificates.

- **List brokers.** Private companies sell lists of both businesses and consumers, sorted virtually every conceivable way. You can buy targeted lists of leads by industry, magazines subscribed to, products purchased, schools attended, age, hobbies, even lists of new mothers. I've never bought leads from a private broker, but my recommendation would be to make certain you've very clearly targeted your prospects, and that the list is new and continually updated. Then be sure to track your results so you know whether the list was effective or not.

Cold calling

A "cold" call is a sales call—either on the phone or in person—when the person you're calling hasn't previously indicated any interest in your products or services. Obviously it's tough to make cold calls because you're going to get a lot—and I mean a *lot*—of rejection.

It's not easy to make (or get) cold calls. Who hasn't been deluged with telemarketers for long-distance service calling during dinner or credit card companies interrupting the workday repeatedly? But have you ever stopped and wondered why they keep calling when we all hate them? Here's the dirty little secret: Cold calls work.

What's the secret of cold call success?

- **Change your perspective.** Most of us start out thinking that making a sales call is "bothering" the other person. But if you are offering something you truly believe will meet a real need at a good value, then you're not a bother but a help. My company changed payroll services based on a cold call. We were having problems with our old service, and got a cold call from a reputable firm. The new payroll service solved a problem for us—so the call was a genuine help, not a bother.

- **"Qualify" your leads.** We all really *hate* sales calls when they don't relate to us. So find reasonable ways to narrow down your target list. That saves you time and increases your success rate. What makes a qualified lead? A person or business that is *likely* to need your product or service *now*.

- **Give yourself a quota.** When my sister—who's been a top-notch salesperson for 25 years—started out, she gave herself a quota every day. She put 20 business cards in her pocket and couldn't go home until she gave out all 20 or made a big sale.

- **Come up with a great pitch.** Be clear about what you're offering. Write out your pitch and the most important points well before you make your first call, but don't read it during the call! Introduce yourself right at the beginning of the call. Think about the objections you're likely to hear and have responses ready. You're not going to get it right the first time—or the second or the third. So constantly practice your pitch and refine it.

- **Mind your manners.** If you walk in on someone and they're on the phone, wait until they're free. If you're phoning, and the person says, "Now's not a good time," ask when a good time would be to call back, and get off the phone.

- **Take people literally.** If a prospect says, "I'm not interested right now," believe they mean right *now*. Perhaps they'll be interested another time. My sister called on a company for seven years before they finally bought from her.

- **Don't be obnoxious.** Take no for an answer. If someone's not interested, why waste your time or theirs? Be polite.

- **Stay in practice.** Cold calling is difficult, and it's easy to forget how to do it well. So make calls from time to time—it reminds you what you're offering your customers.

Finally, don't take it personally and don't get discouraged. You've got to kiss a lot of frogs before you find a prince. It took me four years of calling on the business editor at Gannett News Service before I finally got my nationally syndicated column in *USA Today*. And I'm still friends with him!

Up-selling and cross-selling

Getting customers isn't cheap. It takes money and time to attract new customers. Perhaps you advertise, send direct mail, attend trade shows. You put a lot of effort into getting each customer to walk through your door, call you on the phone, or visit your website, and it costs you the same amount of money whether that customer then spends $1 or $1,000. So it's far more profitable if you can make a bigger sale to each customer who comes your way.

An example of "up-selling" occurred when I went to a neighborhood beauty supply store. I was looking for a new eye shadow, and I went straight for what I wanted. One eye shadow—$8. Then, the nice saleswoman came over and advised me—in a very low-key manner—of a much better deal. They had a special: for $25, I could get three eye shadows of my choice, two lipsticks, one nail polish, and a cosmetic carrying case. That seemed to be a lot better deal, and by the time I left, I had a selection of beauty supplies and a $25 charge on my credit card.

When up-selling is done properly, the customer gets a good deal and you get a bigger sale. How could the retailer afford this kind of offer? Because their big expense is tied up in their overhead—rent, salaries, advertising—not in the cost of the eye shadow.

Many retailers try to up-sell their customers. If you've ever been to a warehouse discount store, you'll see that many items are packaged in multiples—I can only buy two bottles of Hershey's chocolate syrup—or in sets, such as selling three related books together. The result is that the customer makes a bigger total purchase on each visit, and it's much more profitable for the retailer.

Up-selling doesn't just occur in retail. If you need to get a will drawn up, don't be surprised if your lawyer offers you a complete estate planning package, which includes a few other documents you should properly prepare at the same time. The one-price package is a good value to you and a better sale for them.

A slightly different approach is "cross-selling"—selling related products or services. Examples of cross-selling include a cloth diaper service that also sells baby care products, a travel agent who books recreation activities at your destination as well as airline reservations, or a computer hardware firm that sells software.

One of the best ways to make more money from each customer is to look for ways to get continuing income rather than just making a one-time sale. Are there products or services your customers use up or use repeatedly—"consumables"—that you can appropriately sell? There's often more money in consumables than in the original product or service. Decades ago, Kodak figured out there was more profit in the film than the camera. The same is true today for inkjet printers.

Service businesses, too, can look for ongoing revenue streams. Accountants frequently offer bookkeeping or bill-paying services—instead of doing clients' income tax returns once a year, they work for them all year long. What could you offer your customers on a continuing or consumable basis?

Of course, there's a risk that if you're too aggressive when you up-sell, cross-sell, or offer consumables that a customer will view you as too pushy and they'll leave.

But if you can honestly provide a more complete product or service or a better value by up-selling or cross-selling, both you and your customer will benefit.

Nurture your contacts

Right from the start, as you try to land your first customer and find leads, start to build your contact list. Every name and email address of customers, prospects, or referral sources is valuable; every new follower on Facebook and Twitter is a potential new client. Names, contacts, and followers are prized company assets and potential leads. The following techniques will help encourage people to give you their names and contact information:

1. **Ask.** The simplest way to capture contacts is to ask people who come to your store or website for their name and email address, and ask people you meet for their business card. Something as simple as a sign ("like us on Facebook") or signup list by the cash register is a start.

2. **Give an incentive.** Offer a one-time discount to those who sign up to receive emails from you or who "like" you on Facebook.

3. **Tell them why they're signing up.** Let them know they'll get notices of sales, discounts, new products, "family and friends" specials. Everyone likes a deal.

4. **Send a newsletter.** Many people will sign up to receive valuable information relating to your products or services. In my company, for example, we email a monthly newsletter with use-it-now tips for small-business owners. And they get a discount for signing up, too!

5. **Hold contests.** Most people love the chance to win something, and will gladly enter their name and contact information. This is a particularly good strategy for building a Facebook following. Hold a monthly Facebook contest where followers can win some free products or services.

The single most important thing to remember to expand your contact list is to set up a system to routinely capture and enter data. During normal day-to-day operations, you'll quickly forget to ask people for their contact information, and that stack of business cards from people you've met won't do you much good just sitting on your desk. Remember, a name is not just a name—it's potential business.

ACCOMPLISHMENT #5:
Hold your grand opening

Now comes the big day. You're ready to "officially" open your business. It's time for a grand opening!

Grand openings aren't just for retail businesses. You can hold an "Open House" at your new office space, a "Launch Party" for even a home-based or virtual business (throw it at a restaurant or other rented or borrowed space), or a "Product Launch" event for a new product or service.

While your grand opening is certainly a celebration of all the work, time, thought, and money you've put in your new business, it's primarily a marketing event. Draw up an invitation list of all those you want to know about your business, even if you know they won't attend the party or are located out-of-town. This should include potential customers, suppliers, friends, business reporters, trade association or community organization leaders—and of course your family and employees' families.

While up-selling and cross-selling are legal sales techniques, "bait-and-switch" methods are illegal in most states and under some federal laws. "Bait-and-switch" is the practice of using an advertisement or promotion to lure a customer (the "bait") but when the customer requests the promoted item, the salesperson tells them that it is unavailable or inappropriate for their needs and suggests a more expensive option (the "switch"). If you use a low-cost promotion to bring in customers, make certain you have reasonable quantities available and be careful not to be too aggressive in suggesting other, more expensive products instead.

Print up an invitation that not only lists the time, date, and place of the grand opening but also describes what your business does. Remember, this is a chance to let the world know about your business, not just invite them to a party.

Follow up with an email. The least intrusive marketing material you can send someone is an invitation to a party. After all, you're not trying to sell them anything—not yet, at least!

To top it off, write up a press release announcing your new business and send it to the business reporters of your local newspaper and any industry publications. Call them to follow up and ask them to attend. They probably won't, but you'll let them know you exist and that will make it easier to pitch future stories to them.

And don't forget to take a moment to appreciate all that you've accomplished. You should be proud of yourself.

ACCOMPLISHMENT #6:
Look toward the future

You've come a long way! Think about where you were when you first purchased this book—and look at where you are now. Wow! What a transformation!

I wish I could tell you that from here, you'll cruise along with ease, that now you can sit back, a tall glass of lemonade in your hand, and watch the cash roll in. Unfortunately, that's just not the case…at least not yet. Certainly, getting a business up and running is one of the most difficult periods for an entrepreneur. But if you're like most businesses, the next year or two will continue to be a significant challenge for you.

You'll spend a lot of time in the coming months looking for and serving customers, streamlining operations, figuring out which products or services are actually profitable and which are underperforming, reworking your financial projections to better align them with the reality of your business and market, worrying about cash, and keeping yourself energized, motivated, and confident about the choices you've made.

You'll probably have some sleepless nights, questioning your ability to make the business work, worrying about details, customers, products, and mistakes. You may find that the tenuous support you initially had from family members wavers as some things don't work out as you planned. In fact, there may times that you want to ditch the whole business, heed your father-in-law's advice, and "go get a real job."

If so, congratulations! You are a perfectly normal entrepreneur! In fact, self-doubt isn't just a normal feeling that comes with starting a business, it's a necessary one. Many successful business owners are perfectly willing to admit that fear of failure is one of their single biggest motivators.

While it's true that you need to be self-confident about what you're doing, you also need to be able to analyze your choices, learn from your mistakes, and be honest with yourself about how you can change, adapt, and grow. Don't let your negative thoughts paralyze you—instead, harness that energy toward a positive purpose. In other words, turn those self-doubting thoughts into positive actions that will help you move forward. Fear, when used as a catalyst for positive action, is a good thing!

Part of helping yourself overcome fears of failure and getting through difficult times is recognizing that what you are doing is worthwhile and important. Instead of seeing yourself as a struggling self-employee, recognize that you're the leader of a new but growing enterprise.

Feeling like the C.E.O.

Here's a quiz: When you meet someone new, what's the second question you're most likely to be asked? Answer: "What do you do?" People don't ask this question just to figure out whether you're a welder or a writer—

it's to determine how important you are. For the self-employed, that question can be tough on the ego.

Most of us associate status with our jobs. We feel good about having a fancy office or an important job title. Even if ours is an entry-level job, if we work with a big company, we often feel a sense of reflected status ("I'm a bottle-washer at IBM").

So when you go from employee to entrepreneur, giving up those trappings of status and success can be tough.

Even good things can make you feel awkward: wearing very casual clothes everyday, going to your child's school performance in the middle of the day, not having to report to anyone. When you've been used to suits or supervisors, not having external recognition can be unsettling.

Even more frustrating—though you'll get over it—is that when you make a lot of money, often no one knows how well you're doing. After all, you still work at home and wear jeans. I had worked for myself for seven years before my friends took me seriously. What changed their impression? I got my first overseas client. Trust me: When someone pays you to go to Australia, you suddenly get respect.

But I knew I was serious long before that. Although I had given up a job where I had a private office, two assistants, and an expense account, I didn't miss any of that (well, maybe the expense account). Part of the reason is that, early on, I realized I had to take some steps to make me feel good about being self-employed.

I set up a part of my living room as my "office," printed up business cards and stationery, and changed the way I answered my phone (from "Hello," to "Rhonda Abrams speaking"). More importantly, I found a symbol to remind me of my importance.

For me, it was flowers. My first couple of years in business, I didn't have much money and every penny counted. I lived on cheap spaghetti I bought in bulk. But every week, I bought flowers for my desk. Somehow, looking at a bouquet made me feel like I'd arrived at a "real" office.

Little things matter. You can't afford the assistant, you won't necessarily have a separate room for your office, and believe me, when you travel, you're going to fly economy instead of business class. See what kind of symbols help you feel good about being in business day-in and day-out.

Here are a few you might try:

- **Business cards.** Absolutely! You can't exist without them.
- **Get dressed every day.** No, of course, I didn't think you were going to work nude. But how about getting out of those sweats?
- **Set up an "office" and decorate it.**
- **Get a gadget.** Hey, many of us judge ourselves by our toys. Having a smartphone or a cool computer can make you feel you've arrived.
- **Give yourself a title.** You really can grow up to be President!

When is it time to grow?

I know it's hard to think about growing your business when you've just opened your doors. But if you've done most of the things in this book—and have a little luck—pretty soon you'll find yourself dealing with the issue of growth.

Most entrepreneurs hope one day their small business will get bigger, but how do you know when it's time for your business to expand? Even if customers are beating a path to your door, you must make an active choice to hire employees, add locations, or extend product lines. What makes the decision more difficult is that growth rarely occurs in a straight line; you can go along for years with a healthy one-person, or 20-person business, when suddenly business booms, and you're faced with choosing how to handle it.

You'll begin to get the itch to grow when you:

- **Can't get out from under your paperwork**
- **Can't find time to send invoices to your customers**
- **Have more work than you can handle**
- **Need to add products, services, or locations to retain your current customer base**
- **Want to take your business in new directions without ending your current activities**
- **See a significant opportunity in the market**
- **Want to or need to substantially increase your income**
- **Require someone with specialized skills critical to your business**

Perhaps the hardest step is deciding to hire your first employee. It took me almost a decade before I hired my first full-time permanent employee. I'm sorry now that I waited so long, but having an employee represents a huge change in how you do your day-to-day work, and like many entrepreneurs, I was reluctant to have both the responsibility and another person underfoot.

The next critical juncture comes when your company reaches roughly 10 employees. At this point, many customers may not have direct contact with you. This can make you very nervous or it may be liberating. Not all businesses can make the transition—many service businesses depend on the abilities or charisma of the founder, so expansion stops when they're no longer immediately involved.

At around 20 employees, you'll face another major turning point. This is the stage where you can no longer supervise or regularly interact with all employees, and you need managers. Many entrepreneurs consciously choose to stop their growth at this point because they want to run an enterprise where they know and manage everyone who works for them.

The final transformation from small company to big business comes at approximately 100 employees. This is when a company needs substantial outside financing to expand. Do you really want to be a public company, maintain high bank debt, or have outside investors? Although these choices greatly reduce your ability to control your own company, they enable you to compete in much larger arenas.

With any growth comes a transition period in which you have to redefine your own job responsibilities and learn to delegate more authority to other people.

You may want to keep your business to a one-person shop or grow to hundreds of employees. Who knows?

You've given yourself—and your business—a great foundation. From that solid foundation, you can build a future of excitement, opportunity, and success.

Go for it. You can make your dreams a reality. After all, look how far you've come in just six weeks.

 **Index**

customer contact information and,
298–299
customer loyalty programs and, 261
ecommerce sites and, 264
leads, 290, 291, 293–295
vs. marketing, 242
one-page sales sheet, 288–289, 290, 292
pitch, 281, 284, 287
point-of-sale tracking, 170
presentations, 284, 286, 288
product distribution and, 57, 185–189
projections, 219–220, 222
remote sales, defined, 97
responding to prospects, 290–291
revenues, as funding source, 232
techniques and tips, 280–281
up-selling and cross-selling, 297–298, 300
See also Marketing
Sales representatives, 57, 67, 186, 188
Sales taxes, 95, 96–98, 141, 228
Salesforce.com, 43, 174
Schedulicity, 264
Search engine marketing (SEM), 269–270
Search engine optimization (SEO),
267–269, 270
S.E.C. Edgar database, 53
Self-employment, fears/frustrations of,
300–303
Service businesses
believing in what you offer, 281
growth limitations of, 304
introductory giveaways and discounts,
279–280
marketplace needs, identifying, 15
ongoing revenue streams, 298
online appointment bookings, 264
pricing, 212–213
responding to prospects, 290–291
strategic partnerships and, 70
strategic position and, 17–18
Service Corps of Retired Executives
(SCORE), 25
Servicemarks, 31, 32, 100
Shared spaces, 132, 151–152
Shipping
facilities layout and, 152
from home office, 144
location of facilities and, 132, 135,
136–137
order fulfillment, 67, 191, 193, 221
production process and, 155
Shopping carts, online, 97, 174, 184
Showrooming, 62
Sick leave, 115, 116, 122
Size of business. *See* Growth
Skype, 177
Slogans. *See* Taglines
Small Business Administration, 25, 108,
207, 233
Small Business Development Centers
(SBDCs)
industry/market research and, 53

legal and licensing assistance from, 81,
95, 96
meeting with SBDC counselor, 25–26
networking and, 72
Small Business Online Payroll Service, 230
SmugMug, 183
Social media
building online connections with, 75–76,
266, 275, 298
marketing on, 270–273, 282–283
strategy worksheet, 282
Social responsibility, 9, 10
Social Security Number, 94
Social Security taxes, 110
Software
for basic business functions, 42, 177–178,
183
for bookkeeping, 44, 170, 174, 178,
210–211
for customer relationship management
(CRM), 43, 170, 174, 180
intellectual property rights and, 101
purchases, 172–173, 177–180
templates and, 191
Sole proprietorships, 5, 83, 84–85, 86
Sperling's Best Places, 136
Springwise.com, 75
Square, 218
Squarespace, 266
Staff. *See* Employees
StartupNation, 75
State business portals, 81
State websites, guide to, 95
Statements of work (SOWs), 98
Stationery, 27, 37
Stock
convertible debt and, 231
distribution worksheets, 88–89
employee stock options, 87, 90, 121
initial public offerings (IPOs), 23
legal implications of, 87, 90
Strategic partnerships, 69–70, 236,
262–264
Strauss, Levi, 23
Successful Business Plan: Secrets & Strategies
(PlanningShop), 238, 259
Successful Marketing: Secrets & Strategies
(PlanningShop), 242
SugarCRM, 43
Suppliers
comparison chart, 166
online forums and, 75
price markups and, 214
questions to ask, 165
researching and finding, 51, 53, 67–68
trade associations and, 49, 68
Support structure
Advisory Committee, 104
Board of Directors, 104–105
business buddies/mentors, 102, 104
competitors, as resources, 66, 280, 293
SBDC counselors, 25–26, 81, 95

virtual company, 262–264
worksheet on, 103
See also Accountant, meeting with;
Attorney, meeting with

T

Taglines, 27, 37
Target Corporation, 35, 36
Target market. *See* Market, target
TaxCloud, 97
Taxes
accounting method and, 211
bookkeeping and, 44
business expense deductions, 207, 228,
253
corporate structure and, 83–86
double taxation, 82–83, 84, 85, 86
equipment purchases and, 158, 159, 228
home office deductions, 144–146
identification numbers, 92, 94
independent contractors and, 110,
112–114
payroll taxes, 109, 110, 141, 230
questions to ask accountant, 204
sales taxes, 95, 96–98, 141, 228
stock issuance and, 87
understanding tax obligations, 221,
228–230
Tech support services, 179, 181, 184, 185
Technology. *See* Computers and technology
Telephone. *See* Phones
Tenant improvements, 138, 158
ThomasNet, 53, 68
Trade associations
distributors and, 68, 186
financial forecasting and, 220
industry/market research and, 49, 52,
53, 65
insurance and, 194
networking and, 71, 72, 74, 293
online forums and, 76
pricing of services and, 213
suppliers and, 49, 68
Trade secrets, 99
Trade shows
financial forecasting and, 219, 220
industry/market research and, 49, 53,
54, 65
sales leads and, 293
sales sheet handouts at, 288
Trade Show News Network, 53, 248
Tradekey B2B directory, 53, 68
Trademarks
business name selection and, 28, 31,
33–34, 99, 100
domain name availability and, 34–35,
100
legal rights/restrictions of, 31–33
Trans Union, 207
Transaction fees, 215, 217–218
TripAdvisor, 275

Every successful business starts with a plan.

If you're starting a business, you need to make sure you've accurately assessed your market potential, costs, revenue, competition, legal issues, employee needs, and exit strategy *before* you start investing your (or someone else's) money.

Fortunately, *Successful Business Plan: Secrets & Strategies* by Rhonda Abrams will show you how to develop a well-crafted, clear, meaningful business plan—step-by-step—that will help ensure you don't end up facing any costly surprises down the road!

Named by *Inc.* and *Forbes* magazines as one of the top ten essential books for small business, *Successful Business Plan* is the best-selling business plan guide on the market, used in the nation's top business schools and by hundreds of thousands of successful entrepreneurs.

Whether you're seeking funds from outside investors or bankrolling your start-up on your own, *Successful Business Plan* will be your guide to planning your business in a sound, profitable manner.

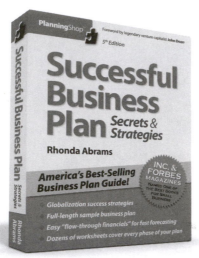

Book features:

• Over 100 worksheets to help you get started quickly, taking you through every critical section of a successful business plan

• Sample business plan offering guidance on length, style, formatting and language

• The Abrams Method of Flow-Through Financials, which makes easy work of number crunching—even if you're a numbers novice

• New in this edition: feasibility analysis, social media, globalization, social responsibility, and more

• 150 real-life insider secrets from top venture capitalists and successful CEOs

"User-friendly and exhaustive...highly recommended."
Forbes Magazine

"There are plenty of decent business plan guides out there, but Abrams' is a cut above the others..."
Inc. Magazine

Available at
www.PlanningShop.com

PlanningShop™